PROFESSIONAL PAPER 14
FINANCIAL STRATEGY

First edition January 1994

ISBN 0 7517 0965 4

British Library Cataloguing-in-Publication Data

A catalogue record for this book
is available from the British Library

Printed in Great Britain by
Ashford Colour Press, Gosport, Hampshire

Published by

BPP Publishing Limited
Aldine House, Aldine Place
London W12 8AW

All rights reserved. No part of this publication may be reproduced, stored in a retrieval system or transmitted, in any form or by any means, electronic, mechanical, photocopying, recording or otherwise, without the prior permission of BPP Publishing Limited.

We are grateful to the Chartered Association of Certified Accountants for permission to reproduce in this text the syllabus, teaching guide and pilot paper questions of which the Association holds the copyright. We are also grateful to the Chartered Association of Certified Accountants, the Chartered Institute of Management Accountants and the Institute of Chartered Secretaries and Administrators for permission to reproduce past examination questions. The suggested solutions to both the pilot paper questions and the past examination questions have been prepared by BPP Publishing Limited.

©

BPP Publishing Limited

1994

CONTENTS

	Page
PREFACE	(v)
INTRODUCTION	
How to use this Kit	(vi)
Syllabus	(vii)
The examination paper	(x)
Formulae you need to know	(xiv)
Updating notes	(xvii)
Practice and revision checklist	(xxiii)
Tables	(xxiv)
INDEX TO QUESTIONS AND SUGGESTED SOLUTIONS	1
QUESTIONS	5
SUGGESTED SOLUTIONS	65
TEST YOUR KNOWLEDGE	
Questions	188
Answers	194
TEST PAPER	
Pilot paper	201
Pilot paper suggested solutions	207
FURTHER READING	219
REVIEW FORM	220

PREFACE

The examination syllabus of the Chartered Association of Certified Accountants is changing radically with effect from the June 1994 examination. The new syllabus will be a demanding test of each student's knowledge and skills.

BPP's Practice & Revision Kits are designed to supplement BPP's Study Texts with study material for practice and revision. The aim is to improve both knowledge and exam technique by providing plenty of opportunity for structured practice of relevant questions designed to reflect the new examination scheme.

The 1994 first edition of the Paper 14 *Financial Strategy* Kit includes the following features.

(a)   Guidance on how to use this Kit

(b)   The syllabus

(c)   An analysis of recent relevant examination papers (up to and including December 1993), plus summaries of examiners' comments on the exams

(d)   Updating notes

(e)   A checklist for you to plan your study and keep tabs on your progress

(f)   An indexed question bank divided into topic areas containing:

    (i)   'Do you know?' checklists identifying essential knowledge on each topic;

    (ii)   a total of 16 tutorial questions to warm you up on key techniques before starting the examination standard questions;

    (iii)   a total of 58 examination standard questions, many of which come from past examinations under the old syllabus. The bank includes a number of shorter questions to allow coverage of a wide range of topics in the study time available;

(g)   A test your knowledge quiz

(h)   A full test paper consisting of the ACCA pilot paper for the subject

All questions, including the pilot paper, are provided with full suggested solutions prepared by BPP, plus tutorial notes where relevant. Many of the tutorial notes to past examination questions contain summaries of the examiner's comments.

If you attempt all the examination standard questions in the Kit, together with the test paper, and write good answers to all of them, you should be well prepared for anything you meet in the examination itself. Good luck!

BPP Publishing
January 1994

Should you wish to send in your comments on this Kit please turn to page 220. An order form for other relevant BPP titles may be found on page 219.

HOW TO USE THIS KIT

Using this Kit in revision

It is vital to have an organised approach to your study and revision. You may find the following approach useful, once you have been through your Study Text for the first time.

(a) Select an area and revise it from your text and notes.

(b) Go through the *'Do you know?' checklist* which is included in the question bank at the beginning of the questions on each topic area. If you are not sure about any of the points in the checklist, revise them again from your Study Text.

(c) When you are happy that you are ready to try some questions, have a go at a selection of questions in the topic area selected, without looking at the answers for any help at all. The *tutorial questions* in this Kit are designed to make the transition from pure study to examination standard question practice a bit easier. Each such question is followed by guidance notes, showing you how to tackle the question. You should not worry about the time it takes to do these questions, but should concentrate on producing good answers. Of the examination style (non-tutorial) questions, a number of shorter questions are included to ensure that you can achieve wide coverage of syllabus topics within the study time available to you.

(d) Mark your answers, as if you were the examiner.

(e) If you did badly, try more questions on the same topic.

(f) Record the date you complete your study of that area on the practice and revision checklist (on page (xxiii)). It is a useful morale booster to see how much you can cover in a few weeks.

(g) When you have covered the whole syllabus, try to identify your weaker topics, and do more questions on them.

(h) Complete the test paper at the end of this Kit, under examination conditions.

Examination technique

As well as learning the material and practising questions, you must ensure that you do yourself full justice in the actual examination. Note the following points, as well as the examiner's comments reproduced in the analysis of past papers above.

(a) *Timing*. Each mark is worth 1.8 minutes. This includes time for selecting and reading questions. For example, you must limit your time to no more than 54 minutes on a 30 mark question, or no more than 9 minutes on a 5 mark part of a question.

(b) *Relevance*. Be sure to answer the precise question set. To this end, always plan your answer, then before starting to write check that what is in your plan is all relevant to the question.

(c) *Tidiness*. You are a professional. Make sure it shows in the presentation of your work.

SYLLABUS

Introduction

While Paper 8 *Managerial Finance* examines finance at an introductory level, Paper 14 goes further to explore the strategic implications of financial decisions which are made at a fairly senior management level.

The following areas receive special emphasis in the Paper 14 syllabus:

(a) modern treasury management techniques, such as the management of risk using options, swaps, futures and other methods;

(b) the international dimension of financial management.

The detailed syllabus as published by the ACCA is set out below.

1. Corporate governance

(a) The aims and objectives of an organisation and the goals of the different interest groups involved, the significance of these for business planning.

(b) The relationship between shareholders, bondholders, bankers and directors, the potential for conflicts of interest. The contribution of agency theory to the debate on governance.

(c) The concept of goal congruence and how it may be achieved.

(d) The role of executive share option schemes (ESOPs), non-executive directors, management buy-outs and buy-ins, administrators etc.

2. Business planning

(a) Proposing, evaluating and implementing ways to meet short and medium-term financial objectives (eg, budgeting, monitoring and controlling cash flow, pricing, raising finance, repaying debt).

(b) Advising on the purpose and benefits of setting short-term objectives consistent with long-term strategy.

(c) Seeking, clarifying and confirming information relevant to the determination of business objectives (eg information on current business position and past performance by ratio and other analysis, planned changes, systems and processes used).

(d) Developing and analysing business plans to meet agreed objectives, including risk assessment of plans and all aspects of the business that they will influence, analysis to include measures of value, profit, optimisation, and utility.

(e) Long-term financial planning including:

    (i) the issues to be considered in the decision whether to expand through organic growth or through acquisition

    (ii) advising clients on the strategies a company might use in order to expand or maintain its current market position

(iii)   the techniques for valuing individual shares and other securities and for valuing a business, the application of these techniques in merger and acquisition situations

(iv)   the arguments for and against mergers and acquisitions

(v)   methods of financing an acquisition

(vi)   advising clients on appropriate merger and acquisition strategies and tactics

(vii)   tactics to follow when defending against a takeover bid

(viii)   planning for post-merger success and post-merger audit

(ix)   identifying schemes for financial restructuring and the issues involved in the decision process; methods of restructuring: buyouts, buyins, going private, share repurchases, rescheduling debts, and joint ventures.

3.   Further issues relating to long term investments

(a)   The relationship of investment decisions to long-term financial planning.

(b)   Portfolio theory and its relevance to decision making and financial management practice.

(c)   The capital asset pricing model and its uses in financial management.

(d)   Calculating the cost of capital, the significance of the dividend-based model and the capital asset pricing model in such calculations. The cost of various forms of debt. The use of the weighted average cost of capital approach.

(e)   The adjusted present value approach and its application in decision-making.

(f)   The factors to take into account in deciding upon a dividend policy. Taxation and dividends. The impact of dividends on share prices. The concept of signalling.

4.   Treasury management

(a)   Optimising the flow of financial assets for an organisation/individual.

(b)   Risk management and cost saving within the organisation by use of:

    (i)   options, including caps, floors and collars
    (ii)   futures
    (iii)   swaps
    (iv)   the scope and benefits of financial engineering.

(c)   Foreign exchange markets and hedging against foreign exchange risk.

5.   Economic influences on international financial management decisions

(a)   International factors affecting business developments. Trends in global competition with particular reference to the role of Japan and the USA.

(b)   The role of multinational companies in the world economy.

(c)   The theory and practice of free trade and problems of protectionism.

(d)   Balance of payments and implications of policies to achieve equilibrium.

(e)   Trade agreements and areas, GATT, EFTA etc.

6.   International financial management decisions

(a)   Advising clients on the alternative methods of financing imports and exports.

(b)   Workings of the international money and capital markets and the opportunities that they offer to companies as a source of finance, and as a repository for the investment of funds.

(c)   The management of financial resources within a group of companies including

  (i)   payments between companies
  (ii)   cash management
  (iii)   transfer pricing
  (iv)   judging the performance of companies within a group
  (v)   the financial control of a group of companies.

(d)   The appraisal of international capital investments, applying the appropriate techniques, and the consideration of the major issues in the decision-making process including

  (i)   strategic objectives
  (ii)   the principle of home country versus host country returns
  (iii)   the form of foreign investment, branch versus subsidiary, European Economic Interest Groups (EEIGs)
  (iv)   the effect of taxation on the foreign investment decision (basic principles only)
  (v)   discounted cash flows
  (vi)   adjusted present value
  (vii)   political risk analysis
  (viii) an analysis of the different methods of financing the investment.

THE EXAMINATION PAPER

Paper format

The paper will consist of 3 questions of 30 to 40 marks each - all of them *compulsory*.

The time allowed is 3 hours.

A formula sheet will be provided (see page (xxvi)). Calculators are essential.

Notes on the content of the paper

There will be an emphasis on problem-solving and scenario analysis, including the 'what if ...' type of question requiring students to look at different assumptions underpinning decisions.

Questions could be in the form of a report and for a specific audience, eg a non-expert. Candidates will be provided with a problem set in a context and will have to use their own judgement of the appropriate techniques to be used. For example, rather than being told to estimate an NPV, candidates could instead be asked to decide whether it is necessary to do this.

Two sections of the syllabus will have less emphasis: *corporate governance* and *economic influences*. These should be studied as an underpinning to strategic financial decisions. There will be no complete question on economics.

Analysis of Pilot Paper

The analysis below show the topics which have been set in the ACCA Pilot Paper for the subject. (The ACCA Pilot Paper forms the test paper at the end of this Kit, and so only an outline of its contents is given here.)

1   Appraisal of an international joint venture (30 marks)
2   Appraisal of the financial position of a group of companies (40 marks)
3   Report on interest rate risk management for a company (40 marks)

Analysis of past papers

Paper 14 *Financial Strategy* is the successor at the ACCA Professional stage to the old 3.2 *Financial Management* paper.

An analysis of the topics set in examination papers for the 3.2 examination from June 1991 to December 1993 inclusive is shown below.

Much of the Paper 14 syllabus - particularly the international aspects and the extended treatment of risk management techniques - is new. Although a shift in emphasis towards the new topics has been evident in recent 3.2 papers, the analysis below should not be taken as indicative of the balance of questions in the new Paper 14.

In the analysis below, the number of questions included in this Kit is indicated, or, in the case of 1993 questions, the number of a question in the Kit which covers the same topic as the question set. Selected comments of the examiner on particular papers are shown below the analysis for the relevant paper.

		Question number in this kit
December 1993		
1	Appraisal of mutually exclusive investments	-
2	Evaluation of alternative sources of finance	-
3	Cost of capital and application of MM theory	-
4	Calculations and explanations on inventory management	-
5	Financial strategies and sources of finance for a multinational	-
6	Valuations of a company for a potential purchaser	-

Examiner's comments were not available at the time of preparation of this Kit.

June 1993

1	Relevant incremental cash flows for a capital investment project	-
2	Cash management in a small company	-
3	The OTC market and selection of an investment portfolio	19
4	Evaluate feasibility of restructuring a company in financial difficulty	-
5	Gearing, its estimation and practical problems in maintaining a desired level of gearing	-
6	Any two of:	
	(a) foreign exchange risk policies	57
	(b) discussion of maximisation of shareholder wealth as a company objective	1
	(c) report advising a company seeking a loan	-

Examiner's comments

Candidates' overall performance was disappointing. Many candidates only displayed superficial knowledge of financial management, and did not appear to have prepared thoroughly for the paper. A number of candidates failed to gain marks because they did not read the requirements of questions, they ignored these requirements and chose to write answers to associated topics which they had prepared more carefully, although such discussion was not relevant.

December 1992

1	Internal rate of return and investment appraisal	-
2	Interest rate swaps and currency swaps	67
3	Overtrading and the operating cycle	-
4	Selection of an appropriate discount rate	10
5	Takeover bid alternatives; implications for shareholders	39
6	Any two of:	
	(a) discussion of government assistance for companies	-
	(b) discussion of corporate planning	26
	(c) calculations and explanations relating to a privatisation	-

Examiner's comments

Part (b) of Question 2 was poorly answered. Many answers to Question 4 lacked explanation of the principles involved in calculations. Weaknesses in answers to Question 5 were a failure to *explain* as required in part (a) and superficial discussion for part (c).

		Question number in this kit
June 1992		

1	Evaluation of the sale of a division by a company, using DCF analysis. Discussion of reasons for divestment	41
2	Discussion of possible changes for a company: factoring of debts; settlement discount; advertising. Explanation of forfaiting	-
3	A proposed issue of shares. Estimation of expected share price	-
4	Report and discussion on possible disposal of shares in a company by a multinational	72
5	Explanation of criteria used by venture capital companies, and their exit routes for their investment. Capital rationing problem using linear programming	-
6	Any two of:	
	(a) discussion of City Code on Takeovers and Mergers	33
	(b) discussion of differences between financial management in a plc and in government	-
	(c) explanation and calculations on traded foreign currency options	-

Examiner's comments

In Question 2, a frequent error was to confuse forfaiting and factoring. Analysis was mainly superficial in part (a) of Question 4, although part (b) was quite well answered. Part (a) of Question 6 was generally well answered.

December 1991

1	Appraisal of proposed joint venture in a country with very high inflation. Discount rate for the project.	-
2	Fundamental analysis and technical analysis. Dividend growth model. Efficient markets hypothesis.	22
3	Sources of finance: venture capital or loans, including foreign currency loan.	-
4	Advice on implications of a three-year financial plan and on medium-term financial planning techniques.	30
5	Cost of capital calculations. Effects on change in capital structure using MM assumptions. Weaknesses of traditional and MM theories.	11
6	Interest rate risk management: discussion and calculations.	-

Examiner's comments

Although international investment has been examined in the past, most candidates' calculations for Question 1 were poor. In question 2, candidates had more problems with part (b)(i) than the other parts. Many candidates with little knowledge of the topic covered unwisely attempted Question 6.

*Question
number in
this kit*

June 1991

1   Factors determining net present value (NPV) of a project and evaluation of a NPV estimate — -

2   Working capital management and its implications for companies' financing costs — -

3   Relative merits of leasing and hire purchase; numerical evaluation of financing methods — 6

4   Debt or equity finance decision for a company; explain mezzanine finance — -

5   Unlisted Securities Market; valuation of a company for a USM listing — -

6   Discussion of practices in a company: monitoring shareholders' register; performance evaluation using return on investment; use of Z scores — -

Examiner's comments

The main weaknesses exhibited by candidates at this examination session were:

(a)   lack of knowledge of new financial instruments and financing methods. Candidates are strongly advised to use only the most recent editions of books or manuals in their preparations for this examination;

(b)   failure to read the question carefully to see what the question requires;

(c)   over-simplistic answers to parts of questions carrying 8 to 10 marks. Marks are allocated roughly in proportion to the work required. Very brief answers, especially to discursive sections, are unlikely to contain depth of analysis to earn high marks;

(d)   unnecessary calculations. These can waste vital minutes and 'short-cuts' should be used whenever possible.

FORMULAE YOU NEED TO KNOW

There are various formulae that you need to know: here are the important ones. Some formulae are provided in the examination: see page (xxvi).

(1)   Dividend valuation model: no dividend growth

$$MV \text{ ex div} = \frac{d}{r}$$

Where   d   is the annual dividend and
            r   is the annual return required by shareholders, expressed as a proportion

(2)   Dividend growth valuation model

$$MV \text{ ex div} = \frac{d_0(1 + g)}{(r - g)}$$

Where d_0 is the current year's dividend
            g   is the dividend growth rate pa

(3)   PV of cash flow £C pa in perpetuity

$$\frac{£C}{r}$$

Where   r   is the cost of capital as a proportion.

(4)   Real cost of capital and money cost of capital

$$(1 + R) \times (1 + I) = (1 + M)$$

Where   R   is the real cost of capital as a proportion
            I   is the annual rate of inflation as a proportion
            M   is the money cost of capital as a proportion

(5)   Modigliani-Miller formula, ignoring taxation

(a) $K_g = K_u + [(K_u - K_d) \times \dfrac{D}{V_{eg}}]$

Where K_g is the cost of equity in a geared company
            K_u is the cost of equity in a similar ungeared company
            K_d is the cost of debt capital
            D   is the market value of the debt capital (irredeemable debt) in the geared company
            V_{eg} is the market value of the equity in a geared company
            $D + V_{eg}$ is therefore the total market value of the geared company

(b)   If the total market value of a similar ungeared company is V_u

$$V_u = D + V_{eg}$$

(6) **Modigliani-Miller formula, taking taxation into account**

(a) $K_g = K_u + [(K_u - K_d) \times \dfrac{D}{V_{eg}}] (1 - t)$

(b) $V_g = V_u + Dt$

(c) $\rho_L = \rho_u [1 - \dfrac{tD}{(D + V_{eg})}]$

        Where ρ_L is the WACC of the firm if it is levered (geared)
                         ρ_u is the WACC of the firm if it is unlevered (ungeared)
                         t   is the rate of taxation.

(7) **Capital Asset Pricing Model**

$$R_p = R_f + \beta (R_m - R_f)$$

   Where R_p is the return required from a share (or portfolio of shares)
                     R_f is the risk free rate of return
                     R_m is the market rate of return
                     β is the beta factor of the share (or portfolio of shares)

(8) **Formulae for calculating a beta factor**

(a) $\beta = \dfrac{\text{cov } x, y}{\text{var } x}$

Where cov x,y is the covariance of returns on an individual company's shares (y) with returns for the market as a whole (x) and var x is the variance of returns for the market as a whole.

(b) $\beta = \dfrac{\sigma_s \rho_{sm}}{\sigma_m}$

       Where σ_s is the standard deviation of the returns on the shares of a company
                     σ_m is the standard deviation of market returns
                     ρ_{sm} is the correlation coefficient between market returns and the returns on the company's shares.

(9) **Beta values and the effect of gearing: geared betas and ungeared betas**

The connection between MM theory and the CAPM means that it is also possible to establish a mathematical relationship between the β value of an ungeared company and the β value of a similar, but geared, company.

The β value of a geared company will be higher than the β value of a company identical in every respect except that it is all-equity financed. This is because of the extra financial risk.

The mathematical relationship between the 'ungeared' and 'geared' betas is:

$$\beta_u = \frac{\beta_g}{[1 + \dfrac{D(1 - t)}{V_{eg}}]}$$

where β_u is the beta factor of an ungeared company: the 'ungeared beta'
           β_g is the beta factor of a similar, but geared company: the 'geared beta'
           D   is the market value of the debt capital in the geared company
           V_{eg} is the market value of the equity capital in the geared company
           t   is the rate of corporation tax

(10) **The cost of forward exchange cover**
There is an implied interest rate in the cost of forward cover. The approximate cost (as an *interest percentage*) of forward exchange cover may be found by means of the following formula:

$$\frac{\text{Premium or discount} \times 12 \text{ months} \times 100}{\text{Number of months forward cover is taken} \times \text{the forward rate}}$$

(11) **Purchasing power parity theory**
There is a theory that in the long run, the exchange rate between the currencies of any two countries, country A and country B, will change in line with the relative rates of inflation in the two countries, so that, for example

$$\text{Future exchange rate US\$/£} = \text{Current US\$/£ exchange rate} \times \left[\frac{1 + \text{inflation rate in USA}}{1 + \text{inflation rate in UK}}\right]$$

Thus if the US$/£ exchange rate is $1.45 to £1 and if the cost of living then goes up by 4% in the USA and 10% in the UK, the exchange rate will change, with the US dollar strengthening to

$$\$1.45 \times \frac{1.04}{1.10} = \$1.37 \text{ to } £1$$

UPDATING NOTES

Options

A graphical approach to options

1. The notes which follow use a graphical approach to options, which may help you to understand options more fully and may provide a means of illustrating options in answers to exam questions.

2. The examples illustrated below generally refer to share prices. In the case of other types of option (eg index options or currency options), then it will be the value or price of the particular underlying investment (eg the stock index or the currency) which is relevant.

3. The first example shows the position of a call option holder.

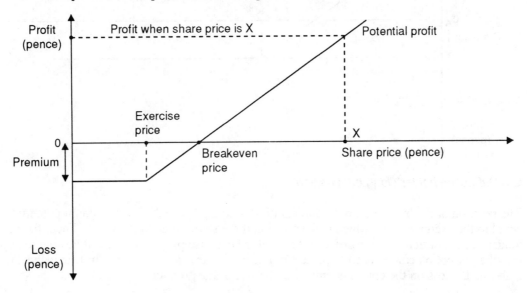

Figure 1 Call option holder ('long call position')

4. The holder of the call option will not exercise the option unless the share price is at least equal to the *exercise price* (or 'strike price') at the exercise date. If the share price is above that level, he can cut his losses (up to the break-even price) or make profits (if the share price is above the break-even price). *Holding* a call option is called having a 'long position' in the option.

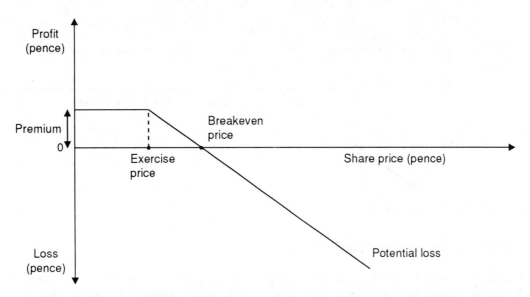

Figure 2 Call option writer ('short call position')

5. Any profit made by the holder of the option is reflected by the loss of the other party to the transaction - the writer of the option. Accordingly, Figure 2, illustrating the potential outcomes for the writer of the option, looks like a 'mirror image' of Figure 1. Selling or writing a call option is called 'taking a short call position'. It can be seen that the writer of the call option is exposed to potentially unlimited losses.

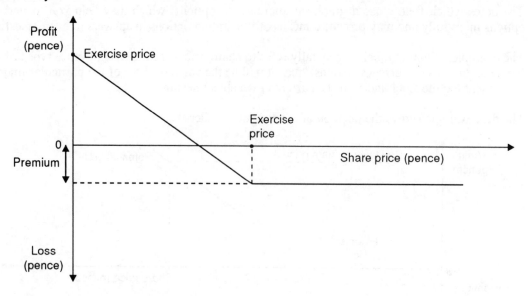

Figure 3 Put option holder ('long put position')

6. The position of the buyer of a put option is illustrated in Figure 3. The maximum potential profit is equal to the exercise price, which is the position if the share price falls to zero. Then, the put option holder has the option to sell worthless shares at the exercise price. You should be able to appreciate that the put option can be used to protect a holder of shares against a fall in their value. As Figure 3 shows, the loss on the option is limited to the size of the premium.

   You will probably by now be able to guess what a graph illustrating the position of a put option writer will look like (see if you can sketch such a graph and then look at Figure 4).

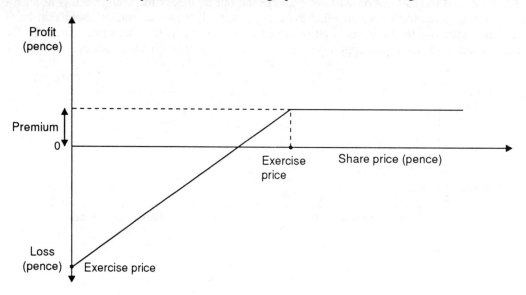

Figure 4 Put option writer ('short put position')

8. Reasoning from what you have already learned about options, check that you can explain Figure 4. Note that the maximum loss for the writer or seller of the put option is the exercise price.

9. Figures 1 to 4 illustrate the basic positions which can be taken in options. It is also possible to combine different option positions in various ways, depending on the combination of risks and returns which are sought from different outcomes. Examination of the various strategies which are possible is beyond the scope of the Paper 14 syllabus.

Time value and valuation of options

10. We also need to consider the *time value* of an option. Holding a call option can be seen effectively as the deferred purchase of the underlying asset (eg shares), since the exercise price does not have to be paid until a later date.

11. The time value of an option will be affected by the level of interest rates. The higher the level of interest rates, the higher will be the value of the option as the present value of the exercise price of the option will be correspondingly lower. The longer the time to expiration, the higher will the value of the option be, as its present value will be lower. Furthermore, the longer is the period to expiration, the more opportunity there is for volatility in the markets to lead to higher share values. These determinants of the value of an option are recognised in the Black-Scholes model, which is outlined in the BPP Paper 14 Study Text.

12. We can illustrate the limits of valuation of options graphically (Figure 5).

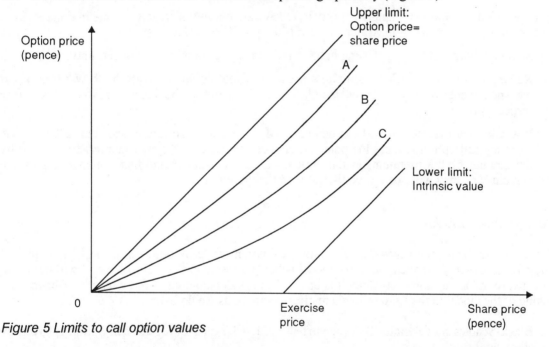

Figure 5 Limits to call option values

13. An upper limit to the value of an option is the value of the underlying share (or other asset). It will never be worthwhile to pay more for an option than the price of the asset which the option enables you to buy.

14. The lower limit to the value of an option shown on Figure 5 represents the intrinsic value of the option - ie the extent to which it is 'in the money'. This lower limit is zero up to the exercise price and at higher share prices is the difference between the share price and the exercise price.

15. In practice, the value of most options will lie somewhere between these limits, as illustrated by lines A, B and C in Figure 5.

Graphical illustration of currency options

16. Above, we have used options on shares as the main type of example, but a similar graphical approach can be used to illustrate other kinds of options, for example currency options.

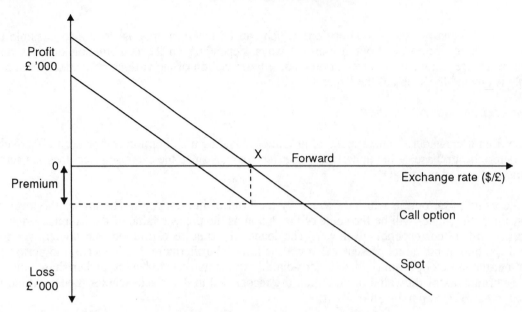

Figure 6 Currency call option, forward and spot markets: profit/loss profile

17. Suppose that a UK-based company expects to receive an amount of export income in dollars ($) in three months' time. Figure 6 illustrates the profit/loss profile of different strategies.

    (a) Selling dollars and buying sterling in the forward market eliminates all uncertainty.

    (b) Relying on the spot market results in a net gain or loss compared with the forward market if the spot exchange rate in three months' time turns out to be below or above $X per £ respectively.

    (c) If a call option is used, it will not be exercised if the exchange rate is less than $X per £. A currency call option reduces the potential gain compared with the spot market strategy (b) by the amount of the premium on the option, but has the advantage that potential losses are contained as they will not exceed the value of the premium.

The Black-Scholes model

18. As mentioned above, the Black-Scholes option valuation model is outlined in the BPP Paper 14 Study Text. Although application of the model is beyond the scope of the syllabus, it will be useful to be aware of the variables on which it is based. Your understanding of these may be enhanced by looking at the model in the form of mathematical notation, as we do below.

19. The Black-Scholes model states that the current value (P_0) of a European call option is given by the following formula:

$$P_0 = P_s N(d_1) - \frac{E}{e^{rt}} N(d_2)$$

where:
$$d_1 = \frac{\log_n(P_s / E) + (r + \frac{1}{2}\sigma^2)t}{\sigma\sqrt{t}}$$

d_2	=	$d_1 - \sigma\sqrt{t}$
P_s	=	the current price of the share
E	=	the exercise price of the option
r	=	the compound risk-free rate of return (as a decimal)
σ	=	the standard deviation of the rate of return on the share
e	=	the exponential constant 2.7183
t	=	the time in years to expiration of the option
$\log_n(P_s/E)$	=	the natural logarithm of P_s/E

$N(d)$ = the probability that a deviation of less than d will occur in a normal distribution with a mean of zero and a standard deviation of 1

20. The formula may well seem daunting, but you do not need to learn it. As already mentioned, what is important is to be aware of the variables which it includes.

21. The determinants of the equilibrium value of an option according to the Black-Scholes model were set out in the BPP Study Text. The corresponding notation for these variables in the above formulae are indicated below.

22. The option value depends upon:

(a) *the current share price* (P_s): if the share price rises, the value of a call option will increase. (For *currency options,* the relevant 'price' is the exchange rate.)

(b) *the exercise price of the option* (E): the higher the exercise price, the lower is the call option value.

(c) *the standard deviation of the return on the underlying share* (σ): the higher the standard deviation of the return, the higher is the value of the option;

(d) *the time to expiration of the option* (t): the longer the period to expiration, the higher is the value of the option;

(e) *the risk-free rate of interest* (r): the higher the risk-free rate of interest, the higher is the option value. (In the case of *currency options,* the risk-free interest rate differential between the currencies involved is a relevant factor).

The delta value

23. If we accept the Black-Scholes model, the value of $N(d_1)$ can be used to indicate the amount of the underlying shares (or other instrument) which the writer of an option should hold in order to hedge (eliminate the risk of) the option position.

24. The appropriate 'hedge ratio' $N(d_1)$ is referred to as the *delta value*: hence the term 'delta hedge'. The delta value is valid if the price changes are small.

Delta = Change in call option price ÷ Change in the price of the underlying share

25. For example, if a change in share price of 3 pence results in a change in the option price of 1 pence, then:

Delta = 1p ÷ 3p = $^1/_3$

26. The writer of the option needs to hold one-third of the number of shares on which there are options in order to achieve a delta hedge. If the writer loses 1 pence per share on the option, this will be offset by 1 pence gain on the share held.

27. The delta value is liable to change during the period of the option, and so the option writer may need to change his holding of the underlying share from time to time in order to maintain a delta hedge position.

Example

28. How can the writer of a 3 month call option on 10,000 shares in R plc with an exercise price of 384 pence achieve a delta hedge?

The delta value is given by $N(d_1)$, whose value is 0.745.

Solution

29. A delta hedge would be achieved by holding the following number of shares:

    $10,000 \times 0.745 = 7,450$ shares.

30. Note also the following points about delta values.

    (a) If an option is 'at the money' (ie if the share price equals the exercise price) then the delta value is approximately 0.5.

    (b) As an option moves 'out of the money' (ie the share price moves below the exercise price), the delta value falls towards zero. Delta will be zero when the share price is zero: the shares are then worthless.

    (c) As an option moves further 'into the money', the delta hedge ratio increase towards a value of 1.

31. The factors influencing delta when the option is either in the money or out of the money can be appreciated by looking at the variables in the $N(d_1)$ formula given earlier. These factors are:

    (a) the exercise price of the option relative to the share price (ie its intrinsic value);
    (b) the time to expiration;
    (c) the risk-free rate of return;
    (d) the volatility of returns on the share.

The gamma value

32. The gamma value measures the amount by which the delta value changes as the share price changes:

    Gamma = Change in delta value ÷ Change in the price of the underlying share

33. The higher the gamma value, the more difficult it is for the option writer to maintain a delta hedge. As a result, a higher gamma value will mean that the option will carry a higher premium.

34. Gamma values will be highest for a share which is close to expiry and is 'at the money'.

    For example, suppose that an option has an exercise price of 340 pence and is due to expire in a few minutes' time.

    (a) If the share price is 338 pence, there is a very low chance of the option being exercised. The delta hedge ratio will be approximately zero: in other words, no hedge is necessary.

    (b) If the share price rises suddenly to 342 pence, it becomes highly probable that the option will be exercised and the delta hedge ratio will approximate to 1, suggesting the need to hedge through holding the underlying shares.

35. This example illustrates how a small change in the share price can result in a large change in the delta value.

PRACTICE AND REVISION CHECKLIST

This checklist is designed to help you chart your progress through this Practice and Revision Kit and thus through the Association's syllabus. By this stage you should have worked through the Study Text, including the illustrative questions at the back of it. You can now tick off each topic as you revise and try questions on it, either of the tutorial type or of the full examination type. Insert the question numbers and the dates you complete them in the relevant boxes. You will thus ensure that you are on track to complete your revision before the exam.

The checklist is arranged in topic order, and follows the content of this Practice and Revision Kit and the corresponding BPP Study Text.

	Revision of Study Text chapter(s) Ch No/Date Comp	Tutorial question in Kit Ques No/Date Comp	Examination style questions Ques No/Date Comp
THE NATURE AND SCOPE OF FINANCIAL STRATEGY			
INVESTMENT DECISIONS AND CAPITAL STRUCTURE Financial returns and market efficiency			
The cost of capital and capital structure			
Portfolio theory and the CAPM			
Dividend policy			
BUSINESS PLANNING Planning and company performance			
Amalgamations and financial restructuring			
THE INTERNATIONAL ENVIRONMENT International trade and international finance			
Risk management			
INTERNATIONAL OPERATIONS			

	Date completed
Test paper	

TABLES

Present value table

Present value of £1 $(1 + r)^{-n}$ where r = discount rate, n= number of periods until payment.

Discount rates (r)

Periods (n)	*1%*	*2%*	*3%*	*4%*	*5%*	*6%*	*7%*	*8%*	*9%*	*10%*	
1	0.990	0.980	0.971	0.962	0.952	0.943	0.935	0.926	0.917	0.909	1
2	0.980	0.961	0.943	0.925	0.907	0.890	0.873	0.857	0.842	0.826	2
3	0.971	0.942	0.915	0.889	0.864	0.840	0.816	0.794	0.772	0.751	3
4	0.961	0.924	0.888	0.855	0.823	0.792	0.763	0.735	0.708	0.683	4
5	0.951	0.906	0.863	0.822	0.784	0.747	0.713	0.681	0.650	0.621	5
6	0.942	0.888	0.837	0.790	0.746	0.705	0.666	0.630	0.596	0.564	6
7	0.933	0.871	0.813	0.760	0.711	0.665	0.623	0.583	0.547	0.513	7
8	0.923	0.853	0.789	0.731	0.677	0.627	0.582	0.540	0.502	0.467	8
9	0.914	0.837	0.766	0.703	0.645	0.592	0.544	0.500	0.460	0.424	9
10	0.905	0.820	0.744	0.676	0.614	0.558	0.508	0.463	0.422	0.386	10
11	0.896	0.804	0.722	0.650	0.585	0.527	0.475	0.429	0.388	0.350	11
12	0.887	0.788	0.702	0.625	0.557	0.497	0.444	0.397	0.356	0.319	12
13	0.879	0.773	0.681	0.601	0.530	0.469	0.415	0.368	0.326	0.290	13
14	0.870	0.758	0.661	0.577	0.505	0.442	0.388	0.340	0.299	0.263	14
15	0.861	0.743	0.642	0.555	0.481	0.417	0.362	0.315	0.275	0.239	15

	11%	*12%*	*13%*	*14%*	*15%*	*16%*	*17%*	*18%*	*19%*	*20%*	
1	0.901	0.893	0.885	0.877	0.870	0.862	0.855	0.847	0.840	0.833	1
2	0.812	0.797	0.783	0.769	0.756	0.743	0.731	0.718	0.706	0.694	2
3	0.731	0.712	0.693	0.675	0.658	0.641	0.624	0.609	0.593	0.579	3
4	0.659	0.636	0.613	0.592	0.572	0.552	0.534	0.516	0.499	0.482	4
5	0.593	0.567	0.543	0.519	0.497	0.476	0.456	0.437	0.419	0.402	5
6	0.535	0.507	0.480	0.456	0.432	0.410	0.390	0.370	0.352	0.335	6
7	0.482	0.452	0.425	0.400	0.376	0.354	0.333	0.314	0.296	0.279	7
8	0.434	0.404	0.376	0.351	0.327	0.305	0.285	0.266	0.249	0.233	8
9	0.391	0.361	0.333	0.308	0.284	0.263	0.243	0.225	0.209	0.194	9
10	0.352	0.322	0.295	0.270	0.247	0.227	0.208	0.191	0.176	0.162	10
11	0.317	0.287	0.261	0.237	0.215	0.195	0.178	0.162	0.148	0.135	11
12	0.286	0.257	0.231	0.208	0.187	0.168	0.152	0.137	0.124	0.112	12
13	0.258	0.229	0.204	0.182	0.163	0.145	0.130	0.116	0.104	0.093	13
14	0.232	0.205	0.181	0.160	0.141	0.125	0.111	0.099	0.088	0.078	14
15	0.209	0.183	0.160	0.140	0.123	0.108	0.095	0.084	0.074	0.065	15

Annuity table

Present value of an annuity of £1 = $\frac{1-(1+r)^{-n}}{r}$ where r = interest rate, n = number of periods.

Interest rates (r)

Periods (n)	*1%*	*2%*	*3%*	*4%*	*5%*	*6%*	*7%*	*8%*	*9%*	*10%*	
1	0.990	0.980	0.971	0.962	0.952	0.943	0.935	0.926	0.917	0.909	1
2	1.970	1.942	1.913	1.886	1.859	1.833	1.808	1.783	1.759	1.736	2
3	2.941	2.884	2.829	2.775	2.723	2.673	2.624	2.577	2.531	2.487	3
4	3.902	3.808	3.717	3.630	3.546	3.465	3.387	3.312	3.240	3.170	4
5	4.853	4.713	4.580	4.452	4.329	4.212	4.100	3.993	3.890	3.791	5
6	5.795	5.601	5.417	5.242	5.076	4.917	4.767	4.623	4.486	4.355	6
7	6.728	6.472	6.230	6.002	5.786	5.582	5.389	5.206	5.033	4.868	7
8	7.652	7.325	7.020	6.733	6.463	6.210	5.971	5.747	5.535	5.335	8
9	8.566	8.162	7.786	7.435	7.108	6.802	6.515	6.247	5.995	5.759	9
10	9.471	8.983	8.530	8.111	7.722	7.360	7.024	6.710	6.418	6.145	10
11	10.37	9.787	9.253	8.760	8.306	7.887	7.499	7.139	6.805	6.495	11
12	11.26	10.58	9.954	9.385	8.863	8.384	7.943	7.536	7.161	6.814	12
13	12.13	11.35	10.63	9.986	9.394	8.853	8.358	7.904	7.487	7.103	13
14	13.00	12.11	11.30	10.56	9.899	9.295	8.745	8.244	7.786	7.367	14
15	13.87	12.85	11.94	11.12	10.38	9.712	9.108	8.559	8.061	7.606	15

Periods (n)	*11%*	*12%*	*13%*	*14%*	*15%*	*16%*	*17%*	*18%*	*19%*	*20%*	
1	0.901	0.893	0.885	0.877	0.870	0.862	0.855	0.847	0.840	0.833	1
2	1.713	1.690	1.668	1.647	1.626	1.605	1.585	1.566	1.547	1.528	2
3	2.444	2.402	2.361	2.322	2.283	2.246	2.210	2.174	2.140	2.106	3
4	3.102	3.037	2.974	2.914	2.855	2.798	2.743	2.690	2.639	2.589	4
5	3.696	3.605	3.517	3.433	3.352	3.274	3.199	3.127	3.058	2.991	5
6	4.231	4.111	3.998	3.889	3.784	3.685	3.589	3.498	3.410	3.326	6
7	4.712	4.567	4.423	4.288	4.160	4.039	3.922	3.812	3.706	3.605	7
8	5.146	4.968	4.799	4.639	4.487	4.344	4.207	4.078	3.954	3.837	8
9	5.537	5.328	5.132	4.946	4.772	4.607	4.451	4.303	4.163	4.031	9
10	5.889	5.650	5.426	5.216	5.019	4.833	4.659	4.494	4.339	4.192	10
11	6.207	5.938	5.687	5.453	5.234	5.209	4.836	4.656	4.486	4.327	11
12	6.492	6.194	5.918	5.660	5.421	5.197	4.988	4.793	4.611	4.439	12
13	6.750	6.424	6.122	5.842	5.583	5.342	5.118	4.910	4.715	4.533	13
14	6.982	6.628	6.302	6.002	5.724	5.468	5.229	5.008	4.802	4.611	14
15	7.191	6.811	6.462	6.142	5.847	5.575	5.324	5.092	4.876	4.675	15

Formula sheet

The formula sheet included in the ACCA Pilot Paper for Paper 14 is as set out below.

Ke   (i) $E(r_j) = r_f + [E(r_m) - r_f]\beta_j$

             (ii) $\dfrac{D_1}{p_0} + g$

WACC $Ke_g \dfrac{E}{E+D} + Kd(1-t)\dfrac{D}{E+D}$

           or $Ke_u \left[1 - \dfrac{Dt}{E+D}\right]$

2 asset portfolio $\sigma_p = \sqrt{\sigma_a^2 x^2 + \sigma_b^2 (1-x)^2 + 2x(1-x)p_{ab}\sigma_a\sigma_b}$

Purchasing power parity $\dfrac{i_f - i_{uk}}{1 + i_{uk}}$

The dates after question titles indicate ACCA 3.2 examinations from which the questions are taken.

		Question	Suggested solution
PART A: THE NATURE AND SCOPE OF FINANCIAL STRATEGY			
1	Financial objective	6	65
2	*Tutorial question: Managerial reward*	6	65
3	Corporate governance	6	66
PART B: INVESTMENT DECISIONS AND CAPITAL STRUCTURE			
Financial returns and market efficiency			
4	Yield curve	8	67
5	*Tutorial question: Efficient market hypothesis*	8	68
6	Nebeng (3.2, 6/91)	8	69
7	Share valuation methods	9	72
8	Mala Vita	9	75
The cost of capital and capital structure			
9	*Tutorial question: Financing expansion*	9	76
10	Crestlee (3.2, 12/92)	11	78
11	Berlan and Canalot (3.2, 12/91)	11	82
Portfolio theory and the CAPM			
12	*Tutorial question: Cost of equity*	12	85
13	Short questions	13	86
14	*Tutorial question: Share prices and returns*	13	86
15	*Tutorial question: Beta factors*	14	88
16	Portfolio risk	15	89
17	Capital market line	15	90
18	Investor	16	92
19	OTC investments	16	94
20	Slohill (3.2, 12/89)	17	96
21	Nelson (3.2, 12/84)	18	98
22	Univo (3.2, 12/91)	19	99
Dividend policy			
23	ABC (3.2, 12/87)	20	102
24	*Tutorial question: Dividend valuation model and dividend policy*	20	104
25	Deerwood (3.2, 12/89)	21	105
PART C: BUSINESS PLANNING			
Planning and company performance			
26	Corporate planning (3.2, 12/92, part question)	24	106
27	Aggressive, moderate or conservative	24	107
28	*Tutorial question: Improving cash flow*	24	108
29	Oxold (3.2, 12/86, part question)	25	110
30	Adsum (3.2, 12/91)	26	111
31	*Tutorial question: Report on a subsidiary*	27	115
32	XQ plc	28	117

BPP Publishing

		Question	*Suggested solution*
Amalgamations and financial restructuring			
33	City Code (3.2, 6/92, part question)	29	119
34	Management buyouts	29	120
35	M and C	29	121
36	Justifications	30	122
37	*Tutorial question: Bid calculations*	30	123
38	*Tutorial question: Bases of valuation*	31	124
39	Takeover (3.2, 12/92)	33	126
40	Woppit (3.2, 12/90)	34	129
41	Apcon (3.2, 6/92)	35	130
42	Divestment plc	36	132
43	*Tutorial question: Financial reconstruction*	38	136
44	Goodsleep (3.2, 12/89)	39	139
45	Rock Bottom	41	140

PART D: THE INTERNATIONAL ENVIRONMENT

International trade and international finance			
46	Common market	43	142
47	Eurocurrencies	43	143
48	New export markets	43	144
49	Tintinnabulum Ltd	43	145
50	Frame-up Ltd	43	146
51	Blanc et Blanc	44	147
52	Heavy Engineering plc	44	150
53	Foreign exchange rate forecasts	44	152
54	*Tutorial question: Financing strategies*	45	153
55	Bolar (3.2, 12/90)	46	155

Risk management			
56	International group	47	158
57	Foreign exchange risk strategies	47	159
58	Foreign currency options	48	160
59	*Tutorial question: Sales to the USA*	48	161
60	Freimarks	49	161
61	Exchange rates	50	162
62	Oxlake (3.2, 12/87)	50	164
63	Bid (3.2, 12/90)	51	166
64	*Tutorial question: Interest rate risks*	52	168
65	Capit (3.2, 6/90)	53	169
66	Manling (3.2, 6/90)	53	171
67	Swaps (3.2, 12/92)	54	173

PART E: INTERNATIONAL OPERATIONS

68	*Tutorial question: Multinational investment appraisal*	56	175
69	Transfer pricing	57	177
70	British company in Ruritania	57	177
71	Ranek (3.2, 6/90)	58	180
72	Passem (3.2, 6/92)	59	182
73	Cash with order	61	185
74	The treasury function	61	185

BPP Publishing

QUESTIONS

4

DO YOU KNOW? - THE NATURE AND SCOPE OF FINANCIAL STRATEGY

- *Check that you know the following basic points before you attempt any questions. If in doubt, go back to your Study Text and revise first.*

- *Strategy* - whether short-term or long-term - involves action to achieve a specific objective. The decisions falling within the scope of *financial strategy* include those relating to the sources from which funds are obtained, the amount which should be paid out by a company in dividends, financial aspects of asset replacement, and a company's policies on allowing and taking up discounts.

- The theory of company finance is based on the assumption that the objective of management is to maximise the market value of the company. More specifically, the main objective of a company should be to maximise the wealth of its ordinary shareholders.

- Possible bases of valuation are:
  - o balance sheet (going concern) valuation
  - o break-up basis
  - o market value of shares

- Financial targets may include targets for:
  - o earnings
  - o earnings per share
  - o dividend per share
  - o gearing level
  - o profit retention
  - o operating profitability

- Non-financial objectives may include:
  - o employee welfare
  - o management welfare
  - o the welfare of society
  - o service provision objectives
  - o fulfilment of responsibilities to customers and suppliers

- Nationalised industries are given rate-of-return targets by government.

- Not-for-profit organisations pursue non-financial objectives but are subject to financial constraints.

- There is the potential for conflict between owners, directors, managers and other interest groups. Agency theory sees employees and shareholders as individuals, each with their own objectives. Where different people's objectives can be met together, there is said to be goal congruence.

- The system of corporate governance - a responsibility of the directors - should seek to ensure congruence between the objectives of the organisation and those of its teams or departments and individual team members.

- In the UK, the Cadbury Report has clarified a number of contentious issues of corporate governance and has set standards of best practice in relation to financial reporting and accountability.

- *Key questions*

  1 *Financial objective*

  3 *Corporate governance*

BPP Publishing

1 FINANCIAL OBJECTIVE (12½ marks)

'The objective of financial management is to maximise the value of the firm.'

Required

Discuss how the achievement of this objective might be compromised by the conflicts which may arise between the various stakeholders in an organisation.

2 TUTORIAL QUESTION: MANAGERIAL REWARD

To what extent is it in the interests of the shareholders of publicly quoted companies to make the remuneration of managers largely dependent upon the financial success of the firm?

Specify the ways in which such a policy could be implemented and outline the merits and disadvantages of each of these ways.

Guidance notes

1   This question is asking you to consider the different types of incentive which may be given to managers to induce them to manage a company in the best interests of shareholders. One of the problems with some forms of incentive is that managers are often in a position to manipulate the criteria on which the incentives are based.

2   Consider: issuing shares to managers, deferred equity, and basing pay or bonuses on achievement of targets.

3   The question was allocated just 12 marks when set in an exam. At 1.8 marks per minute, 12 marks deserve 20 minutes of your time.

3 CORPORATE GOVERNANCE (15 marks)

Required

(a) Describe the main recommendations of the final report of the Committee on the Financial Aspects of Corporate Governance (the Cadbury report) published in December 1992.

(8 marks)

(b) Discuss the arguments for and against the introduction of statutory controls on corporate governance.

(7 marks)

DO YOU KNOW? - INVESTMENT DECISIONS AND CAPITAL STRUCTURE

- *Check that you know the following basic points before you attempt any questions. If in doubt, go back to your Study Text and revise first.*

- Stock markets bring companies and investors together. Different views about share price movements are the fundamental analysis theory; technical analysis (chartist theory); random walk theory.

- The efficient market hypothesis can be proposed in different forms.

  o *Weak form*: share prices reflect all information about companies contained in the record of past share prices.

  o *Semi-strong form*: share prices *also* reflect all publicly available information.

  o *Strong form*: share prices *also* reflect all the information that can be obtained from thorough fundamental analysis of companies and the economy.

- All funds have a cost: equity holders require dividends and/or capital growth; lenders require interest payments.

- The cost of equity can be calculated using either the dividend growth model or the Capital Asset Pricing Model.

- The cost of loan capital is not simply the nominal interest rate. We must take account of the market value of the loan capital.

- A weighted average cost of capital may be computed, usually weighting the sources of finance by their market values.

- The proportion of a company's long-term finance in the form of loan capital (the company's *gearing*) is limited by lenders' reluctance to lend to a company without an adequate equity base. As gearing increases, the volatility of returns to equity increases.

  o The traditional view is that there is an optimum level of gearing for each company which will minimise its weighted average cost of capital.

  o The Modigliani-Miller view is that in the absence of taxation, gearing does not affect the value of a company. With taxation, the company's value is increased by the tax relief on the debt.

- A portfolio of investments will have a risk and an expected return. Some portfolios will be better than others, and those which give the best possible return for their levels of risk lie on the efficient frontier.

- By holding a diversified portfolio an investor can avoid unsystematic risk, but he must still accept systematic risk. Systematic risk is the risk of a rise or fall in returns because of a general rise or fall in the market.

- A security's beta factor measures its volatility relative to that of the market. Risk-free securities have a beta factor of 0; the market as a whole has a beta factor of 1.

- The Capital Asset Pricing Model formula shows how the systematic risk of a security, measured by its beta factor, is related to the rate of return required from it by investors.

- Beta factors may be given for projects as well as for securities, and used to find required rates of return for projects.

- Dividend policy may be affected by the desire to have a stable policy; the availability of cash; the company's tax position; shareholders' preferences for income or capital gains.

- *Key questions*

  6   Nebeng

  11 Berlan and Canalot

  12 Tutorial question: Cost of equity

  22 Univo

  25 Deerwood

BPP Publishing

4 YIELD CURVE (25 marks)

(a) What is a yield curve? (5 marks)

(b) Why is an upward sloping yield curve considered normal? (10 marks)

(c) To what extent does the shape of the yield curve depend on expectations about the future?

(10 marks)

5 TUTORIAL QUESTION: EFFICIENT MARKET HYPOTHESIS

A number of investigations have been undertaken into the use made by shareholders of the annual reports of companies in which they have invested. Several of these show that the annual report is regarded as an important source of information for making decisions on equity investment.

Other types of study indicate that the market price of the shares in a company does not react in the short term to the publication of the company's annual report.

How would you reconcile these findings with each other, and with the efficient market hypothesis?

Guidance notes

1 You should start by outlining the efficient market hypothesis in general, and you should then distinguish the three forms of the hypothesis.

2 You should then identify the form of the hypothesis relevant to published information such as companies' annual reports.

3 Finally, if you feel that form does not explain the observed facts set out in the question, consider whether another form, or some other facts, might do so.

6 NEBENG (25 marks) 3.2, 6/91

The finance director of Nebeng Ltd wishes to know whether to install a new machine. The machine would either be purchased for cash, or on hire-purchase terms, or would be leased. The purchase cost of the machine is £142,500. It has an expected life of four years and, if purchased, will be sold at the end of year four leading to a balancing charge or allowance. The realisable value at the end of four years is expected to be £22,500. The new machine is expected to generate after-tax net cash flows of £40,000 per year for four years; this estimate excludes the tax effects of financing and writing-down allowances. If hire-purchase is used an initial 20% deposit is payable, followed by four equal annual year end payments covering both the interest and principal elements of the payment. The four equal payments are expected to yield the lessor an interest return of 20% per year in present value terms. Leasing would involve an annual rental payment of £45,000 payable in advance.

The company pays tax at the rate of 35% per year, one year in arrears and a 25% writing down allowance is available on the machinery, on a reducing balance basis.

Nebeng Ltd would finance the outright purchase of the machine with a loan repayable in full after four years. The 20% initial deposit on the hire-purchase deal would be financed in the same way. The company's cost of debt is estimated to be 16% per year and equity 22% per year. Three per cent of the 22% cost of equity is due to the company's financial risk (gearing), and the current project is of a similar risk to the company's other activities. The risk free rate is 14% per year, and the market return is 21% per year.

Required

(a) Discuss the relative advantages to the lessee or borrower of leasing and hire purchase.

(8 marks)

(b) Using adjusted present values, evaluate whether the machine should be installed and, if so, which means of financing should be chosen.

State clearly any assumptions that you make. (17 marks)

7   SHARE VALUATION METHODS   (30 marks)

The financial director of a listed company has recently been reading a textbook on the subject of stock market investment. In various parts of the text he found references to several methods which might be used in the valuation of shares:

(i)   Book value of assets per share;
(ii)   Current cost of assets per share;
(iii)   Break-up value of assets per share;
(iv)   Capital asset pricing model;
(v)   Price-earnings ratio;
(vi)   Dividends valuation model;
(vii)   Discounted cash flow;
(viii) Number of years purchase of earnings.

Required

(a) Define each of the above methods giving, where appropriate, the formula to be used in its calculation.   (16 marks)

(b) Prepare a report for the financial director which compares the strengths, weaknesses and objectives of these various methods.   (14 marks)

8   MALA VITA   (30 marks)

Mala Vita, an Italian conglomerate, is considering the possibility of floating off one of its subsidiary companies, La Cena delle Beffe, an Italian restaurant chain, on the UK Stock Exchange.

The profits of the subsidiary are £3.2 million per annum and these are expected to increase at 5% per annum. The book value of the net assets is £15 million and their market value is £20 million. The proposed annual dividend is 20 pence for each of the 10 million shares of 50 pence. The company has a beta factor of 1.2. The risk-free rate of interest is 8% and the price-earnings ratio on the market portfolio is 8.

Required

(a) Suggest five different bases for valuing the shares of the subsidiary on the basis of the above information showing clearly the value calculated on each basis.   (20 marks)

(b) Explain fully which basis is regarded as most appropriate.   (10 marks)

9   TUTORIAL QUESTION: FINANCING EXPANSION

Mosgiel plc is currently financed by four million ordinary shares each of £1.00 par value. The shares have a market value of £3.50 each ex div. No debt finance has ever been used by the company and the share price currently reflects the market's belief that debt will never be used.

The newly appointed managing director wishes to undertake a major expansion project and to finance the cost of the project entirely by fixed interest debt finance.

The after tax operating cash flows relating to the project are:

Cost   £5,000,000
Benefit   £600,000 a year in perpetuity

The managing director proposes that the project be financed by the issue of £5,000,000 of 10% irredeemable debentures to be issued at par. 10% is the current competitive market rate of interest for long term debt and Mosgiel's ability to obtain finance at that rate reflects its good credit rating. Mosgiel's financial advisors have indicated that 'It is only possible to obtain debt finance equal to the entire cost of the project as Mosgiel has previously been all equity financed and has, therefore, considerable unused borrowing capacity. Our calculations show that after obtaining the debt finance and undertaking this project Mosgiel will be at a level of gearing which we believe to be optimum for the company; we measure gearing in terms of expected market values of debt and

9

equity. If Mosgiel had been at this optimum level of gearing before proposing this project then the amount of borrowing justified by the project would be restricted to the optimum level, again measured in terms of market, rather than book, values'.

Mosgiel's management team are, in principle, in favour of expansion but there is considerable opposition to the use of debt finance and it is suggested that the project be funded by an issue of shares at their full market price. It is agreed that it is not likely that Mosgiel will have any other opportunities for expansion in the foreseeable future if the proposed project is rejected and that it is not feasible to alter the capital structure of Mosgiel unless a large expansion project is simultaneously undertaken.

Mosgiel's current after tax cost of equity capital is 15% and the new project has the same risk characteristics as the firm's existing activities. Mosgiel pursues a full dividend payment policy whereby no earnings are retained. This policy will continue.

The tax rate is 40%, debt interest is a tax deductible expense and there is no delay in receiving the benefit of tax relief.

Issue costs may be ignored.

Required

(a) Using maximisation of the wealth of existing shareholders as the objective, determine whether the project should be undertaken:

(i) if it is all equity financed;

(ii) if it is financed by the proposed debenture issue. Calculate the change in the wealth of the existing shareholders, and the new market values of debt and equity, if the project is undertaken and financed by the debenture;

(iii) if Mosgiel were previously at the level of gearing implied in (ii) above and would remain at this gearing level after undertaking the project.

(b) Assuming the project is undertaken and financed by the debenture issue, calculate Mosgiel's:

(i) weighted average cost of capital after undertaking the project; and
(ii) incremental cost of capital when compared with its previous all equity state.

Use the results to support the conclusions reached in (ii) and (iii) of part (a) above.

(c) Explain whether the project is worthwhile and whether it should be undertaken if financed by the debenture. Fully analyse the reasons for the change in shareholders' wealth if the project, financed by the debenture, is undertaken.

You may assume that leverage has an effect on the firm's valuation only through the tax implications of debt interest.

Guidance notes

1   You must first establish the net present value of the project, applying the perpetuity formula.

2   In part (a)(ii), you need to calculate the new total value of the company, taking account of the effect of gearing. The formula you need is $V_g = V_u + Dt$. The term Dt is the value of tax relief on debt interest.

3   In part (a)(iii) the same formula should be used, but should be applied to the project only. This is because the project will make no difference to the value of the existing business, as the project will not affect the gearing of the existing business.

4   In part (b)(i), the WACC can be found as the total return to investors divided by the firm's total market value. The total return is made up of the existing return and the return from the new project.

5   The incremental cost of capital is the return from the new project divided by the increase it causes in the firm's value.

6   In part (c), the overall gain to equity from the project is to be analysed into the NPV of the project if all equity financed, the effect of gearing with regard to the project, and the general effect of gearing. These should add up to the net gain to equity found in part (a)(ii).

10   CRESTLEE (25 marks)   3.2, 12/92

It is now 19X2. Crestlee plc is evaluating two projects. The first involves a £4.725 million expenditure on new machinery to expand the company's existing operations in the textile industry. The second is a diversification into the packaging industry, and will cost £9.275 million.

Crestlee's summarised balance sheet, and those of Canall and Sealalot plc two quoted companies in the packaging industry, are shown below. *Packaging*

	Crestlee plc £m	Canall plc £m	Sealalot plc £m
Fixed assets	96	42	76
Current assets	95	82	65
Less current liabilities	(70)	(72)	(48)
	121	52	93
Financed by:			
Ordinary shares[1]	15	10	30
Reserves	50	27	50
Medium and long-term loans[2]	56	15	13
	121	52	93
Ordinary share price (pence)	380	180	230
Debenture price (£)	104	112	-
Equity beta	1.2	1.3	1.2

[1]Crestlee and Sealalot 50 pence par value, Canall 25 pence par value.

[2]Crestlee 12% debentures 19X8-19Y0, Canall 14% debentures 19Y3, Sealalot medium-term bank loan.

Crestlee proposes to finance the expansion of textile operations with a £4.725 million 11% loan stock issue, and the packaging investment with a £9.275 million rights issue at a discount of 10% on the current market price. Issue costs may be ignored.

Crestlee's managers are proposing to use a discount rate of 15% per year to evaluate each of these projects.

The risk free rate of interest is estimated to be 6% per year and the market return 14% per year. Corporate tax is at a rate of 33% per year.

Required

(a) Determine whether 15% per year is an appropriate discount rate to use for each of these projects. Explain your answer and state clearly any assumptions that you make.

                                                           (19 marks)

(b) Crestlee's marketing director suggests that it is incorrect to use the same discount rate each year for the investment in packaging as the early stages of the investment are more risky, and should be discounted at a higher rate. Another board member disagrees saying that more distant cash flows are riskier and should be discounted at a higher rate. Discuss the validity of the views of each of the directors.   (6 marks)

11   BERLAN AND CANALOT (25 marks)   3.2, 12/91

(a) Berlan plc has annual earnings before interest and tax of £15 million. These earnings are expected to remain constant. The market price of the company's ordinary shares is 86 pence per share cum div and of debentures £105.50 per debenture ex interest. An interim dividend of six pence per share has been declared. Corporate tax is at the rate of 35% and all available earnings are distributed as dividends.

Berlan's long term capital structure is shown below.

	£'000
Ordinary shares (25 pence par value)	12,500
Reserves	24,300
	36,800
16% debenture 31.12.X4 (£100 par value)	23,697
	60,497

Required

Calculate the cost of capital of Berlan plc according to the traditional theory of capital structure. Assume that it is now 31 December 19X1. (8 marks)

(b) Canalot plc is an all equity company with an equilibrium market value of £32.5 million and a cost of capital of 18% per year.

The company proposed to repurchase £5 million of equity and to replace it with 13% irredeemable loan stock.

Canalot's earnings before interest and tax are expected to be constant for the foreseeable future. Corporate tax is at the rate of 35%. All profits are paid out as dividends.

Required

Using the assumptions of Modigliani and Miller explain and demonstrate how this change in capital structure will affect:

(i) the market value
(ii) the cost of equity
(iii) the cost of capital

of Canalot plc. (7 marks)

(c) Explain any weaknesses of both the traditional and Modigliani and Miller theories and discuss how useful they might be in the determination of the appropriate capital structure for a company. (10 marks)

12 TUTORIAL QUESTION: COST OF EQUITY

It is commonly accepted that a crucial factor in the financial decisions of a company, including the evaluation of capital investment proposals, is the cost of capital.

Required

(a) Explain in simple terms what is meant by the 'cost of equity capital' for a particular company.

(b) Calculate the cost of equity capital for X plc from the data given below, using two alternative methods:

(i) a dividend growth model;

(ii) the Capital Asset Pricing Model.

Data

X plc:	current price per share on the Stock Exchange	£1.20
	current annual gross dividend per share	£0.10
	expected average annual growth rate of dividends	7%
	beta coefficient for X plc shares	0.5
Expected rate of return on risk-free securities		8%
Expected return on the market portfolio		12%

(c) State, for each model separately, the main simplifying assumptions made and express your opinion whether, in view of these assumptions, the models yield results that can be used safely in practice.

Guidance notes

1   The first part of this question tests your understanding of the basic idea of the cost of equity capital. Your answer need not be long, but it should be carefully thought out. Try writing an answer, and then go back and revise it to produce the best answer you can.

2   Part (b) can be answered by selecting the appropriate data and putting them into the formulae. To help you without making the question too easy, here are the formulae without definitions of the variables.

   (i)   The dividend growth model: $\dfrac{D_0(1 + g)}{MV} + g$

   (ii) The CAPM: $r_f + \beta\,(r_m - r_f)$

3   To answer part (c), you need to be aware of the theories underlying the formulae. At an early stage in your studies, you may do better simply to read the answer, and to think about how it relates to your answer to part (b).

13   SHORT QUESTIONS   (12 marks)

(a) What formula should be used to express the ordinary shareholder's cost of capital on the assumption that the company's rate of dividend growth will be constant in perpetuity and given that 'D' is the dividend in Year 1?   (4 marks)

(b) What is the meaning of 'systematic risk' in relation to the Capital Asset Pricing Model?
                                                                                          (4 marks)

(c) What is meant by the procedure of 'arbitrage' assumed by Modigliani and Miller in their 1958 paper on the capital structure of firms, and what factors might invalidate this procedure in practice?   (4 marks)

14   TUTORIAL QUESTION: SHARE PRICES AND RETURNS

(a) Page plc is an all equity company whose shares have a beta value of 1.2. The managing director has commented that the actual share price behaviour is frequently inconsistent with that value of beta. Three examples are given. In each case, the risk free rate of return was 2%.

Case 1

In a month when a dividend of 15p per share was paid the share price and stock market all share index values were as follows.

	Share price	Index
At the start of the month	100p	300
At the end of the month	93p	316
Return based on opening and closing price levels	(7%)	5.333%

Case 2

In a month when a 1 for 2 bonus issue was made, but no dividend was paid, the share price and stock market all share index values were as follows.

	Share price	Index
At the start of the month	200p	360
At the end of the month	120p	325.2
Return based on opening and closing price levels	(40%)	(9.667%)

BPP Publishing

Case 3

In many months, when no dividends were paid or bonus issues etc made, the actual share price movement was considerably different from, and sometimes in the opposite direction to that expected of a share with a beta of 1.2.

Required

Comment on each of the cases, explaining the extent to which the share price behaviour is in reality inconsistent with the beta value given. For cases 1 and 2 show the end of month share price which would have occurred if share price behaviour had in those circumstances been exactly as expected given a beta of 1.2.

(b) Cee and Dee are identical in all operating and risk characteristics. Company Cee is all equity financed whereas company Dee's capital structure, at market values, is

	%
Debt	20
Equity	80

Cee's beta is 0.9.

Required

Comment on the view that as the companies are of equal risk then Dee's equity beta will equal 0.9. Estimate the likely value of Dee's equity beta if taxation is assessed at a rate of:

(i)   zero;
(ii)   40%.

Assume that Dee's debt is virtually risk free.

Guidance notes

1   In part (a), cases 1 and 2, we must first recalculate the actual returns achieved. When a dividend is paid, the dividend must be included in the returns to shareholders. When a bonus issue is made, extra shares are issued without an increase in the company's resources, so the share price will fall in proportion to the new shares issued, and the share price after the issue must be adjusted for this.

2   We must then use the CAPM formula, $r_f + \beta (r_m - r_f)$, to work out the return which should have been achieved. From that we can work out what the share price at the end of each month should have been, as the opening price $\times$ (1 + return as a proportion), with an adjustment for the dividend or the bonus issue.

3   In part (b) you are required to find the beta of a geared company (Dee) from that of an ungeared company. The formula (without definitions of the variables) is $\beta_u(1 + (1 - t)D/E)$.

15   TUTORIAL QUESTION: BETA FACTORS

Company A has one project lasting one year. Company B has three projects each lasting one year and in different industries.

The net cash flows and beta factors associated with the projects are as follows.

		£'000	*Beta factor*
Company A		200	1.2
Company B	Project 1	50	1.5
	Project 2	50	1.5
	Project 3	100	0.9

The market return is 10% and the risk free rate of interest is 5%.

Required

(a) Calculate the total present value of projects undertaken by:

    (i)   Company A;
    (ii)   Company B.

(b) Determine the overall beta factor of Company B assuming that all projects are undertaken.

(c) Based upon this information only discuss which company is likely to be valued more highly by an investor.

Guidance notes

1   Part (a) requires you to apply the CAPM formula to find required rates of return, and then to apply those rates to find present values.

2   Part (b) can be answered by calculating a weighted average of beta factors. The weighting should be based on the present values found in part (a)(ii).

3   Part (c) requires you to consider which company is likely to be more highly valued. You could make a decision based on present values and levels of risk, though you would find that such a decision is by no means clear cut. Another consideration is the diversification achieved by company B. To what extent is that relevant?

16 PORTFOLIO RISK (25 marks)

(a) For an investment portfolio consisting of a large number of securities, the important feature determining the riskiness of the portfolio is the way in which the returns on the individual securities vary together.

Illustrate this statement by making calculations from the simplified data given in the table below in relation to a portfolio comprising 40% of Security A and 60% of Security B. You may ignore the possibility of no correlation between the rates of return.

Probability	Predicted return Security A %	Predicted return Security B %
0.2	12	15
0.6	15	20
0.2	18	25

(10 marks)

(b) An investor in risky securities is presumed to select an investment portfolio which is on the efficient frontier and touches one of his *indifference curves* at a tangent.

Required

    (i)   Give a detailed explanation of the above statement, with particular attention to the expressions in italics.

    (ii)   Illustrate your answers with a relevant diagram.   (15 marks)

17 CAPITAL MARKET LINE (13 marks)

Two investors, X and Y, have portfolios which lie on the Capital Market Line. X has one third of his funds invested at the risk-free rate, which is 12%, and the remainder in a market portfolio of equities. The expected return on his total portfolio is 18% with a standard deviation of 12%. Y's expected return on his total portfolio is 24%. Both investors can lend and borrow at the risk-free rate.

BPP Publishing

Required

(a) Explain, with supporting calculations, the composition of the expected return of both portfolios in terms of equity returns and fixed interest. (6 marks)

(b) Give a freehand graphical representation of the Capital Market Line showing the position of each investor's portfolio. (4 marks)

(c) On the assumption that X wishes to keep his portfolio on the Capital Market Line, calculate what standard deviation he would have to accept in order to increase his expected return to 20% and explain how the composition of his portfolio would change. (3 marks)

18 INVESTOR (30 marks)

An investor has a portfolio of shares in five listed companies:

Company	Number of shares held
Ace plc	5,000 shares of 1p
Black plc	8,000 shares of 50p
Club plc	10,000 shares of 25p
Diamond plc	12,000 shares of 20p
Eight plc	15,000 shares of 10p

The following data is given regarding the shares:

	Market price per share	Current dividend yield	Beta factor	Actual expected return during next year
Ace plc	250p	3.2%	1.35	17.5%
Black plc	225p	4.1%	1.25	15.0%
Club plc	180p	5.2%	0.90	13.2%
Diamond plc	150p	2.7%	1.10	15.1%
Eight plc	80p	1.9%	0.85	12.7%

At present the risk-free rate of return is 9%, while the return on the market is 15%.

Required

(a) Calculate the beta factor for the portfolio and the required return on the portfolio.
(10 marks)

(b) Explain whether the individual shares in the portfolio appear to be over- or under-valued. What action would this imply for the portfolio manager? (10 marks)

(c) Explain the relevance of portfolio theory to a real-world portfolio manager. (10 marks)

19 OTC INVESTMENTS (25 marks)

A company is planning to make investments of £250,000 in each of two companies which have no main market listing. The investments will form part of a portfolio of medium-term investments totalling approximately £28 million for use when acquisitions are made in the future. The management of the company has drawn up a short-list of three possible investments, called A, B and C below. The following information is available on the investments.

	A	B	C
Expected return	17%	16%	14%
Standard deviation of returns	6.4	4.3	2.5

	A & C	B & C	A & B
Covariances of returns	12.6	8.4	4.4

It has been proposed that investments B and C should be chosen, on the basis that together they have the most efficient risk/return profile.

BPP Publishing

Required

(a) Outline the main characteristics of the OTC market and explain the merits and demerits of the company investing in OTC companies. (5 marks)

(b) Calculate estimated coefficients of correlation between the three investments, explaining the implications for the risk of the portfolio. (5 marks)

(c) Test whether it is the case that investment in B and C together results in the most efficient risk/return profile. (9 marks)

(d) Discuss the proposition that OTC investments should be included in the portfolio because of their particular risk/return profile. (6 marks)

20 SLOHILL PLC (25 marks)   3.2, 12/89

Slohill plc plans to raise finance sometime within the next few months. Slohill's managing director remembers a stock market crash of October 19X7 when share prices fell approximately 30% during one week, and is worried about the possible effects of a further crash on the cost of capital.

SLOHILL PLC
SUMMARISED BALANCE SHEET AS AT 31 MARCH 19X9

	£m	£m
Fixed assets at cost less depreciation		262.20
Current assets		
Stock	69.00	
Debtors	82.80	
Bank	27.60	
	179.40	
Current liabilities		
Creditors	75.31	
Dividend	8.99	
Taxation	26.10	
	110.40	
		69.00
Less 11% debenture, redeemable in 15 years		(138.00)
Net assets		193.20
Ordinary shares (£1 per value)		69.00
Reserves		124.20
		193.20

5 YEAR SUMMARISED PROFIT AND LOSS ACCOUNT

Year ended 31 March	Turnover £m	Profit before tax £m	Tax £m	Profit after tax £m	Dividend £m
19X5	583.7	49.63	19.85	29.78	9.86
19X6	644.6	58.42	20.45	37.97	10.94
19X7	639.5	59.61	20.86	38.75	12.17
19X8	742.3	62.43	21.85	40.58	13.48
19X9	810.6	74.57	26.10	48.47	14.98

The company's current share price is 546 pence ex div, and the debenture price is £93. No new share or debenture capital has been issued during the last five years. Corporate tax is at the rate of 35%.

If another crash were to occur it would lead to increased demand for gilts and other fixed interest stocks and a change of approximately 2% in all interest rates.

BPP Publishing

Required

(a) Estimate what effect a second stock market crash of the same magnitude as in 19X7 might have on Slohill's current weighted average cost of capital if:

  (i)   the crash has negligible effect on the earnings expectations of the company and on the growth rate of the company's earnings;

  (ii) the annual pre-tax growth rate of the company's earnings is expected to fall by 20%.

  State clearly any assumptions that you make.   (16 marks)

(b) If a second stock market crash were to occur, advise the managing director of the likely effect on the cost of capital of raising a substantial amount of new capital:

  (i)   if the capital raised is all equity;
  (ii) if the capital raised is all debt.   (4 marks)

(c) If the capital asset pricing model were to be used to estimate the cost of equity in scenarios (a)(i) and (a)(ii) above explain in which direction the main variables in the model would be likely to move.   (5 marks)

21   NELSON (24 marks)   3.2, 12/84

The management of Nelson plc wish to estimate their firm's equity beta. Nelson has had a stock market quotation for only two months and the financial manager feels that it would be inappropriate to attempt to estimate beta from the actual share price behaviour over such a short period. Instead it is proposed to ascertain, and where necessary adjust, the observed equity betas of other companies operating in the same industry, and with the same operating characteristics as Nelson, as these should be based on similar levels of systematic risk and be capable of providing an accurate estimate of Nelson's beta.

Three companies have been identified as firms having operations in the same industry as Nelson with identical operating characteristics. However, only one company, Oak plc, operates exclusively in the same industry as Nelson. The other two companies have some dissimilar activities or opportunities in addition to those which are the same as those of Nelson.

Details of the three companies are as follows.

(a) Oak plc has an observed equity beta of 1.12. The capital structure at market values is 60% equity, 40% debt.

(b) Beech plc has an observed equity beta of 1.11. It is estimated that 30% of the current market value of Beech is caused by risky growth opportunities which have an estimated beta of 1.9. The growth opportunities are reflected in the observed beta. Beech's other activities are the same as Nelson's. Beech is financed entirely by equity.

(c) Pine plc has an observed equity beta of 1.14. Pine has two divisions, East and West. East's operating characteristics are considered to be identical to those of Nelson. The operating characteristics of West are considered to be 50% more risky than those of East. In terms of financial valuation East is estimated as being twice as valuable as West. The capital structure of Pine at market values is 75% equity, 25% debt.

Nelson is financed entirely by equity. The tax rate is 40%.

Required

(a) Assuming all debt is virtually risk free, make three estimates of the equity beta of Nelson plc. The three estimates should be based, separately, on the information provided for Oak, Beech and Pine.   (12 marks)

(b) Explain why the estimated beta of Nelson, when eventually determined from observed share price movements, may differ from the values derived from the approach employed in (a) above.   (7 marks)

(c) State the reason why a company which has a very volatile share price and is generally considered to be extremely risky can have a lower beta value, and therefore lower financial risk, than an equally geared firm whose share price is much less volatile. (5 marks)

22   UNIVO   (25 marks)   3.2, 12/91

(a) Stock market analysts sometimes use fundamental analysis and sometimes technical analysis to forecast future share prices. What are fundamental analysis and technical analysis?
(6 marks)

(b) Summarised financial data for Univo plc is shown below.

PROFIT AND LOSS ACCOUNTS

	19W9	19X0	19X1[1]
	£'000	£'000	£'000
Turnover	76,270	89,410	102,300
Taxable income	10,140	12,260	14,190
Taxation	3,549	4,291	4,966
	6,591	7,969	9,224
Dividend	2,335	2,557	2,800
Retained earnings	4,256	5,412	6,424

BALANCE SHEET

	19X1[1]
	£'000
Fixed assets	54,200
Current assets	39,500
Current liabilities	(26,200)
	67,500
Ordinary shares (50 pence par value)	20,000
Reserves	32,500
10% debentures 19X6 (£100 par value)	15,000
	67,500

[1] 19X1 figures are unaudited estimates.

As a result of recent capital investment, stock market analysts expect post tax earnings and dividends to increase by 25% for two years and then to revert to the company's existing growth rates.

Univo's asset (overall) beta is 0.763 and beta of debt is 0.20. The risk free rate is 12% and the market return 17%. The current market price of Univo's ordinary shares is 217 pence, cum 19X1 dividend, and the debenture price is £89.50 ex interest. Corporate tax is at the rate of 35%.

Required

(i) Using the dividend growth model estimate what a fundamental analyst might consider to be the intrinsic (or realistic) value of the company's shares. Comment upon the significance of your estimate for the fundamental analyst.

Assume, for this part of the question only, that the cost of equity is not expected to change. The cost of equity may be estimated by using the CAPM. (10 marks)

(ii) If interest rates were to increase by 2% and expected dividend growth to remain unchanged, estimate what effect this would be likely to have on the intrinsic value of the company's shares. (3 marks)

(c) Explain whether your answer to (b)(i) is consistent with the semi-strong and strong forms of the efficient market hypothesis (EMH), and comment upon whether financial analysts serve any useful purpose in an efficient market. (6 marks)

23 ABC (25 marks)   **3.2, 12/87**

(a) Discuss the factors that might influence a company's choice of dividend policy.

(10 marks)

(b) The managing directors of three profitable listed companies discussed their companies' dividend policies at a business lunch.

Company A has deliberately paid no dividends for the last five years.

Company B always pays a dividend of 50% of earnings after taxation.

Company C maintains a low but constant dividend per share (after adjusting for the general price index), and offers regular scrip issues and shareholder concessions.

Each managing director is convinced that his company's policy is maximising shareholder wealth.

Required

What are the advantages and disadvantages of the alternative dividend policies of the three companies? Discuss the circumstances under which each managing director might be correct in his belief that his company's dividend policy is maximising shareholder wealth. State clearly any assumptions that you make.   (15 marks)

24 TUTORIAL QUESTION: DIVIDEND VALUATION MODEL AND DIVIDEND POLICY

The following financial data relate to RG plc.

Year	Earnings per share (Pence)	Net dividend per share (Pence)	Share price (Pence)
19X7	42	17	252
19X8	46	18	184
19X9	51	20	255
19Y0	55	22	275
19Y1	62	25	372

A firm of market analysts which specialises in the industry in which RG plc operates has recently re-evaluated the company's future profits. The analysts estimate that RG plc's earnings and dividends will grow at 25% for the next two years. Thereafter, earnings are likely to increase at a lower annual rate of 10%. If this reduction in earnings growth occurs, the analysts consider that the dividend payout ratio will be increased to 50%.

RG plc is all equity financed and has one million ordinary shares in issue.

The tax rate of 33% is not expected to change in the foreseeable future.

Required

(a) Calculate the estimate share price and P/E ratio which the analysts now expect for RG plc, using the dividend valuation model, and comment briefly on the method of valuation you have just used. Assume a constant post-tax cost of capital of 18 per cent.

(b) Comment on whether the dividend policy being considered by the analysts would be appropriate for the company in the following two sets of circumstances:

(i)   the company's shareholders are mainly financial institutions; and
(ii) the company's shareholders are mainly small private investors.

(c) Describe briefly *three* other dividend policies which RG plc could consider.

Guidance notes

1   Part (a) requires the dividend valuation model to be applied in circumstances where there is a change in the growth rate. A DCF approach to each of the first three years should be used, with the standard formula being applied for the subsequent periods. Do not forget to discount the dividend figure to be used in the formula as well as the figures for the previous years.

2   Part (b) provides the opportunity to display your knowledge of recent developments in the discussion of dividend policy from the financial press. Examples of the more extreme policies can be given, together with examples of pronouncements made by some of the institutions.

3   When this question was set (in a CIMA examination), it was allocated 25 marks in total (10 for part (a); 8 for part (b); 7 for part (c)).

25   DEERWOOD PLC   (25 marks) 3.2, 12/89

The board of directors of Deerwood plc are arguing about the company's dividend policy.

Director A is in favour of financing all investment by retained earnings and other internally generated funds. He argues that a high level of retentions will save issue costs, and that declaring dividends always results in a fall in share price when the shares are traded ex div.

Director B believes that the dividend policy depends upon the type of shareholders that the company has, and that dividends should be paid according to shareholders' needs. She presents data to the board relating to studies of dividend policy in the USA six years ago, and a breakdown of the company's current shareholders.

Company group (10 companies per group)	US dividend research Mean dividend yield %	Average marginal tax rate of shareholders %
1	7.02	16
2	5.18	22
3	4.17	25
4	3.52	33
5	1.26	45

DEERWOOD PLC: ANALYSIS OF SHAREHOLDINGS

	Number of shareholders	Shares held (million)	% of total shares held
Pension funds	203	38.4	25.1
Insurance companies	41	7.8	5.1
Unit and investment trusts	53	18.6	12.1
Nominees	490	32.4	21.2
Individuals	44,620	55.9	36.5
	45,407	153.1	100.0

She argues that the company's shareholder 'clientèle' must be identified, and dividends fixed according to their marginal tax rates.

Director C agrees that shareholders are important, but points out that many institutional shareholders and private individuals rely on dividends to satisfy their current income requirements, and prefer a known dividend now to an uncertain capital gain in the future.

Director D considers the discussion to be a waste of time. He believes that any one dividend policy is as good as any other, and that dividend policy has no effect on the company's share price. In support of his case he cites the equation by Modigliani and Miller.

$$nP_0 = \frac{1}{1+\rho} \; [(n+m)P_1 - I + X]$$

Where P_0 = market price at time 0
        P_1 = market price at time 1

BPP Publishing

n = number of shares at time 0
m = number of new shares sold at time 1
ρ = capitalisation rate for the company
I = total new investments during period 1
X = total profit of the company during period 1

Required

Critically discuss the arguments of each of the four directors using both the information provided and other evidence on the effect of dividend policy on share price that you consider to be relevant.

BPP Publishing

DO YOU KNOW? - BUSINESS PLANNING

- *Check that you know the following basic points before you attempt any questions. If in doubt, go back to your Study Text and revise first.*

- Plans are made within a framework of objectives. These may include maximising shareholder wealth; maximising turnover; improving conditions for management and staff.

- The performance of a company is primarily assessed using trends and ratios. *Time series* of turnover and profits indicate whether a company is growing or declining. *Ratios* facilitate comparisons over time or between companies.

- The main ratios include: return on capital employed; profit:sales; sales:capital employed; cost of sales:sales; other expenses:sales; debtors:sales; current ratio; quick ratio; debt:equity; interest cover; dividend cover.

- Other sources of information should also be used in appraising a company's performance. These include the following.
  o Information in the accounts and in the notes to the accounts
  o The chairman's report
  o The directors' report
  o Press comments on the company or on the industry in which it operates
  o Published statistics on output and profitability in the relevant industry

- A takeover (subject to the City Code) may involve an offer to shareholders in the target company of any or all of cash; shares; loan stock.

- In a share exchange, the ratio of exchange (for example two shares for five) must be acceptable to the shareholders of both companies.
  o Shareholders will be particularly concerned about post-takeover earnings per share and post-merger asset backing.
  o Holders of the shares valued on the lower P/E ratio will suffer a loss of earnings.
  o This loss of earnings may be compensated for by an increase in overall earnings because of synergy.

- In a management buyout, a division of a company or the whole company is sold to a management team.
  o Substantial external finance is often required, leaving the bought-out business with a heavy burden of interest payments.

- There are many different ways of valuing a company, including the following.
  o Balance sheet value
  o Replacement cost of assets
  o Realisable values of assets
  o The dividend growth model
  o The P/E ratio model

- These methods are likely to yield different values for the same company. The choice of method will depend on the purpose of the valuation.

- To use the P/E ratio method, we must first establish a P/E ratio using listed companies in the same industry. Such a ratio may need adjusting, for example if the company being valued is unlisted.

- A scheme of capitalisation is a scheme to finance a company or a substantial project with a source of finance or a mixture of sources.

- *Key questions*

  29 *Oxold*
  30 *Adsum*
  31 *Tutorial question: Report on a subsidiary*
  38 *Tutorial question: Bases of valuation*
  41 *Apcon*
  44 *Goodsleep*

BPP Publishing

26 CORPORATE PLANNING (12½ marks) 3.2, 12/92, part question

You have been asked to advise on how to develop the planning process for a company. Discuss what stages the company is likely to go through in its corporate planning.

27 AGGRESSIVE, MODERATE OR CONSERVATIVE (10 marks)

Two aspects of working capital policy which require managerial decisions are the level of current assets and the manner in which they are financed.

Required

Discuss aggressive, moderate and conservative policies in these areas.

28 TUTORIAL QUESTION: IMPROVING CASH FLOW

B Ltd is a wholly owned subsidiary of A plc and currently depends entirely on the parent company for any necessary finance.

A plc, however, has its own cash flow problems and cannot permit B Ltd temporary loan facilities in excess of £50,000 at any time, even though the business of B Ltd is highly seasonal and is in a period of growth.

B Ltd has just prepared its cash budget for the year ahead, details of which are as follows. All figures are in thousand of pounds.

Month	1	2	3	4	5	6	7	8	9	10	11	12
Collections from customers	230	250	120	50	60	75	80	90	110	150	220	320
Dividend on investment							45					
Total inflows	230	250	120	50	60	75	125	90	110	150	220	320
Payments to suppliers		80		80		88		88		88		92
Wages and other expenses	102	77	58	103	79	59	105	80	62	108	83	63
Payments for fixed assets				70	10		15				5	
Dividend payable			80									
Corporation tax									120			
Total outflows	102	157	138	253	89	147	120	168	182	196	88	155
Net in or (out)	128	93	(18)	(203)	(29)	(72)	5	(78)	(72)	(46)	132	165
Bank balance/ (overdraft):												
Opening	30	158	251	233	30	1	(71)	(66)	(144)	(216)	(262)	(130)
Closing	158	251	233	30	1	(71)	(66)	(144)	(216)	(262)	(130)	35

The following supplementary information is provided.

(a) Two months credit on average is granted to customers.

(b) Production is scheduled evenly throughout the year. Year-end stocks of finished goods are forecast to be £114,000 higher than at the beginning of the year.

(c) Purchases of raw materials are made at two-monthly intervals. Three months' credit, on average, is taken from suppliers.

(d) The capital expenditure budget comprises:

New equipment for planned production	Month 4	£70,000
Routine replacement of motor vehicles	Month 5	£10,000
Progress payment on building extensions	Month 7	£15,000
Office furniture and equipment	Month 11	£5,000

Required

Review this information and advise the board of B Ltd on possible actions it might take to improve its budgeted cash flow for the year and to avoid any difficulties you can foresee.

Guidance notes

1   A cash budget has been prepared for you, and you are required to analyse it. It is obvious from the closing balances in the latter half of the year that there is a problem. Your task is to read the budget and the supplementary information carefully and to work out precisely why the problem arises. It is important to ask yourself the right questions.

2   It is unlikely that much can be done about the seasonal nature of sales. Do you think that the running of the business could be better adapted to this seasonal pattern?

3   What do you think of the credit periods granted and taken? Are any of them too long or too short?

4   Which of the payments which are not made every month do you think could be reduced or moved, and by how much?

5   Is there anything else which could be done?

29   OXOLD   (10 marks)   3.2, 12/86, part question

Oxold Ltd uses linear programming to asset in its financial planning. The company wishes to estimate its investment and borrowing levels for the next year.

Divisible investment opportunities exist that would require funds of up to £2,000,000. These investment opportunities are all expected to produce perpetual annual cash flows (after tax) with an internal rate of return of 15% a year. The stock market is expected to capitalise these project cash flows at a rate of 17% a year.

Oxold has £1,500,000 cash available. Any surplus cash, after investments have been undertaken, will be paid out as dividends. The company does not wish to issue new equity capital, but is prepared to finance up to 40% of any investment with new long-term debt which may be assumed to result in a permanent increase in the company's capital. The company pays tax at 35%.

Oxold Ltd wishes to maximise the total value of the company.

Required

(a)   Formulate a linear programming model which could be used to estimate the optimum levels of investment and borrowing for the next year. (Modigliani and Miller's formula for the valuation of a company in a world with taxation might be helpful in this process.) Do not calculate the optimal solution.

(b)   Discuss briefly whether Oxold Ltd is likely to undertake any investment during the next year:

(i)   if no new funds are borrowed;
(ii)   if the company borrows funds through new long-term loans.

30 ADSUM (25 marks) 3.2, 12/91

The directors of Adsum Ltd are working on a three year financial plan. Sales during the period will depend upon the state of the economy.

		Sales at current prices		
Economic state	*Probability*	*Year 1*	*Year 2*	*Year 3*
		£'000	£'000	£'000
Slow growth	0.6	5,300	5,500	5,800
Rapid growth	0.4	6,000	7,100	8,200

If slow growth occurs inflation is expected to be 12% per year and if rapid growth occurs 5% per year. Return on sales (profit before tax to sales) is estimated to be 12% per year in both economic states.

In year 1 assets to the value of £200,000 (after all tax effects) will be disposed of, and in years 2 and 3 new fixed assets costing £1.7 million and £800,000 respectively will be purchased. Disposal and purchase values have been estimated at current prices.

Stock is expected to increase by 80% of the percentage increase in sales, debtors by 90% and creditors by 95%. For example, if sales in year 1 increase by 16% from current financial accounts values, stock at the end of year 1 is expected to increase by 16% × 80% = 12.8% of the current balance sheet value. Sales prices and dividends will be increased in line with inflation, except if this would lead to dividends being less than 22% or greater than 35% of before tax profits, in which case a minimum of 22% or a maximum of 35% respectively would be payable.

Corporate tax is at the rate of 35% and is payable at the end of the year in which profit arises. Capital allowances are expected to be £450,000, £530,000 and £620,000 for years 1, 2 and 3 respectively.

Adsum is not planning to raise external funds by equity or long-term debt issues. A £600,000 overdraft facility exists, which is expected to be available for the three year period, but cannot be increased due to the company's level of gearing.

Summarised current financial accounts of Adsum are shown below.

BALANCE SHEET

	£'000
Fixed assets	4,400
Stock	2,130
Debtors	2,920
Cash	80
	9,530
Creditors	(3,210)
Overdraft	(420)
	5,900
Financed by:	
Ordinary shares (25 pence par)	500
Reserves	2,400
12% seven year term loan	3,000
	5,900

PROFIT AND LOSS ACCOUNT

	£'000
Sales	5,000
Profit before tax	600
Tax	210
	390
Dividend	150
Retained earnings	240

Required

(a) Acting as a consultant to Adsum Limited advise the company on the financial implications of its forecasts as presented. Relevant calculations must be shown. Interest on cash balances or on additional overdraft may be ignored.

State clearly any assumptions that you make. (11 marks)

(b) Discuss possible remedies for any problems that you identify. (5 marks)

(c) Advise Adsum Limited on other techniques that might be useful in the company's medium-term financial planning process and comment upon the assumptions that Adsum has used in its plans. (9 marks)

31   TUTORIAL QUESTION: REPORT ON A SUBSIDIARY

The directors of ABC plc, a conglomerate listed on a stock exchange, are appraising one of their wholly-owned subsidiaries, XYZ Limited, with a view to disinvestment. The subsidiary is primarily involved in the manufacture and distribution of car care products.

Financial data for XYZ Ltd are shown below.

SUMMARY ACCOUNTS FOR XYZ LTD

Balance sheet at 31 December

		19X2 £'000	19X1 £'000
Cash and marketable securities		195	162
Debtors		765	476
Stock and work-in-progress		1,250	893
Other current assets		150	91
Total current assets		2,360	1,622
Plant and equipment		2,650	2,255
Other long-term assets	(Note 1)	750	675
Total assets		5,760	4,552
Current liabilities		715	644
Long-term debt		2,250	1,976
Other long-term liabilities	(Note 2)	275	206
Shareholders' funds		2,520	1,726
Total liabilities		5,760	4,552

Extracts from the profit and loss accounts for the years ended 31 December

		19X2 £'000	19X1 £'000
Turnover		6,575	5,918
Cost of goods sold		5,918	5,444
Other expenses		658	592
Other income		23	20
Earnings before interest and tax (EBIT)		22	(98)
Interest		395	339
Tax on ordinary activities	(Note 3)	(120)	(149)
Net loss		(253)	(288)

Notes

1   Other long-term assets are motor vehicles and office equipment.
2   Other long-term liabilities are finance leases.
3   The tax shown in the 19X1 profit and loss extract will be recovered in 19X2.

Other financial information

	£'000
Depreciation 19X2	175
Net realisable value of stock	1,091
Net realisable value of plant and equipment	3,907
Stock and work-in-progress at 1 January 19X1	850
Debtors at 1 January 19X1	435

Required

(a) Calculate *five* ratios for *each* of the *two* years 19X1 and 19X2 which you consider to be appropriate for the evaluation of the subsidiary's efficiency, profitability and liquidity over the two-year period. Your selection of ratios should ensure measurement of the company's performance in all three areas.

(b) Prepare a report for the management of ABC plc. This report should discuss the following:

(i) the performance of the subsidiary during the past two years, using the ratios calculated in part (a) to guide your comments;

(ii) the limitations of the type of historical data you have just provided;

(iii) suggestions for the parent company's future course of action in respect of the subsidiary, including comment on an appropriate procedure for valuing the company;

(iv) other, non-financial information which would be useful to the directors of ABC plc before they make any decision.

Guidance notes

1   In calculating the ratios, make clear the basis being used and any assumptions made in arriving at the figures.

2   A report format should be used in part (b) of the question. Do not forget to take account of the wider operating environment of the firm as well as the internal information which is provided.

3   In part (b) try to assess what strategy has been pursued over the last two years before coming to any conclusions about divestment.

4   When this question was set (in a CIMA examination), it was allocated 30 marks (10 for part (a); 20 for part (b)).

32   XQ PLC (40 marks)

The directors of XQ plc formally disclosed their overriding objective at a recent annual general meeting when the chairman announced:

'We aim for incrementation of our equity value in the stock markets without taking undue risks.'

This announcement displeased the employee representatives on the Works Council. They have argued that the company's management should favour growth both of profits and of turnover, so providing additional employment opportunities.

The company disclosed the following five-year summary of results in its recently published annual report.

	19X6	19X7	19X8	19X9	19Y0
	£'000	£'000	£'000	£'000	£'000
Turnover	156,826	164,220	167,844	176,408	180,913
Interest charges	5,100	5,100	5,100	7,650	7,650
Profit after taxation	27,251	30,458	28,650	30,612	32,193
Dividend	50 pence	60 pence	70 pence	70 pence	80 pence
PE ratio*	5.7	5.3	6.0	5.5	6.5
Number of employees at year end	1,960	1,723	1,587	1,432	1,157

* based on market prices immediately after the preliminary announcement of annual results.

There were 30 million shares in issue throughout the above five-year period.

Required

(a) Assess whether the directors have, thus far, met their stated objective. (10 marks)

(b) Advise the directors how the apparently conflicting views held by themselves and by the employee representatives should be reconciled. (10 marks)

(c) Advise the employee representatives of what information they would require:

(i) from the company's published annual report and accounts; and
(ii) from the directors, in the event of the information in (i) being insufficient;

in order to support the purchase by employees of the company's shares in a forthcoming issue. (10 marks)

(d) Agency theory presents the firm as a combination of competing interest groups, two of which are shareholders and management.

Required

Discuss how the firm's attitude to risk might vary depending on whether shareholder objectives or management-oriented goals predominate in the firm's planning. (10 marks)

33 CITY CODE (12½ marks)   3.2, 6/92, part question

(a) Briefly discuss the nature and purpose of the City Code on Takeovers and Mergers.

(Discussion of detailed rules is not required.) (5 marks)

(b) Discuss and illustrate how the City Code might influence the behaviour of a financial manager defending a company against an unwelcome takeover bid. (7½ marks)

34 MANAGEMENT BUYOUTS (20 marks)

(a) Define what is meant by a 'management buyout'. (4 marks)

(b) State the purpose of management buyouts and their particular advantages for this purpose. (5 marks)

(c) Describe the possible problems and pitfalls that might be encountered by the managers involved, both in achieving the buyout and subsequently. (6 marks)

(d) Outline various possible sources of finance to assist the buyout. (5 marks)

35 M AND C (15 marks)

M plc is an expanding supermarket company. It has an issued ordinary share capital of 20 million shares. Its earnings before tax were £2,300,000 in the most recent year but an interim profit statement indicates that these should rise to £4,800,000 in the current year. Thereafter, profits are forecast to rise by 20% a year.

C plc, a stores and confectionery group, has an issued ordinary share capital of 42.6 million shares. Last year's pre-tax profits were £6,600,000. No growth is forecast for the current year but growth of about 5% a year is predicted thereafter.

M plc has just approached the shareholders of C plc with an offer of two new shares in M plc for every five C plc shares now held. There is a cash alternative of £1.28 a share.

Following the announcement of the bid, the market price of M plc shares fell from £2.90 to £2.60 whilst the price of C plc shares rose from £1.30 to £1.50. Extracts from the shares service statistics in the financial press, including three other companies in the food retailing sector (H, S and T) were then as follows.

| Previous year | | | | Increase or | Dividend | |
High	Low	Company	Price	decrease	yield %	P/E
290	164	M	260	–30	3.4	14
204	130	C	150	+20	3.6	11
187	122	H	187	+ 4½	6.0	12
230	159	S	230	+ 1½	2.4	17
183	150	T	166	nil	2.8	13

The relevant rate of corporation tax is 35%.

Required

(a) Discuss, with appropriate calculations, whether the proposed share-for-share offer is likely to be beneficial to the shareholders in M plc and C plc respectively, both immediately and over the next four years, assuming that the estimates of growth given above are achieved and that no further issues of equity are made. (12 marks)

(b) State in general terms the circumstances under which dilution of earnings per share might be acceptable as a result of a takeover or merger. (3 marks)

36 JUSTIFICATIONS (10 marks)

Discuss the validity of the following reasons that might be advanced by a company to justify a decision to expand the business by way of a takeover or merger.

(a) Economies of scale will be achieved.
(b) Diversification reduces risk.
(c) The shares of the target company are undervalued.

37 TUTORIAL QUESTION: BID CALCULATIONS

Provincial plc is contemplating a bid for the share capital of National plc. The following statistics are available.

	Provincial plc	National plc
Number of shares	14 million	45 million
Share price	840p	166p
Latest equity earnings	£11,850,000	£9,337,500

Provincial plc's plan is to reduce the scale of National plc's operations by selling off a division which accounts for £1,500,000 of National plc's latest earnings, as indicated above. The estimated selling price for the division is £10.2 million.

Earnings in National plc's remaining operations could be increased by an estimated 20% on a permanent basis by the introduction of better management and financial controls. Provincial plc does not anticipate any alteration to National plc's price/earnings multiple as a result of these improvements in earnings.

To avoid duplication, some of Provincial plc's own property could be disposed of at an estimated price of £16 million.

Rationalisation costs are estimated at £4.5 million.

Required

(a) Calculate the effect on the current share price of each company, all other things being equal, of a two for nine share offer by Provincial plc, assuming that Provincial plc's estimates are in line with those of the market.

(b) Offer a rational explanation of why the market might react to the bid by valuing National plc's shares at (i) a higher figure and (ii) a lower figure than that indicated by Provincial plc's offer even though the offer is in line with market estimates of the potential merger synergy.

(c) Assume that Provincial plc is proposing to offer National plc shareholders the choice of the two for nine share exchange or a cash alternative.

Advise Provincial plc whether the cash alternative should be more or less than the current value of the share exchange, giving your reasons.

(d) Assume now that Provincial plc, instead of making a two for nine share exchange offer, wishes to offer an exchange which would give National plc shareholders a 10% gain on the existing value of their shares.

Calculate what share exchange would achieve this effect, assuming the same synergy forecasts as before.

Guidance notes

1 The first part of the question requires the calculation of the theoretical market capitalisation of the new group post merger. This can be derived by calculating the new level of equity earnings in National plc and applying the P/E ratio to find the new value of the earnings.

2 The capital inflows and outflows arising from acquisition can then be included to arrive at the total post merger capitalisation. Since the number of shares in the new group is known, this can then be used to find the theoretical share prices.

3 Parts (b) and (c) require an understanding of the way in which the market reacts to bids in practice, and of factors influencing the way in which investors will react to cash and paper offers.

4 When this question was set in an exam (for the CIMA), it was worth 25 marks (10 marks for part (a); 5 marks for each remaining part).

38 TUTORIAL QUESTION: BASES OF VALUATION

The directors of Carmen plc, a large conglomerate, are considering the acquisition of the entire share capital of Manon Ltd, which manufactures a range of engineering machinery. Neither company has any long-term debt capital. The directors of Carmen plc believe that if Manon is taken over, the business risk of Carmen will not be affected.

The accounting reference date of Manon is 31 July. Its balance sheet as on 31 July 19X4 is expected to be as follows.

	£	£
Fixed assets (net of depreciation)		651,600
Current assets: stocks and work in progress	515,900	
debtors	745,000	
bank balances	158,100	
		1,149,000
		2,070,600
Current liabilities: creditors	753,600	
bank overdraft	862,900	
		1,616,500
		454,100

	£
Capital and reserves: issued ordinary shares of £1 each	50,000
distributable reserves	404,100
	454,100

Manon's summarised financial record for the five years to 31 July 19X4 is as follows.

Year ended 31 July	19X0	19X1	19X2	19X3	19X4 (estimated)
	£	£	£	£	£
Profit before extraordinary items	30,400	69,000	49,400	48,200	53,200
Extraordinary items	2,900	(2,200)	(6,100)	(9,800)	(1,000)
Profit after extraordinary items	33,300	66,800	43,300	38,400	52,200
Less dividends	20,500	22,600	25,000	25,000	25,000
Added to reserves	12,800	44,200	18,300	13,400	27,200

The following additional information is available.

(a) There have been no changes in the issued share capital of Manon Ltd during the past five years.

(b) The estimated values of Manon's fixed assets and stocks and work in progress as on 31 July 19X4 are as follows.

	Replacement cost £	Realisable value £
Fixed assets	725,000	450,000
Stocks and work in progress	550,000	570,000

(c) It is expected that 2% of Manon's debtors at 31 July 19X4 will be uncollectable.

(d) The cost of capital of Carmen plc is 9%. The directors of Manon Ltd estimate that the shareholders of Manon require a minimum return of 12% per annum from their investment in the company.

(e) The current P/E ratio of Carmen plc is 12. Quoted companies with business activities and profitability similar to those of Manon have P/E ratios of approximately 10, although these companies tend to be much larger than Manon.

Required

(a) Estimate the value of the total equity of Manon Ltd as on 31 July 19X4 using each of the following bases:

(i) balance sheet value;
(ii) replacement cost;
(iii) realisable value;
(iv) the Gordon dividend growth model;
(v) the P/E ratio model.

(b) Explain the role and limitations of each of the above five valuation bases in the process by which a price might be agreed for the purchase by Carmen plc of the total equity capital of Manon Ltd.

(c) State and justify briefly the approximate range within which the purchase price is likely to be agreed.

Ignore taxation.

Guidance notes

1 This may at first appear to be a long question, but part (a) is broken down into five small parts, and this will enable you to work through the data systematically.

2   The balance sheet value is simply the value of the shareholders' interest in the business as shown in the balance sheet. The values of certain assets must then be adjusted to get replacement cost (what it would cost to replace them) and realisable value (the amount of cash they could be turned into).

3   The formula for the Gordon dividend growth model is $\dfrac{D_1}{r - g} + D_0$, where D_0 and D_1 are the current dividend and the dividend one year hence respectively, r is the required return and g is the dividend growth rate. In this case, you have to estimate a growth rate. One possibility is to take the average growth rate over 19X0 to 19X4. This is found by taking the fourth root of the fraction 19X4 dividend/19X0 dividend.

4   The P/E ratio valuation is simply earnings × P/E ratio. The problem here is to select an appropriate ratio.

5   In part (b), you must evaluate critically the estimates made in part (a). You should be particularly concerned with the reliability of any estimates or predictions made, and with the relevance of the bases of evaluation to a purchaser intending to run the business as a going concern.

6   In part (c), you should identify the lowest price the vendors might accept and the highest price the purchaser might offer.

39   TAKEOVER   (25 marks)   3.2, 12/92

In a recent meeting of the board of directors of Rayswood plc the chairman proposed the acquisition of Pondhill plc. During his presentation the chairman stated that: 'As a result of this takeover we will diversify our operations and our earnings per share will rise by 13%, bringing great benefits to our shareholders.'

No bid has yet been made, and Rayswood currently owns only 2% of Pondhill.

A bid would be based on a share for share exchange, which would be one Rayswood share for every six Pondhill shares. Financial data for the two companies include the following.

	Rayswood £m	Pondhill £m
Turnover	56.0	42.0
Profit before tax	12.0	10.0
Profit available to ordinary shareholders	7.8	6.5
Dividend	3.2	3.4
Retained earnings	4.6	3.1
Issued ordinary shares [1] (£m)	20	15
Market price per share	320 pence	45 pence

[1]Rayswood 50 pence par value, Pondhill 10 pence par value.

Required

(a) Explain whether you agree with the chairman of Rayswood when he says that the takeover would bring 'great benefits to our investors'.

Support your explanation with relevant calculations. State clearly any assumptions that you make.   (11 marks)

(b) On the basis of the information provided, calculate the likely post acquisition share price of Rayswood if the bid is successful.   (3 marks)

(c) Discuss what alternative forms of payment are available in a bid and what factors a bidder should taken into account when deciding the form of payment.   (11 marks)

40   WOPPIT (25 marks)   3.2, 12/90

(a)   The managing director of Woppit plc is worried about the volatility of the company's traded option price. He considers that such volatility might be seen as financial weakness and make the company more likely to be the target of a takeover bid.

Required

Explain what factors influence the price of a traded option and whether volatility of a company's share option price is necessarily a sign of financial weakness.   (6 marks)

(b)   As a defence against a possible takeover bid the managing director proposes that Woppit make a bid for Grapper plc, in order to increase Woppit's size and, hence, make a bid for Woppit more difficult. The companies are in the same industry.

Woppit's equity beta is 1.2 and Grapper's is 1.05. The risk-free rate and market return are estimated to be 10% and 16% per year respectively. The growth rate of after tax earnings of Woppit in recent years has been 15% per year and of Grapper 12% per year. Both companies maintain an approximately constant dividend payout ratio.

Woppit's directors require information about how much premium above the current market price to offer for Grapper's shares. Two suggestions are:

(i)   the price should be based upon the balance sheet net worth of the company, adjusted for the current value of land and buildings, plus estimated after tax profits for the next five years;

(ii)   the price should be based upon a valuation using the dividend valuation model, using existing growth rate estimates.

Summarised financial data for the two companies are shown below.

MOST RECENT BALANCE SHEETS

	Woppit		Grapper	
	£m	£m	£m	£m
Land and buildings (net)[1]		560		150
Plant and machinery (net)		720		280
Stock	340		240	
Debtors	300		210	
Bank	20		40	
		660		490
Less Trade creditors	200		110	
Overdraft	30		10	
Tax payable	120		40	
Dividends payable	50		40	
		400		200
Total assets less current liabilities		1,540		720
Financed by:				
Ordinary shares[2]		200		100
Share premium		420		220
Other reserves		400		300
		1,020		620
Loans due after one year		520		100
		1,540		720

Notes

[1]   Woppit's land and buildings have been recently revalued. Grapper's have not been revalued for four years, during which time the average value of industrial land and buildings has increased by 25% per year.

[2]   Woppit 10 pence par value, Grapper 25 pence par value.

BPP Publishing

MOST RECENT PROFIT AND LOSS ACCOUNTS

	Woppit	*Grapper*
	£m	*£m*
Turnover	3,500	1,540
Operating profit	700	255
Net interest	120	22
Taxable profit	580	233
Taxation	203	82
Profit attributable to shareholders	377	151
Dividends	113	76
Retained profit	264	75

The current share price of Woppit is 310 pence and of Grapper 470 pence.

Required

(i) Calculate the premium per share above Grapper's current share price that would result from the two suggested valuation methods. Discuss which, if either, of these values should be the bid price.

State clearly any assumptions that you make. (9 marks)

(ii) Assess the managing director's strategy of seeking growth by acquisition in order to make a bid for Woppit more difficult. (3 marks)

(iii) Illustrate how Woppit might achieve benefits through improvements in operational efficiency if it acquires Grapper. (7 marks)

41 APCON (25 marks) 3.2, 6/92

The board of directors of Apcon plc is reviewing the company's operations. There is concern about the performance of the textile division, and the board is considering the divestment of the division. Apcon has received an informal offer of £6 million for the division.

Divisional profits are estimated after the allocation by head office of some central costs and a depreciation charge. The losses for the last two years for the textile division are shown below.

	19X1	*19X2*
	£'000	*£'000*
Turnover	13,500	12,900
Direct costs of production	9,500	9,600
Allocated central overhead	2,320	2,400
Finance charge	1,250	1,600
Depreciation charge	600	500
Loss before tax	(170)	(1,200)
Imputed tax	-	-
Loss after tax	(170)	(1,200)

Balance sheet summaries of the textile division

	19X1	*19X2*
	£'000	*£'000*
Land and buildings	2,100	2,100
Plant and machinery (net)	3,800	3,650
Current assets		
Stock	2,300	2,550
Debtors	1,700	1,900
Cash	40	20
Less current liabilities:		
Trade creditors	(3,200)	(3,750)
Other creditors	(400)	(600)
	6,340	5,870

	19X1 £'000	*19X2* £'000
Finance provided by Apcon's central treasury	6,340	5,870

The division's accountant estimates that 65% of the allocated central overhead has actually been incurred on behalf of the division and would be saved if the division closed. The depreciation charge is currently believed to be at a realistic level to the division's investments, and is expected to remain at approximately this level. Depreciation for tax purposes is the same as the accounting depreciation charge. All finance is provided by Apcon's central treasury, and is charged at a composite rate representing Apcon's estimated weighted average cost of capital which is currently 14% per year in money terms, and 7% per year in real terms. The textile division is believed to be more risky than Apcon's average operations; this extra risk would justify adding 3% per year to both Apcon's money and real discount rate. Turnover of the textile division is expected to grow at 4% per year for the next five years. Direct costs are forecast to increase by 8% per year and central overhead by 10% per year. The central finance charge will remain approximately constant.

At the end of five years the textile division is estimated to have a net of tax disposal value at least equal to the 19X7 market value of land and buildings, plus £1 million. Land and buildings have an estimated current market value 80% above their book value, and plant and machinery 25% below their book value. Both are expected to increase in value by 8% per year. If divestment was to take place Apcon would be responsible for immediate redundancy payments, with an estimated after tax cost of £1.5 million. If divestment does not occur redundancy payments of £0.5 million (after tax) are expected in two years time. Corporate tax is at the rate of 35% per year, payable in the year that it arises.

Assume that it is now December 19X2.

Required

(a) Evaluate whether, on financial grounds, Apcon should accept the offer of £6 million for the textile division. Your evaluation should include a discounted cash flow analysis. State clearly any assumptions that you make. (17 marks)

(b) Discuss possible reasons for a company undertaking divestment. (8 marks)

42 DIVESTMENT PLC (40 marks)

Divestment plc has recently received an offer from the managers of one of its fully-owned subsidiaries for a management buyout of that subsidiary.

The accounts of the subsidiary for the year just ended are as follows.

Profit and loss account

	£'000		£'000
Purchases (stock adjusted)	4,000	Sales	10,000
Wages	3,000		
Depreciation	1,000		
Other expenses	1,500		
Net profit	500		
	10,000		10,000

Balance sheet

	£'000		£'000
Land and buildings		2,000	Ordinary shares of £1	1,000
Plant and machinery			Retained profits	7,000
Cost	6,000			8,000
Depreciation	3,000		Bank overdraft	2,000
		3,000		
		5,000		
Stock	2,000			
Debtors	3,000			
		5,000		
		10,000		10,000

The managers have carried out a feasibility study from which they have learned the following.

(i)   The subsidiary is buying its materials from the parent company and is paying a price 25% higher than that at which the materials could be bought from a competitor. Stockholdings are also too high and could be reduced by one-quarter. Furthermore, the parent company requires payment on delivery, whereas the competitor would give three months credit.

(ii)   The figure for other expenses includes a head office charge of £500,000, which would not be payable if the subsidiary were acquired.

(iii) 20% of the sales are to the parent company which takes six months credit. All sales are made evenly throughout the year and the credit period given to other customers is three months.

(iv) The land and buildings could be sold for £6m, the plant and machinery has a scrap value of £1m, the stock is worth £1m and the debtors would be likely to pay in full.

(v)   If £2m were to be spent on advertising immediately, sales would rise to £12m for the foreseeable future. Material and wages usage would rise proportionately, and 'other expenses' would increase by £200,000.

(vi) The plant and machinery will not require replacement for the foreseeable future.

(vii) A return on capital of 30% would be required for an investment of this sort.

Required

(a)   Write a report which

(i)   explains the highest price which the management team should be prepared to pay for the subsidiary, and   (20 marks)

(ii)   suggests a possible funding package for financing the acquisition.   (10 marks)

Ignore taxation and state clearly any assumptions which you make.

(b)   *Required*

Explain the main reasons for which a company may decide to make a takeover bid.

(10 marks)

BPP Publishing

43 TUTORIAL QUESTION: FINANCIAL RECONSTRUCTION

Nemesis Holdings plc has the following balance sheet at 31 December 19X1.

	£'000	£'000
Goodwill		20,000
Property		90,000
Plant		70,000
		180,000
Stock	50,000	
Debtors	40,000	
		90,000
		270,000
Ordinary shares of £1		100,000
Accumulated losses		(80,000)
		20,000
10% preference shares of £1		20,000
		40,000
14% unsecured debentures 19X5		100,000
		140,000
Trade creditors	60,000	
Bank overdraft (unsecured)	70,000	
		130,000
		270,000

It is believed that the assets would realise the following amounts in the event of a forced sale.

	£'000
Goodwill	-
Property	35,000
Plant	25,000
Stock	30,000
Debtors	30,000
	120,000

The directors of the company feel that trading is about to improve and that if a reconstruction were to be agreed with all interested parties the company would at least be able to break even after payment of all interest charges after the proposed reconstruction but before any new investment. It also has a new project which would generate a return of £6m per annum on an investment of £25m in additional plant.

The following proposals are therefore made.

(a) Goodwill should be written off.

(b) Property and plant are to be written down by 40%.

(c) Debtors are to be written down by 10%.

(d) Both ordinary and preference share capital are to be written down by 90% and the remaining preference shares are to be converted to ordinary shares.

(e) Accumulated losses are to be written off.

(f) Trade creditors are to be written down by 50%.

(g) Debentures are to be written down by 50% and 20m new ordinary shares will be issued to the debenture holders to compensate for this write-down.

(h) A rights issue of 1 for 2 at par is to be made on the share capital after the above adjustments have been made.

(i) The bank overdraft is to be increased by £9m on which interest will be charged at 18%.

BPP Publishing

(j)   £25m is to be invested in additional plant and machinery.

Required

(a) Prepare the balance sheet of the company after the completion of the reconstruction.

(b) Explain whether the reconstruction is in the best interests of:

Ordinary shareholders
Preference shareholders
Debenture holders
Trade creditors
Bank

(c) Explain how your answer would differ if the bank had:

(i)   a fixed charge on the property;
(ii)   a floating charge.

Guidance notes

1   Reconstruction of the balance sheet is quite straightforward, but make clear how the effect of the rights issue is calculated.

2   In part (b) calculate the effect of winding up and reconstruction on the interests of the different parties in order to establish which is the best option for each group.

3   State clearly assumptions made about the source of funds for the additional investment of £25m.

4   In part (c) recalculate the relative returns to the different parties of the two options in the event of a fixed or floating charge being held by the bank. Explain how the interests of the different groups will be affected.

5   When this question was set in an ICSA examination, it was worth 30 marks in total.

44   GOODSLEEP PLC (25 marks)   3.2, 12/89

Three years ago Goodsleep plc invested £6,000,000 in the production of luxury water beds. However, demand was much lower than market research had suggested and the company experienced considerable losses on its investment, leading to a debit balance on the revenue reserves. Water bed production has now ceased, but the project harmed the company's reputation leading to a reduction in sales of other types of bed. The company hopes to improve its profitability and reputation by producing a new 'electronic' bed which automatically (and safely) maintains the bed at a pre-selected temperature. The 'electronic' bed would require new investment totalling £4,000,000.

In view of the company's financial position, the finance director has suggested a scheme of capital reconstruction. The main features of the suggested reconstruction are as follows.

(a) Existing ordinary shares will be cancelled and replaced by 15,000,000 new ordinary shares, with a par value of 50 pence. The shares will be issued for cash at par value.

5,000,000 of the new ordinary shares will be purchased by Growall Capital plc and 2,000,000 by an overseas private investor. Both of these purchasers will require representation on the board of directors. The remaining shares will be offered to existing shareholders on a rights basis. The rights issue will be underwritten.

(b) Existing shareholders will be offered one 5% convertible debenture (£100 nominal value) free of charge for every 500 shares they now own. Conversion into new ordinary shares is available at any time during the next ten years at a conversion rate of 100 shares for every £100 convertible debenture held.

(c) All existing debentures will be repaid at par out of the proceeds of the new ordinary share issue.

(d) Existing preference shares will be redeemed from the proceeds of the new ordinary share issue at a price of 40 pence per share.

(e) The company's bank has indicated that, if the reconstruction occurs, it is willing to provide a £5,500,000 12% secured term loan and a £1,000,000 overdraft facility at an initial cost of 11% a year, to replace the existing loan and overdraft.

(f) No dividends have been paid on ordinary shares or preference shares for the last two years.

(g) Growall Capital plc will purchase £2,000,000 of new 13% debentures at par.

(h) Improved working capital management is expected to provide £150,000 of new funds.

(i) Surplus land and buildings could be disposed of for £1,600,000.

If the new investment does not take place, earnings before tax (after interest payments) are not expected to be more than £50,000 a year during the next three years and losses could occur. If investment takes place forecast first year earnings before interest and tax are:

Probability	£'000
0.3	1,200
0.4	1,800
0.3	2,400

SUMMARISED BALANCE SHEET AS AT 31 MARCH 19X0

	£'000	£'000
Land and buildings		4,200
Plant and machinery		14,600
		18,800
Stock	4,400	
Debtors	3,500	
Cash	200	
Less: bank overdraft (unsecured)	(2,100)	
other creditors	(3,800)	
		2,200
		21,000

	£'000
Ordinary shares (50p par value)	3,000
Share premium	9,000
Revenue reserves	(5,000)
Ordinary shareholders' funds	7,000
8% cumulative preference shares 19X7 (£1 par value)	3,500
10% secured debenture 19X0 (£100 par value)	6,000
Bank term loan (secured)	4,500
	21,000

The current market price of ordinary shares is 20 pence, of preference shares 30 pence and of debentures £96. Corporate tax is at the rate of 35%.

Realisable values of assets upon liquidation are estimated to be as follows.

	£'000
Land and buildings	6,400
Plant and machinery	2,600
Stock	2,200
Debtors	3,000

Required

Prepare a report analysing whether the proposed scheme of reconstruction is likely to be successful. Issue costs and other professional and administrative costs may be ignored. State clearly any assumptions that you make.

45   ROCK BOTTOM PLC   (30 marks)

Rock Bottom plc has suffered many years of losses and its most recent balance sheet is as follows.

	£		£
Ordinary shares of £1	2,000,000	Fixed assets	3,250,000
10% Preference shares	750,000	Stock	1,000,000
15% Debentures (unsecured)	1,000,000	Debtors	500,000
Trade creditors	1,000,000	Accumulated losses	750,000
Bank overdraft	750,000		
	5,500,000		5,500,000

The bank overdraft is secured against the fixed assets.

In the event of a forced sale the assets would probably raise the following amounts.

	£
Fixed assets	1,500,000
Stock	400,000
Debtors	350,000
	2,250,000

However, the company has now reached a break-even position on current trading, before charging debenture interest, and is developing a new product which is expected to generate profits of £400,000 per annum in return for an immediate capital injection of £2,000,000.

The directors are therefore proposing a capital reorganisation of the company on the following basis.

(a)   Ordinary share capital to be written down to 200,000 shares of £1 each.

(b)   Preference share capital to be converted into £150,000 ordinary share capital.

(c)   £650,000 debentures to be converted into ordinary shares, the remainder to be converted into £350,000 10% Debentures.

(d)   Trade creditors to accept a moratorium of six months in payment of amounts currently due. New supplies will be paid for on delivery.

(e)   A two for one rights issue will be made at a price of one pound per share.

(f)   Fixed assets are to be revalued at £2,250,000, stock at £600,000 and debtors at £450,000. The accumulated losses are to be written off.

Required

(a)   Prepare a balance sheet for the company on the assumption that the capital injection takes place.   (8 marks)

(b)   Advise each of the interested parties whether they should encourage the company to continue in existence.   (22 marks)

BPP Publishing

DO YOU KNOW? - THE INTERNATIONAL ENVIRONMENT

- *Check that you know the following basic points before you attempt any questions. If in doubt, go back to your Study Text and revise first.*

- World output of goods and services will increase if countries engage in international trade, specialising in the production of goods/services in which they have a comparative advantage.

- A country can rectify a *balance of payments* deficit by:

  (a) allowing its currency to depreciate or devalue in foreign exchange value;

  (b) imposing protectionist measures or exchange control regulations;

  (c) deflationary economic measures in the domestic economy. (Such measures are usually a precondition of any IMF financial assistance to countries in balance of payments difficulties.)

- The international money and capital markets provide various possibilities in the form of financial instruments which the treasurer of large companies may use for borrowing or for financial investment.

- The IMF was set up partly with the role of providing finance for any countries with temporary balance of payments deficits. The World Bank and the IDA have tried to provide long term finance for *developing countries,* to help them to continue developing.

- There are various methods of providing export and import finance. Export factoring provides all the advantages of factoring generally and is especially useful in assessing credit risk. International credit unions and forfaiting provide medium term finance for imports of capital goods.

- The exporter can obtain finance from the foreign buyer (by insisting on cash with order) and the importer can obtain finance from the foreign supplier (by means of normal trade credit, perhaps evidenced by a term bill of exchange).

- Countertrade is a complex and possibly expensive means of trading with poor and less developed countries.

- When a company has transactions in a foreign currency, it is exposed to the risk of exchange rate fluctuations. A company may avoid this risk by buying or selling currency forward. This fixes the exchange rate for a transaction in the future.

  o The difference between a spot rate (for a transaction now) and a forward rate reflects the difference in interest rates between the two countries concerned.

  o The forward rate is quoted as a spot rate *plus* a discount or *minus* a premium.

- Alternative to forward purchases and sales include currency options and currency futures.

- A variety of financial instruments are available for reducing exposure to interest rate risk.

- An interest rate swap may be used to exchange obligations with another company.

- *Key questions*

  51 *Blanc et Blanc*

  54 *Tutorial question: Financing strategies*

  58 *Foreign currency options*

  62 *Oxlake*

  63 *Bid*

  66 *Manling*

42

46 COMMON MARKET (16 marks)

(a) State the differences between free trade areas, customs unions and common markets.

(6 marks)

(b) What economic benefits might countries gain from forming a common market? (10 marks)

47 EUROCURRENCIES (20 marks)

(a) What is meant by 'eurocurrency loans'? (5 marks)

(b) Discuss the impact of the following on the eurocurrency loan market:

(i)	the debt problem of the developing countries;	(5 marks)
(ii)	securitisation;	(5 marks)
(iii)	liberalisation in the domestic markets.	(5 marks)

48 NEW EXPORT MARKETS (18 marks)

You have been invited to speak at a combined meeting of the Small Business Club and the Export Club. Your subject is: 'What advice and practical help can the small business which is seeking new export markets or endeavouring to enter the export field for the first time expect to receive from its bank?'

Required

Prepare brief notes covering the points you would make.

49 TINTINNABULUM LTD (16 marks)

Tintinnabulum Ltd produce handbells. Recent innovations include the introduction of computer controlled machinery in the company's foundry and manufacturing processes. They have ascertained that they can buy equipment more cheaply from Germany than from the UK, but the suppliers have suggested that payment should be made in advance in deutschmarks. However, Tintinnabulum are not happy with this suggested method of payment.

Mr Clapper, the Financial Director, has called you in to discuss methods by which alternative arrangements can be made to pay for the goods. He informs you that Tintinnabulum Ltd is prepared to make arrangements to offer some form of undertaking to the suppliers, subject to Tintinnabulum being satisfied as to the quality and reliability of the equipment and also being able to establish with a fair degree of certainty the cost of the equipment in sterling terms.

Required

Brief notes covering the following.

(a) An alternative payment method which might be acceptable to the buyers as well as the suppliers. (2 marks)

(b) Suggestion(s) as to how the company could calculate the total cost in sterling terms of this transaction with a reasonable degree of certainty. (6 marks)

(c) If your suggestion(s) under (b) is acceptable, indicate the responsibilities of the parties involved, showing the contractual position in relation to the foreign exchange commitment.

(8 marks)

50 FRAME-UP LTD (20 marks)

Frame-up Ltd manufactures furniture which is sold through retail shops. The furniture is sold in packed-down ready-to-assemble units.

The company has built up a reputation in the UK but it has had little or no experience in overseas markets. As a result of exhibiting at a trade show, it has recently received orders from

BPP Publishing

Scandinavian countries, Holland, Germany and the USA. You understand that the orders were received despite the fact that there is currently a buyer's market in packed-down furniture in these countries.

The sales director, Mr Matchwood, wishes to discuss the various methods by which his salesmen can accept these orders and expand the company's overseas order book. He also wishes to discuss the method by which the company can protect its cashflow options, if it accepts overseas orders.

Required

Describe two appropriate methods of finance which would enable Frame-up Ltd's order book to be expanded and which would also protect the company's cashflow and provide immediate funds/funding.

51   BLANC ET BLANC   (20 marks)

Henri le Blanc is a French national. In view of the European Single Market and the fact that EC and government grants are available, his company Blanc et Blanc SA intends to set up a locally incorporated manufacturing enterprise in the UK to produce bleaching agents.

The bulk of the products are to be sold overseas on a 90 day bill of exchange basis.

Required

Give details of the various methods by which this company can finance its exports.

52   HEAVY ENGINEERING PLC   (20 marks)

Heavy Engineering plc, manufactures and installs heavy plant used in many manufacturing processes. As a result of the freeing of barriers between Eastern and Western Europe, it has decided to try to assist in the reconstruction of heavy industries in Eastern Europe and representatives have attended seminars and trade fairs in Poland, Hungary and Czechoslavakia.

They have discovered that these countries are suffering from a severe shortage of foreign exchange, but they have been told that some of their contacts are willing to provide goods in exchange for plant. The company's export and finance directors, Messrs Blading and Cash, require information on the benefits and disadvantages if the company decides to embark upon any of the schemes you are able to identify.

Required

(a)   Give an explanation of the various schemes currently in use.   (13 marks)
(b)   What disadvantages should Heavy Engineering plc consider?   (3 marks)
(c)   What benefits might accrue to Heavy Engineering plc?   (2 marks)
(d)   Which scheme(s) should Heavy Engineering plc adopt?   (2 marks)

53   FOREIGN EXCHANGE RATE FORECASTS   (25 marks)

Foreign exchange rate forecasts can be used for strategic policy decisions, budgeting and exposure management.

Required

(a)   Outline the following theories of exchange rate determination:

   (i)   purchasing power parity;
   (ii)   the monetary theory.   (7 marks)

(b)   Explain how forecasts would be made using each of the above theories and identify possible problems and weaknesses in each case.   (12 marks)

(c)   Outline the technical analysis approach to exchange rate forecasting and state possible strengths and weaknesses of that approach.   (6 marks)

54 TUTORIAL QUESTION: FINANCING STRATEGIES

It is June 19X1 and Mr Axelot has just inherited the controlling interest in IXT plc. At his first board of directors meeting an item for discussion is the financing of a £5 million expansion scheme. Mr Axelot has read that debt finance is normally cheaper than equity finance and suggests that all external finance during the next five years should be in the form of debt. For the expansion scheme he has suggested using either:

(a) a fixed rate 10 year Swiss Franc bond for 12.25 million francs issued in Zurich at an interest rate of 8% per year; or

(b) a 13% debenture 19Y4-19Y6 issued at par of £100 with warrants to purchase ordinary shares in five years time at a price of 450 pence per share.

A director has challenged Mr Axelot's five year financing strategy, saying that it would be too risky, and has suggested that the £5 million expansion scheme be financed using a placing of new ordinary shares at a price of 245 pence per share.

Financial details of IXT are summarised below. Earnings before interest payable and tax are expected to increase by 20% per year for the next five years, during which time approximately £5 million per year will be required from external financing sources. The company normally uses a dividend payout ratio of 40% and corporate tax rates are not expected to change. IXT's current share price is 250 pence ex div.

The level of inflation in Switzerland is 2% per year and in the United Kingdom 8% per year. The current spot exchange rate is SF2.445-2.450/£.

SUMMARISED BALANCE SHEET AS AT 31 MARCH 19X1

	£'000	£'000
Fixed assets		
Tangible fixed assets		33,000
Investments		4,500
		37,500
Current assets		
Stocks	12,400	
Debtors	9,200	
Bank	1,400	
		23,000
Current liabilities		
Short-term loans	(4,200)	
Overdrafts	(6,400)	
Trade creditors	(10,100)	
Other	(1,800)	
		(22,500)
Creditors falling due after more than one year		
Debentures and loan stock	(5,000)	
Unsecured bank loans	(8,400)	
		(13,400)
		24,600
Capital and reserves		
Called up share capital (25 pence par value)		4,000
Share premium account		3,500
Revaluation reserve		3,900
Profit and loss account		13,200
		24,600

BPP Publishing

SUMMARISED PROFIT AND LOSS ACCOUNT
FOR THE YEAR ENDING 31 MARCH 19X1

	£'000
Turnover	53,500
Trading profit	13,400
Investment income	350
Interest payable	(3,000)
Taxable income	10,750
Taxation	(3,762)
Profit attributable to ordinary shareholders	6,988
Dividend	(2,795)
Profit retained for year	4,193

Required

(a) Explain why the cost of debt finance for a company is normally less than the cost of equity finance.

Relevant calculations should be included to your answers to *both* parts (b) and (c) of this question. State clearly any assumptions that you make.

(b) Appraise Mr Axelot's suggested strategy that all external financing during the next five years should be in the form of debt.

(c) Discuss whether IXT plc should finance the *current* £5m expansion project with the Swiss franc bond, the 13% debenture or the placing.

(d) A non-executive director mentions that his company has recently used mezzanine financing and suggests that IXT might consider this form of financing.

Required

Explain briefly what mezzanine financing is and how it might be useful to IXT.

Guidance notes

1 Part (a) calls for an explanation of the effects of relative risks to holders of equity and debt, and the effect of this on the cost of the different forms of finance to a company.

2 Parts (b) and (c) require an analysis of the effect of the projections on financial performance under the different financing options. State clearly how any ratios are calculated, and assumptions used in making projections. The question also provides the opportunity to demonstrate an understanding of the purchasing power parity theory of exchange rates in evaluating the merits of financing using the Swiss Franc bond.

3 When this question was set in an ACCA examination, it was allocated 25 marks in total.

55 BOLAR (25 marks)   3.2, 12/90

Bolar plc currently has four types of marketable debt in its capital structure.

(a) Unsecured 14% bonds, redemption date 30 June 19X4, with interest payable annually on 31 December. The current market price is £95 ex-interest.

(b) 10% secured debentures, redemption 31 December 19X3-X5 with £5 interest payable per debenture six monthly on 30 June and 31 December. The current market price is £91.50 ex-interest.

(c) 8% unsecured convertible debentures, convertible on either 1 January 19X3, into 40 ordinary shares, or on 1 January 19X5 into 30 ordinary shares. The redemption date is 1 January 20Y1. Interest is payable annually on 1 January and the current market price is £93 cum interest.

(d) 6% unsecured US dollar Eurobonds, interest payable annually on 31 December, redemption date 31 December 19X5, current market price $850 ex-interest.

The sterling debt all has a unit par value of £100, and the Eurobonds each have a par value of $1,000. All of Bolar's marketable debt is redeemable at its par value. The US dollar is expected to strengthen by approximately 3% per year relative to the pound sterling. The current spot mid-rate is $1.60/£.

Assume that it is now 31 December 19X0. Taxation may be ignored.

Required

(a) Calculate the annual redemption yields for each of the four types of debt. For the convertible debenture estimate the annual yield if the company's share price, currently 190 pence, increases by

    (i)   5% per year,
    (ii)   10% per year.

Assume that, if conversion occurs, the shares would immediately be sold, and that the ex-interest value of convertible debentures is expected to be £88.50 on 1 January 19X3 and £92 on 1 January 19X5. (16 marks)

(b) Explain briefly why the redemption yields in your answer to (a) above differ. (4 marks)

(c) What are the advantages and disadvantages of raising finance by issuing Eurobonds?

    (5 marks)

56   INTERNATIONAL GROUP (10 marks)

You have been retained by the management of an international group to advise on the management of its foreign exchange exposure.

Required

(a) Explain the main types of foreign exchange exposure. (4 marks)

(b) Advise on policies which the corporate treasurer could consider to provide valid and relevant methods of reducing exposure to foreign exchange risk. (6 marks)

57   FOREIGN EXCHANGE RISK STRATEGIES (12½ marks)

The currency risk strategies of three companies, A, B and C, are determined by the considerations set out below, which have led the management of each of the companies to conclude that there is no need to take positive action to manage currency risks.

Company A. This company is an exporter with customers in approximately twenty countries spread across Europe, America, Africa and South East Asia. Management argues that the efficiency of foreign exchange markets means that the company is as likely to make foreign exchange gains as losses. It is claimed by management that there is consequently no need to hedge currency risks since there will be costs involved while overall the company will not gain from the hedges.

Company B. Company B is not involved in any foreign trade and because of this sees no need to take foreign exchange rates into account in its financial strategy.

Company C. Company C trades only with countries in the European Union (the European Community) and its management argues that the existence of the exchange rate mechanism (ERM) prevents foreign exchange losses from being suffered.

The management of all three companies A, B and C consider their companies to be risk-averse. All of the companies' export revenues are in foreign currency while imports are paid for in sterling.

Required

Discuss whether the views of management outlined above are valid, considering in turn:

(a) Company A;
(b) Company B;
(c) Company C.

58 FOREIGN CURRENCY OPTIONS (12½ marks)   3.2, 6/92, part question

(a) Explain briefly what is meant by foreign currency options and give examples of the advantages and disadvantages of exchange traded foreign currency options to the financial manager. (5 marks)

(b) Exchange traded foreign currency option prices in Philadelphia for dollar/sterling contracts are shown below.

Sterling (£12,500) contracts

	Calls		Puts	
Exercise price ($)	September	December	September	December
1.90	5.55	7.95	0.42	1.95
1.95	2.75	3.85	4.15	3.80
2.00	0.25	1.00	9.40	-
2.05	-	0.20	-	-

Option prices are in cents per £. The current spot exchange rate is $1.9405 - $1.9425/£.

Required

Assume that you work for a US company that has exported goods to the UK and is due to receive a payment of £1,625,000 in three months time. It is now the end of June.

Calculate and explain whether your company should hedge its sterling exposure on the foreign currency option market if the company's treasurer believes the spot rate in three months time will be:

(i) $1.8950 - $1.8970/£
(ii) $2.0240 - $2.0260/£   (7½ marks)

59 TUTORIAL QUESTION: SALES TO THE USA

(a) A merchant in the UK has agreed to sell goods to an importer in the USA at an invoiced price of $150,000. Of this amount, $60,000 will be payable on shipment, $45,000 one month after shipment and $45,000 three months after shipment.

The quoted foreign exchange rates ($ per £) at the date of shipment are as follows.

Spot	1.690 - 1.692
One month	1.687 - 1.690
Three months	1.680 - 1.684

The merchant decides to enter into appropriate forward exchange contracts through his bank to hedge these transactions.

Required

(i) State what are the presumed advantages of doing this.

(ii) Calculate the sterling amount that the merchant would receive.

(iii) Comment with hindsight on the wisdom of hedging in this instance, assuming that the spot rates at the dates of receipt of the two instalments of $45,000 were as follows.

First instalment	1.694 - 1.696
Second instalment	1.700 - 1.704

(b) (i) Describe how foreign exchange transactions on the London International Financial Futures and Options Exchange would differ from those assumed in part (a) of this question.

(ii) Summarise briefly what other types of contract (apart from those in foreign currencies) are available on the market and how they can assist the financial management of commercial undertakings.

Guidance notes

1 Before making calculations for part (a), you should think about exactly what cash flows will take place and in what currency. The answer is in this case straightforward. All cash flows will take place in dollars, and they are as set out at the start of the question.

2 You must then calculate the sterling the merchant will receive, firstly with hedging and secondly without hedging. All you need to do is divide the dollar cash flow by the appropriate exchange rate for the time of each instalment.

3 You can work out which is the appropriate exchange rate as follows. The merchant is selling dollars for pounds, so the bank is buying dollars. The bank wants to make a profit, so it will want to take in as many dollars as it can for each pound it gives out. It would prefer to take in (say) $1.70 for each pound than $1.65.

4 Part (b) requires a written answer.

60 FREIMARKS (25 marks)

F plc, a merchandising company operating mainly in the UK, undertakes export and import transactions with firms in a less well developed country, Freiland. Many of these transactions are necessarily conducted in the local currency, the Freimark (Fm).

F plc also has a small subsidiary company in Freiland, concerned wholly with servicing equipment sold in that country.

The sterling value of the Freimark has fluctuated frequently over the past 12 months between Fm 12.50 and Fm 27.50 = £1. The exchange rate currently stands at 25.00.

The treasurer of F plc has prepared the following cash flow forecast of transactions in Fm over the next six months.

	Month 1 Fm'000	Month 2 Fm'000	Month 3 Fm'000	Month 4 Fm'000	Month 5 Fm'000	Month 6 Fm'000
Receipts in respect of sales invoiced from the UK	37,400	48,500	35,000	77,300	62,600	46,700
Remittances from subsidiary company: balances in excess of agreed float	3,200	1,600	2,000	2,700	2,400	1,800
Total receipts	40,600	50,100	37,000	80,000	65,000	48,500
Payments for goods imported from Freiland	38,200	55,500	44,200	36,800	53,000	49,500
Purchase of fixed assets in Freiland for subsidiary company				40,000	4,000	
	38,200	55,500	44,200	76,800	57,000	49,500
Net receipts/(payments)	2,400	(5,400)	(7,200)	3,200	8,000	(1,000)

Required

(a) State and explain the various factors that should be taken into account before the company decides to take any action to reduce its foreign exchange transaction exposure. (10 marks)

(b) Describe three techniques of exposure management that might be available to F plc under the circumstances of this question. (10 marks)

BPP Publishing

(c) Explain the meaning of 'economic exposure' and distinguish it from transaction exposure.

(5 marks)

61 EXCHANGE RATES (25 marks)

(a) (i) Describe the European Monetary System and contrast government actions under that system with those applicable to policies of a managed float and of fixed exchange rates.

(ii) Summarise possible advantages and disadvantages of each system from the point of view of a business in the United Kingdom. (15 marks)

(b) An exporter in the UK has invoiced a customer in the USA the sum of $300,000 receivable in one year's time.

He has under consideration two methods of hedging his exchange risk.

(i) He could borrow $300,000 now for one year, convert the amount into sterling, and repay the loan out of the eventual receipts.

(ii) He could enter into a 12-month forward exchange contract to sell the $300,000 and meanwhile borrow an equivalent amount in sterling.

The sterling - US dollar spot rate is 1.8190 - 1.8402.

The 12 months forward rate of dollars against sterling is 1.7915.

Interest rates for 12 months are: USA 6.65%, UK 9.25%.

Required

Calculate the net proceeds in sterling under each alternative and to explain the result you obtain. (10 marks)

62 OXLAKE (25 marks)

3.2, 12/87

Oxlake plc has export orders from a company in Singapore for 250,000 china cups, and from a company in Indonesia for 100,000 china cups. The unit variable cost to Oxlake of producing china cups is 55. The unit sales price to Singapore is Singapore $2.862 and to Indonesia, 2,246 rupiahs. Both orders are subject to credit terms of 60 days, and are payable in the currency of the importers. Past experience suggests that there is 50% chance of the customer in Singapore paying 30 days late. The Indonesian customer has offered to Oxlake the alternative of being paid US $125,000 in 3 months time instead of payment in the Indonesian currency. The Indonesian currency is forecast by Oxlake's bank to depreciate in value during the next year by 30% (from an Indonesian viewpoint) relative to the $US.

Whenever appropriate Oxlake uses option forward foreign exchange contracts.

Foreign exchange rates (mid rates)

	$Singapore/$US	$US/£	Rupiahs/£
Spot	2.1378	1.4875	2,481
1 month forward	2.1132	1.4963	No forward
2 months forward	2.0964	1.5047	market exists
3 months forward	2.0915	1.5105	

Assume that any foreign currency holding in the UK will be immediately converted into sterling.

	Money market rates (% per year)	
	Deposit	*Borrowing*
UK clearing bank	6	11
Singapore bank	4	7
Euro-dollars	7½	12
Indonesian bank	15	Not available
Euro-sterling	6½	10½
US domestic bank	8	12½

50

These interest rates are fixed rates for either immediate deposits or borrowing over a period of two or three months, but the rates are subject to future movement according to economic pressures.

Required

(a) Using what you consider to be the most suitable way of protecting against foreign exchange risk, evaluate the sterling receipts that Oxlake can expect from its sales to Singapore and to Indonesia, without taking any risks.

All contracts, including foreign exchange and money market contracts, may be assumed to be free from the risk of default. Transactions costs may be ignored. (13 marks)

(b) If the Indonesian customer offered another form of payment to Oxlake, immediate payment in $US of the full amount owed in return for a 5% discount on the rupiah unit sales price, calculate whether Oxlake is likely to benefit from this form of payment. (7 marks)

(c) Discuss the advantages and disadvantages to a company of invoicing an export sale in a foreign currency. (5 marks)

63 BID (25 marks) 3.2, 12/90

(a) Briefly discuss five sources of external finance that a medium-sized company might use to finance its export sales. (10 marks)

(b) BID (UK) Ltd trades with several countries. During the next six months export and import receipts and payments are due as a result of business with companies in Australia, North Africa, Eastern Europe and Italy. The transactions are in the currencies specified. It is now 31 December.

	Payment	*Exports*	*Imports*
Australia	31 March	A$120,000	£40,000
Italy	31 March	Lire 400 million	Lire 220 million
North Africa	31 March	Francs 565,000	-
Italy	Between 31 March and 30 June	Lire 500 million	-
Eastern Europe	30 June	Tinned meat	-
Australia	30 June	A$180,000	A$260,000
West Africa	30 June	Coffee	Tinned meat
Italy	30 June	-	Lire 700 million

The exports to Eastern Europe will be paid for by a barter exchange of 100,000 tins of meat. BID has arranged for this tinned meat to be exchanged for 70 tons of coffee by its customer in West Africa where tinned meat is in demand. The West African country's currency is tied to the French franc.

Exchange rates

	A$/£	*Lire/£*	*Franc/£*
Spot	2.1400 - 2.1425	2,208 - 2,210	10.38 - 10.39
3 months forward	2 - 2.5 cents dis	3 - 6 lire dis	5 - 3 centimes pm
6 months forward	3.5 - 4.5 cents dis	5 - 8 lire dis	7 - 5 centimes pm

Commodities	*Futures rate* (£/tonne)
Coffee beans	
March	791
June	860

Interest rates

	Borrowing	*Lending*
UK bank	15%	10.5%
Australian bank	16%	13.0%
Italian bank	Not available	16.0%
French bank	9%	6.0%

Assume that interest rates will not change during the next six months.

BID proposed to invest net sterling proceeds from foreign trade in a UK bank. The company wishes to hedge against all foreign exchange risk, and currently has no surplus cash.

Taxation, transaction costs and margin requirements on futures contracts may be ignored.

Required

Using the forward market, money market or commodity futures market, as appropriate, estimate the maximum size of cash surplus or the minimum size of cash deficit that will result from BID's foreign trade at the end of six months.   (15 marks)

64 TUTORIAL QUESTION: INTEREST RATE RISKS

(a) It is now 31 December 19X1 and the corporate treasurer of Omniown plc is concerned about the volatility of interest rates. His company needs in three months time to borrow £5 million for a six month period. Current interest rates are 14% per year for the type of loan Omniown would use, and the treasurer does not wish to pay more than this.

He is considering using:

(i)   a forward rate agreement (FRA); or
(ii)   interest rate futures; or
(iii)   an interest rate guarantee (short-term cap).

Required

Explain briefly how each of these three alternatives might be useful to Omniown plc.

(b) The corporate treasurer of Omniown plc expects interests rates to increase by 2% during the next three months and has decided to hedge the interest rate risk using interest rate futures.

March sterling three months time deposit futures are currently priced at 86.25. The standard contract size is £500,000 and the minimum price movement is one tick (the value of one tick is 0.01% per year of the contract size).

Required

Show the effect of using the futures market to hedge against interest rate movements:

(i)   if interest rates increase by 2% and the futures market price also moves by 2%;
(ii)   if interest rates increase by 2% and the futures market moves by 1.5%;
(iii)   if interest rates fall by 1% and the futures market moves by 0.75%.

In each case estimate the hedge efficiency.

Taxation, margin requirements, and the time value of money are to be ignored.

(c) If, as an alternative to interest rate futures, the corporate treasurer had been able to purchase interest rate guarantees at 14% for a premium of 0.2% of the size of the loan to be guaranteed, calculate whether the total cost of the loan after hedging in each of the situations (i) to (iii) in (b) above would have been less with the futures hedge or with the guarantee. The guarantee would be effective for the entire six month period of the loan.

Taxation, margin requirements and the time value of money are to be ignored.

Guidance notes

1   Part (a) requires a straightforward description of three of the mechanisms for hedging against interest rate movements.

2   One approach to part (b) is to make all futures calculations in terms of ticks; an alternative would be to calculate the effect of the movements on the prices of futures and then to calculate gains and losses on this basis.

3   Once (b) has been completed, part (c) becomes a matter of comparing the net cost of the loan using futures with the net cost using an interest rate guarantee in each of the three scenarios.

4   When this question was set in an ACCA exam, it was allocated 25 marks (10 marks for part (a); 10 marks for (b); 5 marks for (c)).

65   CAPIT   (12½ marks)   3.2, 6/90, part question

The managers of a small company, Capit Ltd, plan to borrow £200,000 to invest in buildings, equipment, and working capital. It will take more than 18 months before significant cash inflows are generated from the investment. The managers are worried about servicing the interest on the borrowed funds for an 18 month period as interest rates have recently been volatile.

The company's advisors believe that there is an equal chance of interest rates rising or falling by 2% during the first six months. After the first six months there is a 60% chance of rates continuing to move by a further 2% in the same direction as in the first six months in each future six month period and a 40% chance of a 2% movement in the opposite direction. Interest is payable at the end of each six month period.

The managers are undecided whether to borrow the £200,000 in either:

(a) £150,000 short-term floating rate loan at an initial interest rate of 15% per year and renewable every six months, plus a £50,000 five year fixed rate loan at 17% per year; or

(b) £50,000 short-term loan, £150,000 five year loan, both on the same terms as (a) above.

   All loans are secured. Interest rate reviews for floating rate loans are every six months.

   Issue costs/renewal costs are 1% of the loan size for each short-term loan, and £800 for the five year loan. Issue costs are payable at the end of the previous loan period except for the initial loans where issue costs are payable at the start of the loan period. Tax relief is available on interest payments 12 months after the interest has been paid. No tax relief is available on issue costs. Corporate tax is at the rate of 25%. It is expected that £19,500, £18,500 and £15,500 will be available to service the loans in the first, second and third six month periods respectively. Any unused surplus may be carried forward to the next six monthly period.

   Required

(a) Discuss which form of financing Capit Ltd should use.   (5 marks)

(b) Estimate which form of financing is expected to be cheapest for Capit Ltd during the 18 month period. For each financing method calculate the probability of the company being unable to service its interest payments during the 18 month period. Assume that financing will continue to be required after the 18 month period. The time value of money, and any possible income from investing surplus cash between six month periods may be ignored.
                                                                                          (7½ marks)

66   MANLING (25 marks)   3.2, 6/90

(a) Explain and illustrate what is meant by disintermediation and securitisation. How can disintermediation and securitisation help the financial manager?   (8 marks)

(b) Manling plc has £14 million of fixed rate loans at an interest rate of 12% per year which are due to mature in one year. The company's treasurer believes that interest rates are going to fall, but does not wish to redeem the loans because large penalties exist for early redemption. Manling's bank has offered to arrange an interest rate swap for one year with a company that has obtained floating rate finance at London Interbank Offered Rate (LIBOR) plus $1^1/_8$%. The bank will charge each of the companies an arrangement fee of £20,000 and the proposed terms of the swap are that Manling will pay LIBOR plus 1½% to the other company and receive from the company $11^5/_8$%.

   Corporate tax is at 35% per year and the arrangement fee is a tax allowable expense. Manling could issue floating rate debt at LIBOR plus 2% and the other company could issue fixed rate debt at 11¾%. Assume that any tax relief is immediately available.

Required

(i)   Evaluate whether Manling plc would benefit from the interest rate swap:

(1)   if LIBOR remains at 10% for the whole year;
(2)   if LIBOR falls to 9% after six months.   (6 marks)

(ii)   If LIBOR remains at 10% evaluate whether both companies could benefit from the interest rate swap if the terms of the swap were altered. Any benefit would be equally shared.   (6 marks)

(c)   Manling expects to have £1 million surplus funds for three months prior to making a tax payment. Discuss possible short-term investments for these funds.   (5 marks)

67   SWAPS   (25 marks)   3.2, 12/92

(a)   Discuss how interest rate swaps and currency swaps might be of value to the corporate financial manager.   (10 marks)

(b)   Calvold plc has a one year contract to construct factories in a South American country. At the end of the year the factories will be paid for by the local government. The price has been fixed at 2,000 million pesos, payable in the South American currency.

In order to fulfil the contract Calvold will need to invest 1,000 million pesos in the project immediately, and a fixed additional sum of 500 million pesos in six months time.

The government of the South American country has offered Calvold a fixed rate-fixed rate currency swap for *one year* for the full 1,500 million pesos at a swap rate of 20 pesos/£. Net interest of 10% per year would be payable in pesos by Calvold to the government.

There is no forward foreign exchange market for the peso against the pound.

Forecasts of inflation rates for the next year are:

Probability	*UK*		*South American country*
0.25	4%	and	40%
0.50	5%	and	60%
0.25	7%	and	100%

The peso is a freely floating currency which has not recently been subject to major government intervention.

The current spot rate is 25 pesos/£. Calvold's opportunity cost of funds is 12% per year in the UK. The company has no access to funds in the South American country.

Taxation, the risk of default, and discounting to allow for the timing of payments may be ignored.

Required

Evaluate whether it is likely to be beneficial for Calvold plc to agree to the currency swap.

(15 marks)

DO YOU KNOW? - INTERNATIONAL OPERATIONS

- *Check that you know the following basic points before you attempt any questions. If in doubt, go back to your Study Text and revise first.*

- Foreign direct investment (FDI) will generally be undertaken if exporting is more costly than overseas production. However, difficulties in repatriating profits and other political factors complicate the issue.

- Transfer pricing is of importance to multinational companies.

  o There are legal provisions affecting transfer pricing which are aimed at preventing avoidance of tax.

  o Different methods of transfer pricing also have different motivational effects on the cost centres involved.

- International portfolio diversification brings advantages resulting from differences in the economies of different countries.

- The CAPM can be extended to cover international portfolio risk, but in practice foreign exchange fluctuations and market imperfections also need to be considered.

- The appraisal of foreign projects involves a number of complexities which do not arise in the case of domestic projects, including international tax complications and differential rates of inflation.

- The functions of a *treasurer* include all the following:

  o Advising on capital structure

  o Managing cash flows to minimise associated costs

  o Maintaining good banking relationships

  o Managing foreign currency transactions to avoid risk.

- A small company may have little choice but to accept the range of services offered by their bank managers or the facilities offered by overseas suppliers. Larger treasury companies and multinational enterprises are in a position to adopt a more active role in managing deposits, borrowings and foreign debtors.

- *Key questions*

  68 Tutorial question: Multinational investment appraisal

  71 Ranek

  72 Passem

  74 The treasury function

BPP Publishing

68 TUTORIAL QUESTION: MULTINATIONAL INVESTMENT APPRAISAL

Rippentoff Inc is an American multinational which is considering an investment in a subsidiary company in Penuria, a developing country.

The investment would require capital of 50 million local currency units (LCUs) and the current rate of exchange is LCU 5 = $1. Rippentoff would supply capital of LCU 30 million and the remainder would be borrowed locally at a 15% rate of interest. The subsidiary would invest its capital in machinery costing LCU 40 million and inventory of LCU 10 million. Of the machinery, LCU 30 million would be purchased from Rippentoff, consisting of three machines costing LCU 10 million each. One of these machines was scheduled for sale for scrap at $100,000, one would need to be replaced by a machine costing $1.5 million, and one would be bought new for $2.0 million, less a discount of 10%.

One half of the opening inventory and of all subsequent purchases of materials would be bought from Rippentoff, which obtains a 25% contribution on all sales of materials.

It is forecast that the annual income statement of the subsidiary for the foreseeable future will be as follows.

	LCU million	LCU million
Sales		40
Less: Materials	20	
Labour	7	
Interest	3	
Management fee to Rippentoff	5	
		35
Net profit (all paid as dividend)		5

The management fee does not involve Rippentoff in any additional cost.

The cost of equity of the subsidiary is 20%, while Rippentoff's overall cost of capital is 15%. There is no taxation in Penuria.

Required

(a) Calculate whether the proposed investment is worthwhile:

    (i)   from the viewpoint of Rippentoff;
    (ii)   from the viewpoint of the subsidiary company.

(b) Explain the additional factors that Rippentoff would take into account in the appraisal of the investment.

Guidance notes

1   First, calculate the return on investment for each party: in US dollars for the parent company and in the local currency for the subsidiary. Then compare this with the cost of capital. It is important to distinguish which costs and revenues are relevant - in the technical sense - to each party, and to state clearly any assumptions made.

2   Part (b) requires an assessment of the various *risks* of overseas investments by multinationals in the context of the example given.

3   When this question was set in an ICSA exam, it was allocated 30 marks (20 for part (a); 10 for part (b)).

BPP Publishing

69 TRANSFER PRICING (10 marks)

Explain why you agree or disagree with the following statement, made by a finance director.

'Transfer pricing policy is a difficult area which offers considerable scope for dysfunctional behaviour. Decisions about selling prices should be removed from the control of divisional managers and made the responsibility of a head office department.'

70 BRITISH COMPANY IN RURITANIA (35 marks)

A British company is planning to set up a subsidiary company in Ruritania at the start of 19X0 in order to invest in a project which is expected to last for four years.

You are given the following information concerning the project.

(a) Expected exchange rates between the pound and the Ruritanian mark (£:Rm):

	19X0		19X1		19X2		19X3	
Start	Average	End	Average	End	Average	End	Average	End
1:5	1:6	1:7	1:8	1:9	1:10	1:11	1:12	1:13

(b) The expected profits from the project in Rm('000s):

19X0: 21,000   19X1: 22,500   19X2: 22,000   19X3: 26,000

(c) The project has an immediate cost of Rm50 million and will require further investment of Rm18 million at the end of 19X1. At the end of 19X3 the assets of the subsidiary will have a break-up value of Rm13 million.

(d) The entire capital cost of the project consists of the following machinery supplied by the parent company:

	£m			
New machinery	6			
Surplus machinery	2	replacement cost	£2.3m	
		(scrap value £200,000)		
Machine currently in use	2	replacement cost	£2.5m	
		(scrap value £400,000)		

The machinery supplied at the end of 19X1 will be surplus to requirements and will have a scrap value of £500,000 and a replacement cost of £3m.

(e) Three-quarters of the profits may be paid out as a dividend on the last day of the year in which they are earned. The remainder must be invested in interest-free Ruritanian government stock, which may be redeemed at par at the end of the project. There are no other restrictions on the transfer of currency.

(f) The profits are calculated after the following charges (Rm'000s)

	19X0	19X1	19X2	19X3
Purchases from parent company	12,000	16,000	24,000	30,000
Depreciation	10,000	10,000	10,000	10,000
Management fee	7,000	6,300	6,600	6,500
Royalties	7,000	9,000	11,000	13,000

The management fee and the royalties are paid to the parent company on the last day of the year.

The actual cost to the parent company of providing the management services is £100,000 per annum. The goods sold to the subsidiary are supplied evenly throughout the year, for immediate cash. The cost structure for these goods is as follows.

	%
Labour	20
Materials	40
Depreciation	10
Fixed overheads	15
Profit margin	15
	100

(g) The cost of capital of the parent company is 20%.

Required

(a) Prepare a report which explains whether the project is worthwhile from the viewpoint of the British company and discuss the other factors which should be taken into account before arriving at a final decision. (30 marks)

Ignore taxation.

(b) Explain how the control of remittances by a government overseas may affect a foreign investor. (5 marks)

71 RANEK (25 marks)   3.2, 6/90

You have been appointed by Ranek plc to advise on the price that the company should tender for the construction of a small power station in a foreign country, Zmbland.

The company normally charges a price that gives a 20% markup on all directly attributable costs (which includes leasing and the current written-down value of assets less any residual value of assets expected at the end of the contract but excludes any tax effects of such costs).

The power station will take 15 months to construct. All costs are payable in pounds sterling. Wages totalling £380,000 are payable monthly in arrears in pounds sterling. Materials are purchased two months in advance of the month when they are to be used. One month's credit is taken on all materials purchases. Materials usage is expected to be £715,000 per month, payable in sterling. Other direct costs are expected to be £50,000 per month and the company will allocate central overhead to the project at £25,000 per month. No increases in costs are expected during the contract period.

Ranek already owns some plant and equipment that could be used in this project. These assets cost £3 million and have a written-down value of £1.8 million after deduction of tax allowable depreciation at 25% on a reducing balance basis. If the contract is not undertaken the existing plant and equipment will be sold immediately for £2 million. The realisable value of these assets at the end of 15 months is expected to be £900,000. Special equipment for the contract would be obtained through an operating lease at a quarterly cost of £620,000 payable in advance on the first day of the quarter.

Assume that corporate tax in the United Kingdom at the rate of 35% is payable on net cash flows six months after the end of the relevant tax year. No foreign tax liability is expected. Any tax effects associated with the disposal of assets also occur six months after the relevant year end. The end of Ranek's financial year occurs three months after the start of the project.

The tender price for the power station is to be in Zmbland dollars (Z$). Thirty per cent is payable immediately and the balance upon completion. The current exchange rate is Z$45.5-46.0/£ and the Zmbland dollar is expected to steadily depreciate in value relative to the pound by approximately 25% during the next 15 months. No forward foreign exchange market exists.

Ranek's managers estimate that the company's opportunity cost of capital is 1% per month. The company currently has spare capacity.

Required

(a) Estimate the tender price that would result from a 20% markup on sterling direct costs. Ignore the time value of money in the estimate of the required markup. (5 marks)

(b) Estimate the net present value of the proposed project and discuss and recommend the minimum price that the company should tender. State clearly any assumptions that you make. (20 marks)

72 PASSEM (25 marks) 3.2, 6/92

The finance director of a large UK based multinational company is reviewing the multinational's investments. The company has built up a portfolio of over £500 million in shares of UK and European Community companies. The portfolio is held primarily to provide quick access to finance for acquisitions, and to build up a minority equity stake in potential acquisition targets.

The finance director is wondering whether to sell the multinational's holding of two million ordinary shares in Passem plc, a chain of department stores. A 'Z' score for Passem has been purchased, which places Passem in a 'zone of ignorance' between expected corporate failure and expected corporate survival.

The retail sector is currently suffering from an economic recession, which has led to retail sales falling on average by 10% during the past year. Consumer credit has been temporarily constrained by the government which is trying to control inflation. Bank base rates are currently 15.5% per year and have not changed for six months.

Financial data for Passem are summarised below.

BALANCE SHEETS AS AT 31 MARCH

	19X1 £m	19X2 £m
Fixed assets		
Tangible assets	236	252
Goodwill	26	22
	262	274
Current assets		
Stock	125	142
Debtors	12	16
Cash at bank and in hand	2	1
	139	159
Creditors		
Amounts falling due within one year		
Overdrafts	68	84
Trade creditors	95	108
Corporate tax	6	4
Other creditors	38	42
Proposed final dividend	3	-
	210	238
Amounts falling due after more than one year		
9% unsecured convertible loan stock 19Y2-19Y7	20	20
3% unsecured deep discount loan stock 19Z0	30	32
10% fixed rate term loan 19X5 (secured)	40	40
	101	103
Shareholders' funds		
Called up share capital (50 pence par value)	20	23
Share premium account	42	48
Profit and loss account	39	32
	101	103

BPP Publishing

CONSOLIDATED PROFIT AND LOSS ACCOUNTS
FOR THE YEARS ENDING 31 MARCH

	19X1 £m	19X2 £m
Turnover	820	770
Gross profit	45	42
Administration and other expenses	12	13
Operating profit	33	29
Interest payable	14	19
	19	10
Net surplus on sale of properties	4	2
Profit on ordinary activities before tax	23	8
Tax on ordinary activities	8	3
Profit on ordinary activities after tax	15	5
Extraordinary items	-	(7)
Dividends	6	3
Profit retained	9	(5)

Notes

1   No final dividend was paid in the year ending 31 March 19X2.

2   Extraordinary items relate to restructuring and reorganisation costs.

3   Tangible fixed assets (mostly property) have not been revealed for three years and are believed to be undervalued by between 25% and 35%.

4   Passem's current share price is 155 pence.

Market data (all for year ending 31 March)

All data are based upon monthly observations.

	19W8	19W9	19X0	19X1	19X2
Passem: Average share price (pence)	125	130	188	175	150
Passem: Dividend per share (pence)	11	12	13	15	6.5
Average share price for companies in Passem's industry	210	240	280	250	180
Average earnings per share (pence) for companies in Passem's industry	46	50	56	62.5	58
Average dividend per share (pence) for companies in Passem's industry	18	20	22	25	20
Beta equity:					
Passem	1.20	1.20	1.20	1.20	1.20
Average for Passem's industry	1.10	1.10	1.10	1.15	1.15
Risk-free rate (%)	7	7	6	7	8

The market return (capital gain or loss plus dividend yield based upon monthly observations) averaged 12% per year between 19W8 and 19X2.

Required

(a) Using the above information prepare a reasoned report discussing whether the multinational company should dispose of its holding in Passem.

All relevant calculations must be included within the report or as an appendix to the report.

State clearly any assumptions that you make.   (20 marks)

(b) Briefly discuss what other publicly available information would be of value in making the decision on whether or not to sell the holding.   (5 marks)

73 CASH WITH ORDER (10 marks)

Amongst the recent acquisitions of Plant and Machinery Ltd is a small company whose payment terms are 'cash with order'. This has resulted in a large number of cheques, drawn in sterling by buyers in Europe, and in dollars from others in the USA, being paid into the bank for collection.

The parent company is concerned as to the cost and delay involved in obtaining these funds. It is understood that whilst it might be possible to persuade customers in Europe to adopt other methods, any attempt to make a complete change in the USA would seriously affect the business. Their buyers in the USA insist on sending the actual payments in dollars with orders and in a few cases would not be prepared for any alteration whatsoever.

What advice would you give the parent company regarding payments by customers, with a view to reducing cost and delay in the availability of funds:

(a) in Europe;
(b) in the USA?

State any possible disadvantages which your suggestion in relation to (b) might involve.

74 THE TREASURY FUNCTION (20 marks)

P & Q plc is a UK-based manufacturing company having subsidiary companies in the USA and various European countries and also a number of overseas agencies.

The company has been growing rapidly and the finance director has recently put in hand a major reorganisation of the finance department, including the setting up of a separate treasury function.

Required

Draft a report from the finance director to the board:

(a) describing the proposed responsibilities of the treasury function;   (12 marks)
(b) stating the advantages to the company of having such a specialist function.   (8 marks)

BPP Publishing

SUGGESTED SOLUTIONS

1 FINANCIAL OBJECTIVE

At first sight it appears that both managers and owners will benefit from the objective of shareholder wealth maximisation since managers' remuneration is generally linked to the profit performance of the company. However, other factors can come into play which mean that this is not necessarily the case. Firstly, the timescales which concern managers may be different from those which are important to the owners. This may mean that the management aim to maximise short-term profits in order to maximise their personal earnings through bonus schemes etc. It may mean that unacceptably risky projects are undertaken and that long-term investments are neglected. This may have the effect of reducing expectations about future performance and depressing the share price, thereby reducing the wealth of the ordinary shareholders.

Further 'agency' conflicts can arise when the management take other decisions aimed at increasing their own utility, for instance by raising salaries and improving the level of perks. There may also be a tendency to satisfice rather than maximise in decision making. It is now frequently the practice to try to unify the interests of owners and managers by giving managers a stake in the ownership of the company through some form of share ownership (or the means of acquiring ownership).

Many firms now express an increasing level of concern for the physical and social environment within which they operate. Some companies have a clearly defined environmental policy which is regulated by a separate supervisory board, for example Shanks and McEwan. Others second staff to assist on community projects, for example The Body Shop. While such initiatives undoubtedly do contribute to financial performance by building customer support, it is unlikely that the additional revenue generated exceeds the costs incurred.

In practice, firms operate with a number of objectives and constraints. While it is sensible to do as much as possible to reduce agency conflicts, certain non-financial objectives and constraints will always be important. Maximisation of shareholder wealth will undoubtedly remain the primary financial objective, but it will never be possible for it to be fully realised.

2 TUTORIAL QUESTION: MANAGERIAL REWARD

It is generally assumed that the prime corporate objective is the maximisation of shareholder wealth. However since the day-to-day activities of the company are conducted by its management there is no guarantee that, where the interests of managers and shareholders conflict, managers will take decisions to benefit shareholders. It has been suggested therefore that to overcome this problem and to encourage goal congruence, managerial remuneration should depend upon the success of the firm.

The ways this policy could be implemented include the following.

(a) Issuing shares to managers. In this situation the managers become shareholders and therefore should take decisions which will benefit all shareholders. But managerial and shareholder interests can still conflict and that there is no guarantee that, simply because they are shareholders, managers will choose the latter. The managers may get greater personal benefit by ignoring shareholder interests. Furthermore, the company cannot ensure that the managers will retain their shares.

(b) Basing reward upon the achievement of financial targets, such as profit or return on capital. If the achievement of these targets maximises shareholder wealth, then shareholders will benefit as managers endeavour to meet the targets. However, such a policy could well encourage sub-optimal decision making, such as the retention of fully depreciated fixed assets to boost profit and return on capital employed. Furthermore, emphasis is placed on short-term rather than long-term achievement. Managers may hit targets by making short-term decisions and then leave: no long-term commitment to the firm is guaranteed.

(c) Issuing deferred equity to managers. This should encourage concentration on long-term maximisation of the firm's wealth (as long as the date on which the equity is obtained is not too far in the future). However the managerial reward is not directly related to the performance of the company: the share price may be depressed on the day of the reward

BPP Publishing

because of factors beyond managerial control. Furthermore, such a policy will encourage managers to retain profits for future expansion whereas shareholders may want regular distributions of earnings as their reward for investing funds.

3   CORPORATE GOVERNANCE

(a)   The main recommendation of the Cadbury report was that the boards of all listed companies should comply with the 'Code of Best Practice' defined in the report. A 'statement of compliance' with the Code should become a listing requirement and the directors of all UK companies should use the Code for guidance. In accounts for periods ending on or after 31 December 1992, directors should state whether the report and accounts comply with the Code and give reasons for any non-compliance.

Some of the principal items in the Code are as follows.

(i)   The board of directors should meet regularly and monitor the performance of the executive management.

(ii)   There should be a separation of powers at the top of the firm. This should be achieved either by a separation of the posts of chairman and chief executive, or by ensuring that there is a strong independent group present on the board.

(iii) There should be a formal schedule of matters that must be referred to the board such as material acquisitions and disposals, capital investments and borrowings.

(iv)   The board should include a number of fully independent non-executive directors.

(v)   Directors' contracts should normally be for a maximum of three years, and all emoluments should be fully disclosed. Directors' pay should be decided by a separate remuneration committee.

(vi)   An audit committee should be appointed with the authority, resources and access to investigate anything within its terms of reference. It should have at least one meeting a year with the auditors when no executive directors are present.

(vii) The directors should report on the effectiveness of the internal control systems.

(viii) The board should present a clear and balanced assessment of the company's position, together with a going concern statement supported by any necessary assumptions or qualifications.

(b)   It is not totally correct to talk about the *introduction* of statutory control of corporate governance since there has been some degree of control for a considerable time through such instruments as the Companies Acts. An example is the regulations governing the appointment and responsibilities of directors. However, many of the controls commonly accepted by firms are not statutory in nature but are generally agreed codes of practice. An example of this is the City Code on Takeovers and Mergers which has no legal backing but is administered and enforced by the Takeover Panel.

Recent incidents, for example the collapse of the Maxwell Corporation, have increased the pressure for stricter statutory controls. Particular areas of concern include the following.

(i)   Accounting policies which are misleading as to the true financial health of the company, for example in the area of the capitalisation of intangibles.

(ii)   The weakness of the shareholders' control over the directors' investment decisions.

(iii) The lack of clearly defined rules for the governance and investment of pension funds.

From the point of view of the vast majority of firms which try to follow the spirit of the law and abide by such regulations as do exist, further legislation will only add to the burden of overheads. It is also likely that there would be a large increase in the amount of litigation, some of it for the unintentional breaches of detailed rules. This is happening now in the waste management industry which is subject to much more stringent statutory regulation than most other industries. However, unless all firms do comply not only with the letter but also with the spirit of the legislation it is very likely that more legislation will be introduced in the future.

4   YIELD CURVE

(a)   A yield curve is a curve that can be drawn showing the relationship between the yield on an asset (usually long term government stocks) and the term to maturity of that same asset. It shows how the rate of interest (yield) varies with different maturities. To construct a yield curve you need to gather information about the interest rates on short term stocks, medium term stocks and long-term stocks. These rates can then be plotted on a diagram against the maturity dates of those same stocks.

(b)   A normal yield curve looks like Figure 1.

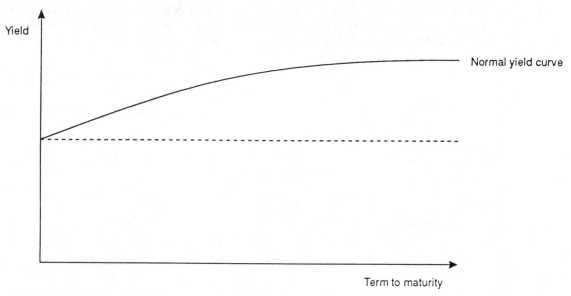

Figure 1

In Figure 1, the longer the time to maturity, the higher is the yield (interest rate). There are several reasons why a normal yield curve looks like this.

(i)   People need to get a reward for tying their money up. This is because they lose the use of this money whilst it is tied up. The longer the period that people lose liquidity in this way, the greater the reward they demand. The only way that borrowers are going to get people to part with the use of their money for long periods of time is to offer them more. The first reason then, for higher yields over longer periods, is to reward people for the loss of their liquidity.

(ii)   The second reason why yields are generally higher for longer terms is due to the increased uncertainty associated with longer time periods. If you tie money up for long periods of time there are many extra uncertainty that you face compared with tying money up for short periods of time in short term assets. The major uncertainty is that inflation over the longer term is more difficult to predict than over a shorter term. Investors are particularly anxious about the effect of inflation on their investments. A yield of 8% may look quite good now, but if you lock into this rate for a long period of time there is considerable risk. In 10 years' time inflation may be much higher and short term interest rates may be 15%. If you are in any doubt that this might happen you would not want to tie up your money at 8% for a 10 year term. This is one main reason why rates for long terms are usually above rates for short terms.

(iii)   If we consider yields on assets other than government stock, there are other risks. The longer the term the greater the risk that the borrower may not repay the loan. To cover this risk of default, rates are usually higher for longer terms.

(iv)   Another problem could be that the investor may wish to cash in his or her investment before maturity. There is a greater risk that this would involve a capital loss on a long-term asset compared with a short-term asset. Short-term government stock for example will trade close to its par value of £100. Long term stock may vary for

BPP Publishing

example between £50 and £200 for each £100 lot. If you have to sell long-term stock in a hurry there is a greater risk of loss.

(c) The shape of the yield curve depends very much on expectations about the future. Reward for loss of liquidity is likely to remain fairly constant. Reward for possible default is likely to remain constant also. Reward for the risk of having to cash in before maturity and suffering a loss are also likely to stay fairly constant. The only factor which will vary widely is expectations - in particular, expectations about future short-term interest rates.

Expectations about the future level of short term interest rates are the most important factor in determining the shape of the yield curve. Although the normal yield curve is upward sloping, expectations of rises in future interest rates can cause the yield curve to be steeper than the normal curve and expectations of falls in interest rates can cause the yield to flatten, or, if substantial falls are expected, to become downward-sloping (Figure 2).

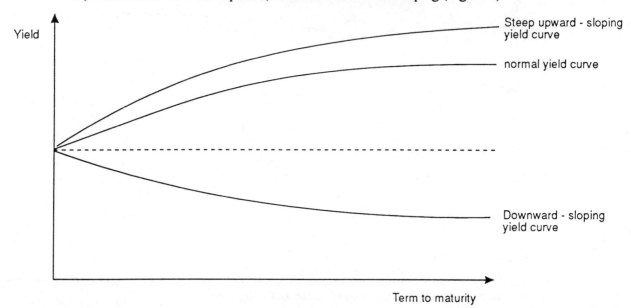

Figure 2

If interest rates are now expected to rise, investors will not wish to lock in to lower interest rates and will therefore sell short. Borrowers will wish to borrow at lower long-term rates to avoid exposure to the higher rates expected in the future. These demand and supply factors will result in a shortage of long-term funds, which will push up long term money market rates, and to an excess supply of short-term funds, which will lead to a reduction in short-term rates. The resulting yield curve will be more steeply upward-sloping than the normal curve.

If there are new expectations that interest rates will fall, investors will prefer to lock in at higher long rates, while borrowers will not wish to be committed to higher long term rates and will prefer to borrow short. There will be an excess supply of funds at long maturities and a shortage of funds at short maturities. This will tend to lower the yield curve, possibly resulting in a flat curve or even in a downward-sloping curve.

Short-term interest rates are in turn determined partly by expectations of inflation rates in the near future. If high inflation is expected, investors will seek higher nominal rates of interest in order to achieve a real return. If people believe that inflation is falling, then they will not require such a high return.

5 TUTORIAL QUESTION: EFFICIENT MARKET HYPOTHESIS

The efficient market hypothesis describes an efficient market as one where security prices fully and speedily reflect available information. This result is the product of the actions of market participants actively competing with each other. The content of any new information becoming available will be quickly digested by market participants and if the information causes them to change their opinion of the security's intrinsic value their subsequent actions will rapidly cause an equivalent change in the security's market price.

The hypothesis takes three forms depending upon the extent of the information deemed available to market participants.

(a) *Weak form.* Information available is restricted to details of past share prices, returns and trading volumes. Hence future prices cannot be predicted from historical price data alone and trading rules based only on such price and volume data, ie the chartist approach, cannot consistently produce excess returns if the hypothesis is correct.

(b) *Semi-strong form.* Share prices reflect all publicly available information. Reaction to public announcements will not produce excess returns as the information content of such announcements is reflected in share prices.

(c) *Strong form.* Share prices reflect all information whether publicly available or not.

Since the question refers to published annual reports it is the semi-strong form of the hypothesis which is in question. This form of the hypothesis is in accord with the results of the first set of investigations, which indicated that the annual report is an important source of information for investment decisions, but appears to conflict with the studies which indicate that market prices of equity do not react in the short term to the publication of the annual report.

There are three factors which may explain the apparent discrepancy.

(a) Much information contained in the annual report will already have been published in the financial press before the report appears.

(b) If the strong form of the hypothesis is valid, share prices may be influenced by information which has not been published. Investors in possession of such information will take action accordingly and if they are large, for example institutional investors, their actions may influence the market price.

(c) It is possible that reactions to the annual report take time to affect share prices. This might be because time is needed to weigh up the contents of the report or because investors need time to gather together the funds necessary to give effect to their reactions. Studies based on the short term would then be inadequate as a guide to the effect of the annual report on market prices.

6   NEBENG

> *Tutorial note.* The APV calculations here are lengthy but not difficult. State clearly the basis of the calculations and the reasons for the selection of the different discount rates for different elements of the cash flow. Also make clear assumptions about the timing of tax allowances.

(a) The benefits of leasing to the lessee are as follows.

    (i) No initial capital payment is required. This is particularly important in the case of very large capital purchases such as aircraft. Instead, the lessee is able to match payments for the use of the equipment with the income generated by it.

    (ii) Where the lessee has insufficient taxable profits to utilise the capital allowances, leasing can be helpful. The lessor will take up the allowances in full and will pass at least part of the benefit on to the lessee in the lease payments. Since 1991, the lessee gets tax relief based on depreciation and interest charged in the profit and loss account.

    (iii) A lease agreement often provides for a secondary period after the term of the primary period has expired. During this secondary period, the lessee pays only a nominal or 'peppercorn' rental but continues to benefit from the use of the asset.

    (iv) When the equipment being leased is likely to become obsolescent very quickly, but at the same time there is an active secondhand market, then leasing provides flexibility.

BPP Publishing

The asset can be leased for a relatively short period and then replaced more cheaply than if it were bought outright. An example of this is computer equipment leasing.

(v) The assets and liabilities associated with operating leases do not have to be shown on the balance sheet, and therefore provide a form of 'off balance sheet' finance. In theory this should make it easier for the company to raise further debt finance; however in practice lenders will look further than the balance sheet in deciding the credit worthiness of a potential borrower.

The relative benefits of hire purchase are as follows.

(i) The hiree obtains ownership of the asset. This may be important if the asset is of key significance in the survival of the business.

(ii) Although there may be a relatively large initial payment, the hiree obtains the benefit of the writing down allowances and is also able to offset the interest element of the annual payments against the tax liability.

(b) The APV technique is a refinement of the NPV approach. Instead of evaluating all the cash flows associated with the project using a single discount rate, the NPV of the basic project is calculated first on the assumption that it is the only project being undertaken by an all equity financed mini-firm. This is known as the 'base case NPV'. The PV of any side effects associated with the project are then calculated using an appropriate discount rate. An example would be the tax relief on debt interest which is discounted at the before-tax interest rate. The APV of the project is the base case APV plus or minus the PV of any side effects. The first step therefore is to calculate the base case NPV of the project. This will be discounted at the cost of equity ie 19% (22% minus the 3% premium due to financial gearing).

Year	Machine cost £	Revenues £	Cash flow £	Discount factor 19%	NPV £
0	(142,500)		(142,500)	1.000	(142,500)
1		40,000	40,000	0.840	33,600
2		40,000	40,000	0.706	28,240
3		40,000	40,000	0.594	23,760
4	22,500	40,000	62,500	0.499	31,188
Base case NPV					(25,712)

The PV of the cash flows associated with each of the different financing options can now be calculated and combined with the base case NPV to determine the APV of each option.

Cash purchase

If Nebeng purchases the equipment, it will benefit from writing-down allowances. It is assumed that these will be claimed from year 1 (ie one year in arrears). The tax saving arising will be discounted at 16% which is the cost of debt, since it is known that the project will be financed by means of a loan. (14%, the risk free rate, could alternatively be used, on the basis that tax savings are virtually risk free.)

Year	NBV £	WDA @ 25% £	Tax cr @ 35% £	Discount factor 16%	NPV @ 16% £
1	142,500	35,625	12,469	0.862	10,748
2	106,875	26,719	9,352	0.743	6,948
3	80,156	20,039	7,014	0.641	4,496
4	60,117	15,029	5,260	0.552	2,904
5	45,088	22,588	7,906	0.476	3,763
PV of tax savings on WDAs					28,859

Note. The WDA in year 5 is calculated as the residual NBV less the residual value (£45,088 – £22,500). Nebeng will also be able to claim tax relief on the interest payments on the loan used to purchase the machine. These too will be discounted at 16%.

It is assumed that tax relief will be claimed from year 1.

Annual interest payment £142,500 × 16% = £22,800

Annual tax relief £22,800 × 35% = £7,980

PV of tax relief for four years (annuity at 16%):
£7,980 × 2.798 = £22,328

The APV of cash purchase can now be calculated:

APV = £28,859 + £22,328 − £25,712 = £25,475

Hire purchase

If Nebeng finances the machine by hire purchase, it will be entitled to writing-down allowances as calculated above (PV = £28,859). It will also be entitled to tax relief on the interest element of the hire purchase payments. The amount of the annual payments can be calculated as follows.

Initial deposit £142,500 × 20% = £ 28,500.00
Balance to be paid over 4 years = £114,000.00

Annual payment £114,000/2.589 = £44,032.44
(2.589 is the value of a four year annuity at 20%)

These annual payments can now be split between capital and interest. The tax relief due on the interest can then be calculated, and this relief discounted at 16% (as above). The interest is calculated as 20% of the capital balance at the end of the previous year.

The new capital balance = old capital balance + interest − payment:

Year	Payment £	Capital balance £	Interest @ 20% £	Tax cr @ 35% £	Discount factor 16%	NPV @ 16% £
0	28,500	114,000				
1	44,032	92,768	22,800	7,980	0.862	6,879
2	44,032	67,290	18,554	6,494	0.743	4,825
3	44,032	36,716	13,458	4,710	0.641	3,019
4	44,032	-	7,343	2,570	0.552	1,419
PV of tax savings on hire purchase interest						16,142

In addition to tax relief on the interest element of the hire purchase payments, Nebeng can also claim tax relief for the four year period on the interest payable on the £28,500 deposit. This too will be calculated at 16%.

Annual interest payment £28,500 × 16% = £4,560
Annual tax relief on interest £4,560 × 35% = £1,596
Discounted value of tax relief (4 year annuity @ 16%) = £4,466

The base NPV must also be adjusted for the different capital cash flows, namely:

Saving in year 0 = £114,000
Additional annual payments years 1 − 4 discounted at 16%:
£44,032 × 2.798 = £123,202

The APV of hire purchase can now be calculated.

APV = £28,859 + £16,142 + £4,466 + £114,000 − £123,202 − £25,712
    = £14,553

Leasing

Annual value of lease payments = £45,000
Assume annual tax relief at 35% from year 1 = £15,750
PV of tax savings at 16% ie £15,750 × annuity for yrs 1–4 (2.798) = £44,069

The base NPV must also be adjusted for the different capital cash flows, namely:

Saving in year 0 = £142,500
Additional annual payments years 0-3 discounted at 16%:
£45,000 × 3.246 = £146,070
Loss of residual value in year 4 £22,500 × 0.499 = £11,228

APV $= £44,069 + £142,500 - £146,070 - £11,228 - £25,712$
$= £3,559$

The APV is positive regardless of the method of financing, and therefore the project should be undertaken. Cash purchase using a £142,500 loan yields the highest APV, and on this basis is the recommended method of financing.

7 SHARE VALUATION METHODS

(a) *Book value of assets per share*. By this method, the shares are valued by taking the net book value of the company's assets that are financed by equity capital, and dividing this by the number of shares in issue. The net book value of fixed assets is their value net of depreciation in the books of account, and the book value of short term assets is total current assets minus total current liabilities.

$$\frac{\text{Net book value of assets minus long term liabilities}}{\text{Number of shares}}$$

Current cost of assets per share. Shares are valued by taking the current cost value of the company's assets that are financed by equity capital, and dividing this by the number of shares in issue. The current cost value of assets is usually their net replacement cost in the case of fixed assets (ie replacement cost minus depreciation) and replacement cost in the case of stocks. However, current cost value might sometimes be net realisable value.

$$\frac{\text{Current cost value of assets minus liabilities}}{\text{Number of shares}}$$

Break-up value of assets per share. By this method, the assets of the company are valued on the basis of what they would sell for if the company were broken up and the assets sold off individually. After providing for the payment of all liabilities and debts, the remaining net sell-off value is divided by the number of shares in issue.

Capital asset pricing model. By this method, a valuation for a share can be derived from the share's estimated beta value. The beta value is used to estimate the expected return from the share (as a percentage annual yield) and this is applied to the actual return in pence to calculate a share price.

Stage 1 $R_s = R_f + \beta (R_m - R_f)$

Stage 2 $MV = \dfrac{\text{Return in pence}}{R_s}$

R_s = return from the share (as a %)
R_f = risk free rate of return
β = the share's estimated beta value
R_m = market rate of return
MV = share price

Price/earnings ratio. For listed companies, the share price is regularly measured as a multiple of the company's earnings per share (EPS), which is simply the ratio of market price to EPS. A share valuation for any company can be reached by multiplying a suitable EPS by a suitable P/E ratio.

$$\text{EPS} \times \text{P/E ratio} = \text{share price.}$$

Dividend valuation model. By this method, a share price is calculated with reference to estimated future annual dividend payments in perpetuity. Given a required annual dividend yield of r (measured as a proportion) the following formulae are used.

(i)   Nil dividend growth: $MV = \dfrac{d}{r}$

(ii)   Estimated annual dividend growth of g: $MV = \dfrac{d(1 + g)}{(r - g)}$

Discounted cash flow. By this method, a valuation for the company's equity is derived by estimating the future annual cash profits (ie profits in cash flow terms), over a 'project period' and discounting these cash flows at an appropriate cost of capital. The resulting net present value of equity can be converted into a share price by dividing this NPV by the number of shares in issue.

Number of years purchase of earnings. By this method, a share is valued on the basis of a certain number of years of earnings, and so it is essentially the same as the price/earnings ratio method.

$$\text{EPS} \times \text{agreed number of years earnings} = \text{share price}$$

Alternatively, it can be used to describe a valuation method whereby shares are valued at, say, the total of the last six years' earnings, or the total of the estimated earnings for the next six years.

(b) **REPORT**

> To: Financial Director
> From: Company Secretary
> Date: 24 March 19X4

Subject: Share valuation methods

This report sets out briefly the objectives of each of eight methods of share valuation, and their strengths and weaknesses.

(i) *Book value of assets per share*

Objective: To relate the value of a share to the company's balance sheet.

Strength: Balance sheet valuations are fairly readily obtainable.

Weaknesses: (1) Balance sheet valuations depend on accounting conventions and might be very different from market valuations.

(2) The value of the company and its shares should come mainly from its profits, not its asset values.

(ii) *Current cost of assets per share*

Objective: To relate the value of a share to the current cost values of the company's assets.

Strength: Balance sheet valuations are less unrealistic than valuations using historical cost accounting, especially in a period of high inflation.

Weakness: The same as in (i) above. A current cost valuation of an asset assumes that the business will continue as a going concern, and so a profit-based valuation of shares must be preferable.

(iii) *Break-up value of assets per share*

Objective: To estimate what the shares would earn if the company's assets were sold off individually.

Strength: This provides a minimum realistic market price for a share. If a share's price falls below this value, it will be profitable to acquire the company and 'strip it' of its assets - ie break it up and sell off the individual assets at a profit.

Weakness: A share's value should normally be well in excess of its break-up value, on the assumption that the company ought to remain a going concern.

(iv) *Capital asset pricing model*

Objective: To estimate a value for a share based on an assessment of its beta value, and the market rate of return and risk-free rate of return.

BPP Publishing

Strengths: (1) It recognises that the value of the share depends on the risk of investing in that share. The assessment of risk is contained within the beta value.

(2) It relates the value of a share to expected returns (both capital gains and dividends).

Weakness: There might be a problem in calculating a beta value. Actual returns on a share will be subjected to 'unexpected' factors, which ought to be taken out in order to calculate a beta value.

(v) *Price/earnings ratio*

Objective: To derive a value for a share based on earnings.

Strengths: (1) Earnings are more significant than dividend for an investor with a controlling interest in the company (eg a parent company), and earnings are used to estimate a share value.

(2) P/E ratios are widely used to assess the market prices of companies whose shares are quoted on the Stock Exchange.

Weaknesses: (1) A P/E valuation for a share depends on estimates of suitable values for EPS and a P/E multiple.

(2) It ignores the likelihood of future changes in EPS from one year to the next.

(vi) *Dividend valuation model*

Objective: To derive a share valuation from estimated future dividend payments on the share.

Strength: Dividends are more relevant to an investor in a minority shareholding than either earnings or asset values.

Weaknesses: (1) Unsuitable for valuations where the shareholder has a controlling interest in the company and can dictate dividends/retentions policy.

(2) Expectations of future dividend growth might be inaccurate.

(3) Possibly inferior to the capital asset pricing model method, which ignores fluctuations in profits and dividends arising from unexpected factors for which the investor can 'diversify away' the risk.

(vii) *Discounted cash flow method*

Objectives: To value a company's shares in terms of cash flows from future earnings and the investor's cost of capital.

Strength: Very useful technique when one company is planning to take over another. It can be used to put a maximum price on the offer price - ie a price where the NPV from the takeover 'project' would be 0.

Weakness: Only useful in takeover situations.

(viii) *Number of years purchase of earnings*

This is essentially similar to the price/earnings ratio method, and the same objectives, strengths and weaknesses apply. Might be used to reach a takeover price where the buyer agrees to pay the seller a multiple of future earnings. For example, a sale price might be 10 times current year earnings of £1 million, with a 'top up' in each of the next 2 years of 10 times the amount by which earnings in those years exceeds £1 million.

BPP Publishing

8 MALA VITA

> *Tutorial note.* In part (a) the market P/E ratio that is provided can be used to derive the market rate of return. This rate of return can then be used as the required rate of return in the dividend yield methods of valuation. However, the assumption that investors will require the market rate must be stated.
>
> In part (b) do not be afraid to come down in favour of one method as being the most appropriate. Do not merely comment on the relative merits of the different approaches.

(a) (i) *Asset value.* The shares can be valued on the basis of the market value of the assets. This provides a measure of the security of the shares, since this method of valuation indicates the amount that the investors might expect to receive if the company was forced into liquidation. It is assumed that there is only one class of shareholders and that therefore all the net assets are attributable to the ordinary shareholders.

Market value of net assets	£20.0m
No of shares in issue	10.0m
Market value of each share	£2.00

(ii) *Earnings basis.* The shares can be valued on the basis of the required price/earnings ratio. It is assumed that investors will expect to receive a similar price/earnings ratio to that which can be obtained on the market portfolio.

Current level of annual earnings	£3.2m
Market P/E ratio	8
Market capitalisation	£25.6m
Market value of each share (3.2 × 8)	£2.56

(iii) *Dividend yield (no growth).* The shares can be valued on the basis of their dividend yield. It is assumed that investors will expect to receive a similar return to that which can be obtained on the market portfolio. This can be calculated as the inverse of the market price/earnings ratio ie $1/8 = 12.5\%$.

$$MV = d/i$$

Current annual dividend (d)	£2.0m
Market rate of return (i)	12.5%
Market capitalisation	£16.0m
Market value of each share	£1.60

(iv) *Dividend yield (including growth).* The dividend yield model used in (c) above can be modified to take into account the rate of growth in dividends that is expected in the future. It is assumed that there will be no change in the payout ratio, and that the rate of growth in dividends will therefore be the same as the projected annual rate of growth in earnings.

$$MV = \frac{d(1 + g)}{(r - g)}$$

where d = current level of dividends
r = required rate of return (assume market rate)
g = projected annual rate of dividend growth

Current annual dividend	£2.0m
Market rate of return	12.5%
Projected rate of growth	5.0%
Market capitalisation	£28.0m
Market value of each share	£2.80

(v) *Capital asset pricing model (CAPM).* The CAPM can be used to calculate a required rate of return specific to the company which takes into account its individual level of

BPP Publishing

risk as expressed through the Beta value. This can then be substituted for the market rate of return in the dividend valuation model including growth ((iv) above) to obtain a valuation of the shares.

$$r = \beta(R_m - R_f) + R_f$$

where
r = required rate of return
β = Beta value (= 1.2)
R_m = Market rate of return (12.5%)
R_f = Risk free rate of return (8.0%)

$$r = 1.2(12.5 - 8.0) + 8.0 = 13.4\%$$

$$MV = \frac{d(1 + g)}{(r - g)}$$

Market capitalisation = £25.0m
Market value of each share = £2.50

(b) The results of the valuation bases applied in part (a) can be summarised as follows.

	Market capitalisation £	Share price £
Asset value	20.0m	2.00
Earnings basis	25.6m	2.56
Dividend yield (no growth)	16.0m	1.60
Dividend yield (including growth)	28.0m	2.80
Capital asset pricing model	25.0m	2.50

The lowest possible price is derived using the dividend valuation model excluding growth. This is out of line with the other results, producing a price which is even lower than the asset-based valuation (the basis which would be expected to produce the most conservative result). Since an annual growth rate of 5% is expected, this version of the dividend valuation model is inappropriate and will be excluded from the discussion.

The remaining approaches suggest a price of between £2.00 and £2.80 per share. The asset value basis is useful in that it indicates the minimum level at which the shares should be priced; if the shares were to be issued at less than £2.00 each, then investors would be obtaining the assets of the company at a discount, and the company's ability to generate income from its assets would be ignored.

The choice then lies between the earnings basis, the dividend yield (with growth) basis and the capital asset pricing model. Of these, the first two approaches are both based on the premise that investors will be looking for a return from the company which is equivalent to the market rate of return. The capital asset pricing model takes into account the element of business risk which is specific to this particular operation. Since the beta-factor for the company is greater than 1.0, the perceived risk attaching to the investment is greater than that for the market portfolio. It is therefore reasonable to assume that investors will wish to see a higher than average return from the firm to compensate them for this higher element of risk. This valuation basis is therefore regarded as being the most appropriate since it is the only one which takes into account that element of risk which is specific to the company, and does not assume that investors are indifferent between risk attaching to alternative securities.

9 TUTORIAL QUESTION: FINANCING EXPANSION

			£m
(a)	(i)	Benefit (0.6/15%)	4
		Cost	5
		Net present value	(1)

The project should not be undertaken as the net present value is negative.

76

(ii) In equilibrium the total market value of a geared company can be derived as follows.

$$V_g = V_u + Dt$$

where V_g = total market value of geared company

V_u = total market value that the same company would have if it was purely equity financed

D = market value of debt

t = rate of corporation tax expressed as a percentage.

For Mosgiel plc:

D = £5,000,000 and t = 40%

V_u = (4,000,000 shares × £3.50) + benefit of project if all equity financed
= £14,000,000 + £4,000,000
= £18,000,000

V_g = 18 + (5 × 0.4) = £20,000,000

D = £5,000,000

The new value of equity after the project is undertaken is £20,000,000 – £5,000,000 = £15,000,000.

This is £1,000,000 more than at present so the project should be undertaken.

(iii) The gearing level in (ii) is 25% (5/20). The formula used in (ii) can again be used but applied this time to the project. V_g is the value of the project (after considering leverage) while D is 25% of V_g (if the gearing level is to be maintained).

$$V_g = (0.6 + 0.15) + (0.4 × 0.25 V_g)$$
$$V_g = 4 + 0.1 V_g$$
$$0.9 \ V_g = 4$$
$$V_g = 4.444444 \text{ (ie £4,444,444)}$$

	£
Benefit of project	4,444,444
Less cost	(5,000,000)
Net present value	(555,556)

The project should not be undertaken because the net present value is negative.

(b) (i) Weighted average cost of capital (WACC) = $\dfrac{\text{Total return to investors}}{\text{Total market value of firm}}$

	£m
Existing return 4 × £3.50 × 15%	2.1

(since cost of capital = $\dfrac{\text{return}}{\text{market value}}$,

return = market value × cost of capital)

	£m
Return from new project	0.6
Total return	2.7
Total market value	20

Therefore WACC = 2.7/20 = 13.5%

(ii) Incremental cost of capital = incremental reward ÷ incremental value of firm
= 0.6/(20 – 14)
= 10%

This figure should confirm the conclusions reached in (a) (ii) and (iii).

The benefit of the project if debt is introduced

	£m
Value of incremental benefit valued at incremental cost of capital (0.6 ÷ 10%)	6
Less cost	5
	1

This is the incremental benefit of the project, financed by the debenture, as calculated in (a) (ii).

The benefit of the project if gearing is already in the capital structure

	£
Value of incremental benefits valued at new WACC (0.6 ÷ 13.5%)	4,444,000
Less cost	5,000,000
Net present value	(555,556)

This is the value calculated in (a) (iii).

(c) The project is not worth undertaking because by itself it has a negative net present value. If the company already had optimal gearing in its capital structure the net present value would remain negative. However, if gearing is to be introduced for the first time (to the optimal level) the worth of existing shareholders will increase. This is because the post-tax cost of the debt reduces the WACC and the advantages from this outweigh the disadvantages of the project.

This can be explained by reference to the following analysis.

	£
NPV of project if financed by equity (a) (i)	(1,000,000)
Favourable effect of gearing (solely with regard to the project itself - W1)	444,444
NPV of project (with gearing considered in relation to the project) (a) (iii)	(555,556)
General benefit of debt (W2)	1,555,556
Net gain by equity (a) (ii)	1,000,000

Workings

W1 The benefit of the project (when gearing already exists and is applied to the project) is £4,444,444 (see (a) (iii)).

The proportion relating to the debt part of the total finance is (25%) £1,111,111.

The post-tax benefit is $1,111,111 \times 40\% = £444,444$.

W2 Let the unused debt capacity be D (but remember that D must comprise 25% of the total firm's value if the optimal gearing level is to be achieved).

$$
\begin{aligned}
V_g &= V_u + Dt \\
&= 14 + (D \times 40\%) \\
&= 14 + (25\% \times V_g \times 40\%) \\
V_g &= 14 + 0.1 V_g \\
0.9\ V_g &= 14 \\
V_g &= £15,555,556 \\
D &= 25\% \times £15,555,556 = £3,888,889
\end{aligned}
$$

Post tax value = $40\% \times £3,888,889 = £1,555,556$

10 CRESTLEE

Tutorial note. When considering the diversification project, you should have taken into account the effect of financial structure on the WACC. You should not have assumed that the WACC of one company can simply be transferred to another for project appraisal.

(a) Consider firstly the expansion of the company's existing operations by the purchase of new machinery. This course of action should not involve any significant change in the risk profile of the company's operations, and therefore no adjustment to take account of variation in risk need be made when calculating the cost of capital to be used in evaluating the expansion.

Probably the best cost of capital to use in investment appraisal is the marginal cost of the funds raised to finance the investment. Provided that the company continues to invest in projects with a similar level of risk, and to finance its investments in such a way as to avoid altering its capital structure in the long term, then the weighted average cost of capital (WACC) gives a reliable guide to the marginal cost of capital.

The WACC for Crestlee can be found as follows.

(i) *The cost of equity*

The two main methods available to calculate the cost of equity are the dividend valuation model and the capital asset pricing model (CAPM). In this case, there is only sufficient information for the CAPM to be used. This can be expressed as follows:

$$R_e = \beta(R_m - R_f) + R_f$$

where
R_e = Cost of equity capital
β = Beta factor for the company (1.2)
R_m = Market rate of return (14%)
R_f = Risk free rate of return (6%)
R_e = $1.2(14\% - 6\%) + 6\% = 15.6\%$

(ii) *The cost of debentures*

It is known that the debentures are trading at £104 per £100. This price can be used to estimate the cost of the stock assuming that it is not redeemed until 19Y0. The after tax cost to the company of servicing this stock is as follows.

Interest (after tax)	8 years × £12 × (1 – 0.33) = 8 years × £8.04
Redemption value year 7	£100

The cost of the debentures can be found by estimating the discount rate which would have to be used in the above situation to provide a NPV of £104. Two rates will be tried, and the actual rate estimated by interpolation.

			£
At 10%:			104.00
Interest	5.335 × £8.04		(42.89)
Redemption	0.467 × £100		(46.70)
NPV			14.41

			£
At 7%:			104.00
Interest	5.971 × £8.04		(48.00)
Redemption	0.582 × £100		(58.20)
NPV			(2.20)

$$R_d = 7\% + \frac{2.20 \times (10\% - 7\%)}{14.41 + 2.20} = 7.4\%$$

(iii) *The WACC*

The WACC can now be found by weighting the cost of the different elements in the capital structure as calculated above on the basis of their market values.

	No in issue	Market price	Market value	Cost	Weighted cost
		p	£m	%	£m
Equity	30m	380	114.00	15.6	17.784
Debentures	56m	104	58.24	7.4	4.310
			172.24		22.094

WACC $= 22.094/172.24 = 12.8\%$

The new debentures will not significantly affect the WACC, since the issue is relatively small.

If the company uses its usual rate of 15% to evaluate this expansion, it would effectively be imposing a premium for risk of 2.2%. Whether such a premium is appropriate will depend on the sensitivities inherent in the expansion plans. However, if the company is satisfied that there will be sufficient demand to support the expansion, then only a low premium should be necessary. A discount rate of 15% therefore seems appropriate.

When considering the rate to apply in appraising the diversification into the packaging industry, it is helpful to take into account the cost of capital of firms carrying out similar operations in the new sector. The WACCs for Canall plc and Sealalot plc can be found as follows.

(i)   Canall plc

(1)   *The cost of equity:*

$$R_e = \beta(R_m - R_f) + R_f$$
$$= 1.3 \times (14\% - 6\%) + 6\% = 16.4\%$$

(2)   *The cost of debentures:*

The debentures will be redeemed in nine years' time. Since the current market price is known, the same technique will be used as in the case of Crestlee plc.

			£
At 10%:			112.00
	Interest	$6.495 \times £14 \times (1 - 0.33)$	(60.92)
	Redemption	$0.350 \times £100$	(35.00)
	NPV		16.08
At 7%:			112.00
	Interest	$7.499 \times £14 \times (1 - 0.33)$	(70.34)
	Redemption	$0.475 \times £100$	(47.50)
	NPV		(5.84)

$$R_d = 7\% + \frac{5.84 \times (10\% - 7\%)}{16.08 + 5.84} = 7.8\%$$

(3)   *The WACC:*

	No in issue	Market price p	Market value £m	Cost %	Weighted cost £m
Equity	20m	180	36.0	16.4	5.904
Debentures	15m	112	16.8	7.8	1.310
			52.8		7.214

WACC $=$ $721.4/52.8 = 13.66\%$

(ii)   Sealalot plc

(1)   *The cost of equity:* $R_e = \beta(R_m - R_f) + R_f$

$$= 1.2 \times (14\% - 6\%) + 6\% = 15.6\%$$

(2)   *The cost of debt:*

The rate of interest being paid on the bank loan is not known. A rate of 10% will be assumed. The cost of debt is therefore 6.7% (10% × 67%).

BPP Publishing

(3) *The WACC*:

	No in issue	*Market price* p	*Market value* £m	*Cost* %	*Weighted cost* £m
Equity	120m	230	276	15.6	43.06
Bank loan	13m	100	13	6.7	0.87
			289		43.93

WACC = 43.93/289 = 15.2%

The effect of the rights issue on Crestlee's WACC can also be calculated. It is assumed that the beta value will remain unchanged and that the cost of the new equity is also 15.6%. For the rights issue to raise £9.275m at an issue price of 342p (380p × 90%), 2.712m shares will need to be issued. No adjustment to the price of the existing shares post-rights will be made since the anticipated effect of the diversification on earnings is not known. The WACC will be as follows.

	No in issue	*Market price* p	*Market value* £m	*Cost* %	*Weighted cost* £m
Rights issue			9.275	15.6	1.447
Equity	30m	380	114.000	15.6	17.784
Debentures	56m	104	58.240	7.4	4.310
			181.515		23.541

WACC = 23.541/181.515 = 12.97%

The WACCs for the three companies are therefore as follows.

	%
Crestlee plc	12.97
Canall plc	13.66
Sealalot plc	15.2

Both Sealalot and Canall have a higher cost of capital than Crestlee. However, the financial structure of the three firms is also quite different. Gearing ratios (Long-term debt : equity) based on book values are as follows.

	%
Crestlee plc (after rights issue)	75.40
Canall plc	40.54
Sealalot plc	16.25

Since the beta values and the after tax cost of debt to the three firms are very similar, the differences in the WACC is a greater reflection of the differences in the level of gearing than of variations in perceived risk. The key question in selecting an appropriate cost of capital for Crestlee to use in its evaluation of the diversification is therefore the likely effect of the project on the volatility of its returns, that is on the beta value. The beta value is a measure of the level of systematic risk in the company, that element of risk which cannot be reduced by diversification. Therefore the fact that this project represents a diversification is irrelevant in setting the criteria for its evaluation. The key question is whether or not the likely volatility in Crestlee's profits will change as a result of its being undertaken. Since the beta values of the three companies are similar, it is unlikely that the volatility will change. Therefore it would seem appropriate to use a similar rate in evaluating the diversification project to that for the expansion project. However, this assumes that the management are confident of their ability to handle the diversification effectively and that they will be able to break into the new market in line with their forecasts.

BPP Publishing

(b) Suggestions that the discount rate should vary over a project's life address the problem of risk in the sense of the likelihood of the actual outcome being different from that anticipated in the forecast cash flows. Such suggestions are based on the risk premium approach. In this approach, a premium is applied to the discount rate used to evaluate the project which reflects the perceived additional risk that will be associated with the project. Normally a single premium is applied to the rate used for each year of the project's life, but in theory the rate could be adjusted for different years.

Consider the view that more distant cash flows are riskier than earlier cash flows. This situation is likely to be true of all forecasts relating to all capital projects. To apply premiums only in respect of diversification projects would therefore be to discriminate against them in favour of other opportunities. Other more appropriate techniques are available to deal with this problem, such as the finite horizon method which requires a project to show a positive NPV based on returns and costs within a given period. Alternatively, the NPV approach can be combined with looking at the payback period to eliminate projects which have a long payback.

If earlier years of a project are more risky than subsequent years, this should be quantifiable in terms of the effect of the project on the beta value. The CAPM, used to estimate the cost of equity, is in theory a single period model, and therefore revised discount rates could be calculated for each year of a project to reflect differences in the level of risk. However, if a project is relatively small in comparison with the overall size of the company, it is doubtful whether such an approach would be appropriate to deal with the problem. It might be more helpful to use sensitivity analysis to calculate the degree of variation in each of the variables that could be tolerated before the project failed to achieve a positive NPV. The benefit of this approach is that it focuses attention on the variables which are of key significance in determining the viability of the project. It is therefore more helpful than simply applying a premium to the discount rate.

11 BERLAN AND CANALOT

> *Tutorial note.* In part (a) remember to use the ex div share price to calculate the market value. Do not be misled into using the interim dividend payment instead of the full payment for the year. Remember also to use the after tax cost of debt when estimating the cost of the debentures. In part (c) the question is asking for a critique of the weaknesses in the two theories and not for an explanation of the theories themselves, on which many candidates wasted valuable time.

(a) The cost of capital of Berlan can be found by calculating the weighted average cost of the debt and equity capital, with weightings based on market values.

Cost of equity

This can be found using the formula $r = d / MV$

where r = cost of equity
d = annual dividend
MV = market price of shares (ex div)

In this case, all earnings are paid out as dividends. The total value of dividends is therefore:

	£
Earnings	15,000,000
Less debenture interest	(3,791,520)
	11,208,480
Less tax at 35%	(3,922,968)
	7,285,512

The market capitalisation is £40,000,000 (50m shares at 80p).

$r = 7,285,512/40,000,000$
$r = 18.21\%$

Cost of debt

The market price of the debentures is £105.50, giving a market capitalisation of £25m. Using traditional theory, this will equate to the income stream to redemption discounted at the cost of capital.

The income stream is made up of three years' interest (after tax) plus the redemption value:

Annual interest = £3,791,520 × 65% = £2,464,488
Redemption value at par = £23,697,000

The cost of capital will be the discount rate at which the NPV of this income equals £25,000. Rates on either side of the cost of capital can be found by trial and error, and the cost of capital then estimated by interpolation.

			£
At 10%:	PV of interest = £2,464,488 × 2.487	=	6,129,181
	PV of redemption value = £23.697m × 0.751	=	17,796,447
	Less market value		(25,000,000)
			(1,074,372)
At 8%:	PV of interest = £2,464,488 × 2.577	=	6,350,986
	PV of redemption value = £23.697m × 0.794	=	18,815,418
	Less market value		(25,000,000)
			166,404

$$\text{Cost of debt} = 8\% + \frac{166,404}{166,404 + 1,074,372} \times 2\% = 8.27\%$$

Weighted average cost of capital

	Market value £	Cost %	Weighted cost £
Equity	40,000,000	18.21	7,284,000
Debt	25,000,000	8.27	2,067,500
	65,000,000		9,351,500

WACC = 9,351,500/65,000,000 = 14.39%

(b) (i) Using Modigliani and Miller's theory, the market value will equal the market value of the company if it were wholly equity financed, plus the present value of tax relief on any debt interest:

$$MV = M_e + Dt$$

where: MV = total market value
M_e = market value if equity financed
D = debt
t = tax rate

In this case:

MV = 32.5m + (5m × 0.35)
MV = 34.25m

The market value will therefore increase by £1.75m (£34.25m − £32.5m).

(ii) It is assumed that the actual cost of debt is 13%. The cost of equity in a geared company can be found using the expression:

$$K_g = K_u + \frac{(1 - t)(K_u - K_d) \times D))}{E_g}$$

83

where K_g = cost of equity in the geared company
K_u = cost of equity when ungeared
t = taxation rate
K_d = cost of debt
D = value of debt
E_g = value of equity in the geared company

In this case:

K_u = 18%
t = 35%
K_d = 13%
D = 35m
E_g = £34.25m – £5m = £29.25m

$$K_g = 18 + \frac{(1 - 0.35)((18 - 13) \times 5)}{29.25} = 18.56\%$$

The cost of equity has therefore risen by 0.56% due to the presence of financial risk.

(iii) The weighted average cost of capital (WACC) can now be found as follows.

The cost of debt = 13% × (1 – 0.35) = 8.45%

	Value £ million	Cost %	Weighted cost £
Equity	29.25	18.56	542.88
Debt	5.00	8.45	42.25
	34.25		585.13

WACC = 585.13/34.25 = 17.08%

The weighted average cost of capital has fallen by 0.92% due to the benefit of tax relief on debt interest payments.

(c) *Traditional theory*

The traditional theory of capital structure contends that there is an optimal mix of debt and equity in a company's financial structure. It is based on the assumption that the introduction of debt into the capital structure initially causes the WACC to fall due to the lower after tax cost of debt; however as the gearing increases, the cost of equity will increase to reflect the rising level of financial risk to the shareholders. Beyond a certain optimal point, the cost of equity will increase at a faster rate and will more than offset the benefits of using debt.

The theory therefore assumes that the cost of equity changes in a non-linear way as gearing rises; it is basically an intuitive theory. It does have some attractions since it is clear that at very high levels of gearing the Modigliani and Miller model breaks down and share prices fall with a rapidly increasing cost of equity. It suggests that there will be at least an optimal range of gearing levels which a company should seek to attain, and this may be useful when making financing decisions. However, it does not provide a precise method of determining what this range is in practice.

Modigliani and Miller theory

This theory is based on the assumption that the total market value of any firm is independent of its capital structure, and can be found by discounting its expected returns at the appropriate rate. However, taken to its logical conclusion and taking into account taxation, the theory would recommend a capital structure wholly made up of debt. It is based on the principle of arbitrage whereby it is assumed that investors are able to adjust their own level of personal gearing and are not reliant on companies in which they invest to do this for them.

Problems with the theory include the following.

(i) The risks faced by an investor may differ between personal gearing and corporate gearing, since if he borrows to invest in a company, he stands to lose his total investment including his debt repayment. If he takes advantage of corporate gearing, then assuming it is a limited liability company, he will only lose his stake in the company.

BPP Publishing

(ii) The interest rate on personal loans is assumed to be the same as on corporate loans and is insensitive to the level of gearing.

(iii) Transaction costs are assumed to be irrelevant.

(iv) It ignores the possibility of bankruptcy at very high levels of gearing, and ignores the effect of restrictive covenants being imposed by lenders at high levels of gearing.

(v) It assumes that the company will be able to use all available tax relief on interest payments. As the gearing level rises this is less likely to be true in practice.

Taking these weaknesses into account, it would be expected that there is an optimal level of gearing which is below 100%. As with the traditional theory, there is no explicit method by which a company can determine what this optimal point or range might be.

To summarise, in practice both theories suggest that there is an optimal range of gearing for a company. However neither of the theories provides a precise method for calculating this range.

12 TUTORIAL QUESTION: COST OF EQUITY

(a) The cost of equity capital for a particular company is the rate of return on investment that appears to be required by the company's ordinary shareholders. The return consists of both dividend and capital gains (ie increases in the share price), and it is expressed as a proportion or percentage of the share's market price.

The returns are expected future returns, not historical returns, and so the returns on equity can be expressed as the anticipated dividends on the shares every year in perpetuity. The cost of equity is then the cost of capital which will equate the current market price of the share with the discounted value of all future dividends in perpetuity.

The cost of equity reflects the opportunity cost of investment for individual shareholders. It will vary from company to company because of the differences in the perceived status (business risk and financial or gearing risk) of different companies.

(b) (i) *Dividend growth model*

$$r = \frac{0.10(1.07)}{1.20} + 0.07$$

$$= 0.159, \text{ or } 15.9\%$$

(ii) *CAPM*

$$r = 8\% + 0.5\,(12\% - 8\%)$$

$$= 8\% + 2\%$$

$$= 10\%$$

(c) *Dividend growth model*

Assumptions in this model are that:

(i) a dividend growth rate can be forecast, and expectations are the same for all shareholders;

(ii) there will be no capital gains in share prices, except those which arise because current dividends increase over time with dividend growth;

(iii) there is a readily-available current market value for the share, which is also a 'free market' price.

None of these assumptions is necessarily correct, and the weakness of assumption (i) is particularly damaging to the credibility of the model.

CAPM

The main assumptions in this model are that:

(i) there is a single risk-free rate of return;

(ii)   an accurate statistical estimate can be made of the beta factor of a company's shares;

(iii)   investors hold well-diversified portfolios;

(iv)   investors are risk-averse, and require higher returns to compensate them for taking risks;

(v)   inflation, and its effect on dividends and capital gains, can be ignored;

(vi)   returns are measured as both dividends and capital gains.

None of the assumptions in the model is unacceptable, in spite of their simplification of reality, but the potential weaknesses are that:

(i)   a statistically reliable beta factor might not exist for some companies' shares;

(ii)   the beta factor is calculated from historical data about dividends and capital growth. Historical data might not provide a good guide to investors' expectations about a company's future, which ought to be the main basis for investment decisions.

13   SHORT QUESTIONS

> *Tutorial note*. With only four marks for each part of this question, answers should be brief and precise.

(a)   The formula to be used is:

$$r = \frac{D}{MV} + g$$

where r = ordinary shareholders' cost of capital,
          D = dividend in year 1,
          MV = market price of share,
          g = growth rate.

(b)   In the Capital Asset Pricing Model, share prices are considered to be subject to two types of risk. Systematic risk is the risk of general market fluctuations, which will affect all shares, and any portfolio however well diversified it may be. Unsystematic risk affects shares in individual companies, reflecting the nature of the companies' businesses, and does not affect a well diversified portfolio as a whole.

(c)   Arbitrage is the process of switching between investments to improve return with no increase in risk, or to reduce risk with no fall in return. According to the theory of Modigliani and Miller, the effect is that a change in a company's gearing does not change its weighted average cost of capital. However, this theory may not apply in practice because individuals and companies differ in borrowing ability and in their tax positions, in particular the availability of tax relief on interest on borrowings.

14   TUTORIAL QUESTION: SHARE PRICES AND RETURNS

(a)   Beta is a measure of systematic risk and found in practice from regression analysis relating returns on a security to market returns. Actual share price behaviour cannot be expected to bear exactly that relationship to market returns in each period. If actual performance were always exactly in accordance to that expected from the beta factor there would be no unsystematic risk at all. The existence of unsystematic risk enables portfolio diversification to reduce risk.

Case 1

Return
$$= \frac{15 - (100 - 93)}{100} = 8\%$$

Index return
$$= \frac{316 - 300}{300} = 5.333\%$$

Expected share return
$$= 2\% + 1.2(5.333\% - 2\%) = 6\%$$

Expected month-end share price
$$= 91p, \text{ ie } (100p \times 1.06 - 15p)$$

The expected price is close to the actual price. The managing director ignored the effect of the dividend payment.

Case 2

1 share at start = 1.5 shares at end.

Return per share held at start
$$= \frac{(120 \times 1.5) - 200}{200} = -10\%$$

Index return
$$= \frac{(325.2 - 360)}{360} = -9.667\%$$

Expected share return
$$= 2\% + 1.2(-9.667\% - 2\%) = -12\%$$

Expected month end share price
$$= \frac{200(1 - 0.12)}{1.5} = 117p$$

The expected price is close to the actual price. The managing director ignored the effect of the bonus issue.

Case 3

The reason for the share price movement being considerably different to that expected of a share with a beta of 1.2 in many months is the existence of the unsystematic risk of the shares.

(b) Given that debt is risk free, the higher gearing in Dee will produce a higher equity beta than in Cee. This reflects the fact that as gearing rises, returns to equity become more volatile.

If: β_g = geared company's beta
β_u = ungeared company's beta
D = market value of debt
E = market value of equity
t = tax rate.

then $\beta_g = \beta_u (1 + (1 - t) D/E)$

β_g for Dee's equity:

(i) with t = 0 $\beta_g = 0.9 \left(1 + \frac{0.2}{0.8}\right) = 1.125$

(ii) with t = 0.4 $\beta_g = 0.9 \left(1 + \frac{0.6 \times 0.2}{0.8}\right) = 1.035$

BPP Publishing

15 TUTORIAL QUESTION: BETA FACTORS

(a) (i) *Company A*

Required return from project = $R_f + \beta (R_m - R_f)$

$= 5 + 1.2 (10 - 5) = 11\%$

Present value of project $= \dfrac{200}{1.11} = £180,180$

(ii) *Company B*

Each of projects 1 and 2

Required return $= 5 + 1.5 (10 - 5) = 12.5\%$

Present value $= \dfrac{50}{1.125} = £44,444$

Project 3

Required return $= 5 + 0.9 (10 - 5) = 9.5\%$

Present value $= \dfrac{100}{1.095} = £91,324$

Total present value of Company B's projects

$= 2 \times £44,444 + £91,324 = £180,212$

(b) Overall β factor of Company B

$$= \left(\frac{2 \times 44,444}{180,212} \times 1.5 \right) + \left(\frac{91,324}{180,212} \times 0.9 \right) = 1.196 \cong 1.2$$

(c) Both companies have very nearly the same expected present value and systematic risk and therefore in an efficient capital market would have about the same market value.

Company B is a diversified company and if investors were not themselves able to hold well-diversified portfolios and thereby reduce as far as possible unsystematic risk then Company B would be likely to be more highly valued by investors. However in large, well developed capital markets such diversification by individual investors is quite easily possible and therefore Company B's own diversification gives it no advantage over Company A.

16 PORTFOLIO RISK

Tutorial note. Among the common errors noted by the CIMA examiner for this question were the following.

Part (a): 'Many candidates ignored the work "riskiness" and merely calculated expected rates of return from the two securities for which no marks were awarded. Others tabulated a probability distribution of returns, implying the nil correlation which they had been told to ignore.'

Part (b): 'A very high percentage of candidates could not answer this question or produced incorrect solutions. Some of them, obviously still thinking about part (a), gave diagrams illustrating the reduction of risk as the number of securities in a portfolio increased, or possible alternative combinations of two securities.'

(a) *Perfect positive correlation from given data*

Probability	Security A:40% expected return	Security B:60% expected return	Combined portfolio (R)	pR	$R - \bar{R}$	$p(R - \bar{R})^2$
0.2	4.8	9.0	13.8	2.76	(4.2)	3.53
0.6	6.0	12.0	18.0	10.80	-	-
0.2	7.2	15.0	22.2	4.44	4.2	3.53
	18.0	36.0		18.00		7.06

$\bar{R} = 18.00$ Standard deviation = $\sqrt{7.06} = 2.66$

Perfect negative correlation from given data

Probability	Security A:40% expected return	Security B:60% expected return	Combined portfolio (R)	pR	$R - \bar{R}$	$p(R - \bar{R})^2$
0.2	4.8	15.0	19.8	3.96	1.8	0.65
0.6	6.0	12.0	18.0	10.80	-	-
0.2	7.2	9.0	16.2	3.24	(1.8)	0.65
	18.0	36.0		18.00		1.30

$\bar{R} = 18.00$ Standard deviation = $\sqrt{1.30} = 1.14$

Thus it can be seen that perfect positive correlation, with movements in expected returns of both securities going in the same direction, gives the highest risk for the portfolio; while perfect negative correlation, with the movements of expected returns on the two securities varying inversely, gives the lowest risk. If there is no discernible correlation, the risk factor will fall somewhere between the standard deviations shown.

(b) (i) Investors want the highest possible returns at the lowest possible risk. There are of course limits to what can be attained, and in general the higher the return, the higher the risk. An investor may be indifferent between certain combinations of risk and return, and if a graph of risk (measured by the standard deviation, σ, of the return on a portfolio) against expected return is plotted, such combinations between which an investor is indifferent fall on an *indifference curve*. Such curves slope up to the right, as higher risk is only acceptable if matched by a higher expected return.

An investor would prefer to have a portfolio on an indifference curve as far to the left as possible (curve A in the diagram below), as that represents high returns and low risks. However, if we plot the actual portfolios available (the crosses in the diagram), we may find that the best obtainable portfolio lies on another indifference curve (curve B). This portfolio, the one lying on the left-most indifference curve which meets any actual portfolios, will be the best available. It is marked * in the diagram. It is clearly preferable to portfolio z, which lies on indifference curve C and offers lower expected returns at higher risk.

The actual portfolios cover an area, of which the left hand boundary is the *efficient frontier*. Any portfolio within the area can be bettered by one on the efficient frontier, either by its offering the same return at lower risk or by its offering a higher return at the same risk. The best portfolio for an investor will therefore always lie on the efficient frontier, at a point where it just touches (is tangential to) an indifference cure. Any indifference curve which crosses the efficient frontier must be further to the right than, and therefore less desirable than, one which only touches the efficient frontier.

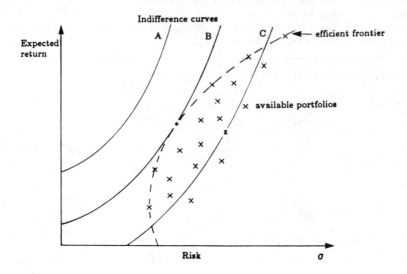

17   CAPITAL MARKET LINE

Tutorial note. The question requires the construction of simple equations to calculate the mix of equities and risk free investments in the two portfolios. It also requires a knowledge of the linear expression which describes the capital market line, since this must be used to calculate the new standard deviation in (c). In (b), the axes of your graph should be labelled clearly.

(a)   X's overall expected return is 18%. We know that one third of his investments are at the risk free rate of 12%. It is therefore possible to calculate the overall return being earned by his equity investments as follows:

Let: Overall expected return $= R$
Return on equities $= R_e$
Risk free returns $= R_f$

$$R = R_f/3 + 2R_e/3$$
$$18 = 4 + 2R_e/3$$
$$14 = 2R_e/3$$
$$R_e = 21\%$$

Assume that the market portfolio held by Y is similar to that of X and yields a return of 21%. For Y to achieve an overall return in excess of this implies that he must be augmenting his funds by borrowing at the risk free rate.

Let: Overall expected return $= R$
Funds borrowed as a proportion of
existing investment $= F$
Return on equities $= R_e$
Risk free returns $= R_f$

BPP Publishing

$$R = R_e(1 + F) - (R_f \times F)$$
$$24 = 21(1 + F) - 12F$$
$$24 = 21 + 21F - 12F$$
$$3 = 9F$$
$$F = 1/3$$

Y has therefore borrowed at 12% to increase his funds by one third. All his funds are invested in equities.

(b)

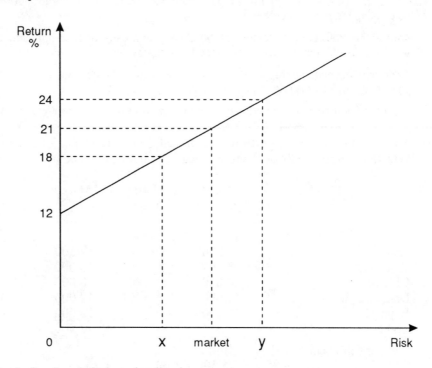

(c) The formula for the capital market line is:

$$Y = R_f + b\sigma$$

Where: Y = Overall rate of return
          R_f = Risk free rate of return
          b = Slope of capital market line
          σ = Standard deviation of portfolio

Using the existing data for the portfolio it is possible to calculate b.

$$18 = 12 + 12b$$
$$b = 0.5$$

This can then be used to calculate the new standard deviation of the portfolio if the required return increases to 20%.

$$Y = R_f + b\sigma$$
$$20 = 12 + 0.5\sigma$$
$$\sigma = 16\%$$

The composition of the new portfolio can also be calculated.

Let: R = Overall rate of return
     R_f = Risk free rate of return
     R_e = Rate of return on equities
     p = Proportion invested in risk free investments

$$R = pR_f + R_e(1 - p)$$
$$20 = 12p + 21(1 - p)$$
$$20 = 12p + 21 - 21p$$
$$9p = 1$$
$$p = 1/9$$

91

Thus the proportion of equities in the portfolio would have to increase to 8/9, with a corresponding rise in the risk (as represented by the standard deviation) of the portfolio, in order to achieve an overall rate of return of 20%.

18   INVESTOR

Tutorial note. Use a weighted average based on market values and not book values when calculating the portfolio beta.

Assess the over-/under-valuation of the shares by means of a comparison of required returns using the CAPM and the actual expected returns provided.

Take into account share price and business variability as well as transaction costs when assessing buy/hold/sell decisions.

In part (c), you need to set portfolio theory in the context of real life investment decisions.

(a)   The beta factor for the portfolio can be calculated by means of a weighted average of the beta values of the individual shares. Market values should be used in weightings.

	No of shares	Market price	Market value (MV) £	Beta factor (β)	MV × β
Ace plc	5,000	250	12,500	1.35	16,875
Black plc	8,000	225	18,000	1.25	22,500
Club plc	10,000	180	18,000	0.90	16,200
Diamond plc	12,000	150	18,000	1.10	19,800
Eight plc	15,000	80	12,000	0.85	10,200
Total			78,500		85,575

The portfolio beta $= (MV \times \beta)/MV$
$= 85,575/78,500 = 1.09$

The required return on the portfolio can be calculated by establishing the required rate of return for each share, and then applying this to the market value of the holding. The formula used is:

$$R = \beta(R_m - R_f) + R_f$$

where: R = Return on the individual share
β = Beta factor
R_m = Market rate of return (15%)
R_f = Risk free rate of return (9%)

	Beta factor	R (%)	Market value (MV) £	R × MV
Ace plc	1.35	17.10	12,500	2,138
Black plc	1.25	16.50	18,000	2,970
Club plc	0.90	14.40	18,000	2,592
Diamond plc	1.10	15.60	18,000	2,808
Eight plc	0.85	14.10	12,000	1,692
Total				12,200

A quicker way to calculate this is to calculate 'R' for the portfolio as a whole using the beta factor previously derived, and then to apply this rate of return to the market value of the portfolio:

$$R = \beta(R_m - R_f) + R_f$$
$$R = 1.09(15 - 9) + 9 = 15.54\%$$

Expected return $= £78,500 \times 15.54\% = £12,200$

(b) It is possible to assess whether an individual share in the portfolio is over- or under-valued by comparing its expected return for the coming period with the required return derived on the basis of its systematic risk (beta factor) calculated above. If the expected return is less than the required return, then the share is over-valued, and vice versa.

	Expected return %	*Required return %*	*Difference*
Ace plc	17.50	17.10	0.40
Black plc	15.00	16.50	(1.50)
Club plc	13.20	14.40	(1.20)
Diamond plc	15.10	15.60	(0.50)
Eight plc	12.70	14.10	(1.40)

It appears that with the exception of Ace plc, the shares in the portfolio are all over-valued since the expected return is less than the required return. The portfolio manager might therefore decide that the shares in Black, Club, Diamond and Eight should be sold. However, it is possible that the manager expects that the market return is also likely to fall in the coming year, and if this is the case then the required returns from the individual shares would also fall. If this is the case, then since the difference between expected and required returns are small, it is unlikely that the shares are in reality over-valued.

In taking the decision as to whether to sell or hold the apparently over-valued shares, the portfolio manager must take into account the likelihood of abnormal events affecting the actual returns that will be achieved, together with the obvious uncertainty about expected returns. He must also take into account the transaction costs that will be involved in trading equities, and should only sell if he is able to obtain a significantly better return elsewhere after taking these costs into account.

(c) Portfolio theory provides the portfolio manager with a formal means of evaluating the systematic risk profile of his portfolio. He can decide the level of risk that he is happy to accept and express this in terms of a target beta factor for his portfolio as a whole. He can then select securities which will provide him with this risk/return profile. As has been demonstrated above, he can also use the theory to indicate whether an individual security is correctly priced in the market, and this will influence his buying and selling decisions.

At the same time, however, the portfolio manager must be aware of the theoretical shortcomings of this form of analysis.

(i) The theory assumes that transaction costs can be ignored. In practice, the costs of buying and selling shares, particularly in relatively small quantities may become significant.

(ii) It further assumes that investors hold a well diversified portfolio and are therefore protected against unsystematic risk and need only be concerned with systematic risk. In practice this is often not the case. The portfolio above contains only five securities, and this is unlikely to provide full protection against unsystematic risk. The portfolio manager must therefore often take this factor into account as well.

(iii) The theory is based upon a single period time horizon. This is unrealistic in terms of the way business decisions within firms are made.

In practice, the portfolio manager must also take other factors into account as well as the risk/return profile. These include the following.

(i) *Liquidity*. The manager must ensure that he always has liquid funds available to meet current commitments. This may mean that the portfolio at any one time contains a higher than predicted element of risk-free securities which are being held in anticipation of a known payment.

(ii) *Purpose*. The purpose for which the portfolio is being held will influence its make-up. For instance, if the overall fund is small and transaction costs are significant, and the fund is being invested with the intention of providing a regular income, then the manager will select high income securities in preference to growth stocks. This may mean that the optimum portfolio from the point of view of the theory may not be the one which should in practice be selected.

(iii) *Investment criteria*. The owners of the fund may lay down investment criteria such as the ethical status of the companies in which they invest, which restrict the choice available to the portfolio manager. Again this may mean that the 'optimum portfolio' is not chosen.

Thus it can be seen that the theory does have relevance to a portfolio manager in his selection of securities, but it does not provide the complete answer to the structuring of a portfolio.

19 OTC INVESTMENTS

Tutorial note. Part (a) is testing your knowledge of the OTC market and also requires you to discuss the value of making an OTC investment in a portfolio of this size and type.

Parts (b) and (c) call for the ability to handle the CAPM formulae and to interpret their results.

Part (d) requires an evaluation of the techniques used in parts (b) and (c) in the context of the overall portfolio selection. Take into account not only the size of the OTC investment, but also its interaction with the overall portfolio and the practical problems associated with the analysis.

(a) An important characteristic of the OTC market is that it is independent of the official Stock Exchange. The UK market developed in the 1970's and is a trading place for the shares of smaller medium size companies through a number of licensed dealers. The dealers try to match buyers' and sellers' requirements and do not work to a common set of rules as is the case in the USM and the full market. Regulations covering accounting and other information are also less stringent.

As a result, investment in OTC companies tends to be more risky than those traded on the other markets, and the 'matching' system means that it can be difficult to dispose of OTC shares. However, the advantage is that the company can gain access to specific investment opportunities that are not available elsewhere.

A further problem in this case is the size of the investment required. Since the majority of OTC companies are small, £250,000 could represent a significant proportion of their capital, and such an investment is likely to be inappropriate for this company. The number of companies in which it could invest will therefore probably be small. However, the portfolio is intended to provide funds for future acquisitions, and it might be that a small investment in an OTC company could pave the way for its takeover at a later date.

(b) The correlation coefficient can be found using the expression:

$$r = \frac{Cov(A,B)}{\sigma a \times \sigma b}$$

where: r   = Correlation coefficient
Cov(A,B) = Covariance of investments A and B
σa   = Standard deviation of returns from A
σb   = Standard deviation of returns from B

The correlation coefficient can range from –1.0, meaning perfect negative correlation, to +1.0 meaning perfect positive correlation. Perfect negative correlation means that there is the maximum unsystematic risk reduction, while perfect positive correlation means that there is no unsystematic risk reduction. Unsystematic risk is that element of risk which can be reduced by diversification.

(i) *A and C*

$$r = \frac{12.6}{6.4 \times 2.5} = 0.79$$

The correlation coefficient of +0.79 between A and C means that there is strong positive correlation and that there will be little reduction in unsystematic risk through combining the two investments in a portfolio.

(ii)   *B and C*

$$r = \frac{8.4}{4.3 \times 2.5} = 0.78$$

The correlation coefficient of +0.78, although a little smaller than that between A and C, is still relatively strong, and there will be little reduction in unsystematic risk if the two investments are combined in a portfolio.

(iii)   *A and B*

$$r = \frac{4.4}{4.3 \times 6.4} = 0.16$$

The correlation coefficient between A and B is much lower than the other two. A much greater reduction in unsystematic risk will be achieved if the two investments are combined in a portfolio.

(c)   The risk/return profile can be assessed by calculating the expected return and the standard deviation of each portfolio. The standard deviation measures the expected variability in portfolio returns, and therefore a lower standard deviation indicates a lower level of risk.

The expected return can be calculated using the expression:

$$R_{ab} = (P_a \times R_a) + (P_b \times R_b)$$

where: R_{ab} = Expected return from portfolio AB
P_a = Proportion of funds invested in A
P_b = Proportion of funds invested in B
R_a = Expected return from investment A
R_b = Expected return from investment B

The standard deviation can be calculated using the expression:

$$\sigma_{ab} = \sqrt{(W_a)^2\sigma_a^2 + (W_b)^2\sigma_b^2 + 2r(W_a)(W_b)(\sigma_a)(\sigma_b)}$$

where: σ_{ab} = Standard deviation of portfolio of A and B
W_a = Weighting (proportion) of investment A
W_b = Weighting (proportion) of investment B
σ_a = Standard deviation of returns from A
σ_b = Standard deviation of returns from B
r = Correlation coefficient of returns from A & B

In all cases the portfolio is made up of equal proportions of the two investments.

A and C

R_{ac} = $(0.5 \times 14\%) + (0.5 \times 17\%) = 15.5\%$

σ_{ac} = $\sqrt{(0.5)^2 2.5^2 + (0.5)^2 6.4^2 + (2 \times 0.79 \times 0.5 \times 0.5 \times 2.5 \times 6.4)}$
= 4.26

B and C

R_{bc} = $(0.5 \times 14\%) + (0.5 \times 16\%) = 15.0\%$

σ_{bc} = $\sqrt{(0.5)^2 2.5^2 + (0.5)^2 4.3^2 + (2 \times 0.78 \times 0.5 \times 0.5 \times 2.5 \times 4.3)}$
= 3.22

A and B

R_{ab} = $(0.5 \times 17\%) + (0.5 \times 16\%) = 16.5\%$

$$\sigma_{ab} = \sqrt{(0.5)^2 6.4^2 + (0.5)^2 4.3^2 + (2 \times 0.16 \times 0.5 \times 0.5 \times 6.4 \times 4.3)}$$
$$= 4.13$$

The results can be summarised as follows.

Portfolio	Expected return	Standard deviation
A and C	15.5%	4.26
B and C	15.0%	3.22
A and B	16.5%	4.13

For one portfolio to be considered more efficient than another it must offer either a higher level of return for a given level of risk or a lower level of risk for a given level of return. In this case, the portfolio comprising A and B is superior to that comprising A and C since it offers a higher expected return plus a lower level of risk. However, it is not possible to determine from the information available whether it is also more efficient than the B/C portfolio since both the expected return and the expected risk are higher.

(d) The calculations made in part (c) only relate to the effect of combining the OTC companies together into a two asset portfolio with a total value of £500,000. This is very small in the context of the total £28m portfolio being constructed. Further, the issue at stake is not the effect of combining the two OTC investments together, but the effect that such investments would have on the risk/return profile of the whole portfolio. Thus it is not valid to include the OTC investments on the basis of the calculations above.

The implication of this is that the entire proposed portfolio, including the various possible combinations of OTC investments should be subjected to risk/return analysis. This is likely to be extremely time consuming in practice. It will also be very difficult to carry this out with any degree of accuracy since all estimates of the risk and return associated with each security will be subject to varying degrees of error.

20 SLOHILL PLC

(a) The cost of capital will be estimated using the dividend valuation model.

$$\text{Cost of equity} = \frac{\text{Dividend one year hence}}{\text{Share price}} + \text{dividend growth rate}$$

Dividend growth rate $= \sqrt[4]{14.98 / 9.86} - 1 = 0.11$

Dividend one year hence $= 1.11 \times 14.98/69 = £0.241$

$$\text{Cost of equity} = \frac{0.241}{5.46} + 0.11 = 0.154 = 15.4\%$$

The cost of debt is r in the equation $£93 = \dfrac{11 \times 0.65}{1 + r} + \dfrac{11 \times 0.65}{(1+r)^2} + ... + \dfrac{11 \times 0.65 + 100}{(1+r)^{15}}$

This must be solved by trial and error: r = 0.08, or 8%, is very close to the exact solution, giving a value for the right hand side of £92.70.

The current weighted average cost of capital is therefore

$$\frac{(15.4\% \times 69 \times 5.46) + (8\% \times 138 \times 0.93)}{(69 \times 5.46) + (138 \times 0.93)} = 13.5\%$$

(i) If the crash has negligible effect on the company's earnings expectations and the growth rate of those earnings, the new cost of equity will be

$$\frac{0.241}{5.46 \times 0.7} + 0.11 = 17.3\%$$

BPP Publishing

The new cost of debt will be about $8 - 2 \times 0.65 = 6.7\%$ (interest rates will fall as investors seek safety in interest-bearing securities), and the new market value of the debt will be approximately:

$$11 \times 0.65 \times 15 \text{ - year annuity factor at } 6.7\% + \frac{100}{1.067^{15}}$$

$$= \quad 11 \times 0.65 \times \frac{1}{0.067}\left[1 - \frac{1}{1.067^{15}}\right] + \frac{100}{1.067^{15}}$$

$$= \quad (7.15 \times 9.283) + 37.8 = 104.2$$

The new weighted average cost of capital will be

$$\frac{(17.3\% \times 69 \times 5.46 \times 0.7) + (6.7\% \times 138 \times 1.042)}{(69 \times 5.46 \times 0.7) + (138 \times 1.042)} = 13.6\%$$

(ii) If the rate of growth in the company's pre-tax earnings falls by 20%, the rate of growth in the company's dividends will probably also fall by 20%, to $0.11 \times 0.8 = 0.088$.

The new cost of equity will be:

$$\frac{1.088 \times 14.98 / 69}{5.46 \times 0.7} + 0.088 = 15\%$$

The new weighted average cost of capital will be

$$\frac{(15\% \times 69 \times 5.46 \times 0.7) + (6.7\% \times 138 \times 1.042)}{(69 \times 5.46 \times 0.7) + (138 \times 1.042)} = 12.1\%$$

(b) REPORT

To: Managing Director
From: A B Accountant
Date: 15 July 19X9
Subject: The effect on the cost of capital of raising new finance and of a stock market crash

(i) *The effect of issuing new equity*

If the expected crash does not affect earnings prospects, the cost of equity will rise slightly. However, the weighted average cost of capital would be increased by an equity issue, because the cost of equity is much higher than the cost of debt. It is extremely unlikely that the fall in gearing would lead to a significant fall in the cost of debt, as (based on market values) gearing is in any case low.

If the expected crash reduces prospective earnings, the cost of equity will fall. While an equity issue would still have the effect of raising the weighted average cost of capital, this increase could well be less than the fall due to the crash, so the final weighted average cost could still be less than the pre-crash weighted average cost.

(ii) *The effect of issuing new debt*

Whatever happens, a fall in the weighted average cost of capital is likely, because of the relatively low cost of debt. The fall will probably be greater if the crash adversely affects earnings prospects, although in that case increases in the cost of both debt and equity are more likely due to concern over gearing. However, a very large amount of debt would have to be issued for gearing to become a serious problem.

(c) Under the capital asset pricing model, $K_e = R_f + (R_m - R_f) \beta_e$,

where K_e = the cost of equity
R_f = the risk-free rate of return
R_m = the market rate of return
β_e = the equity beta for the company

R_f would fall following the crash.

R_m would probably rise if the crash did not affect earnings prospects. If earnings prospects were affected, however, R_m might rise or fall. The larger the adverse impact on earnings prospects, the more likely is a fall in R_m.

β_e is likely to remain constant, unless the company's earnings prospects fall by a different percentage from the market average fall.

21 NELSON

(a) (i) Oak plc has 40% gearing in its capital structure.

Beta of ungeared company

$$= \text{Beta of geared company} \div \left[1 + \frac{(1 - \text{corporate tax rate}) \times \text{market value of debt}}{\text{market value of equity}} \right]$$

$$= 1.12 \div \left[1 + \frac{(1 - 0.4) \times 0.4}{0.6} \right] = 1.12 \div 1.4$$

$$= 0.8$$

(ii) Beech plc's beta is a weighted average of the beta factor relating to risky investments and the beta factor relating to normal investments. Since the latter operating activities are carried out entirely by Nelson plc, its beta factor will be equivalent to this latter beta.

1.11 = (70% × β factor of normal activities) + (30% × 1.9)
1.11 = 70% × β + 0.57
70% × β = 0.54
β = 0.77

(iii) Two calculations have to be carried out for Pine plc, firstly to adjust Pine's beta to what it would be if the company were all equity financed and secondly to eliminate the proportion of the beta relating to the risky investments.

Using the same formula as in (i):

$$\text{ungeared beta} = 1.14 \div \left[1 + \frac{(1 - 0.4) \times 0.25}{0.75} \right]$$

$$= 1.14 \div 1.2 = 0.95$$

This beta is a weighted average of East's beta and West's beta. East comprises 2/3 of the total activities of Pine but West's activities are 50% riskier than East's. We wish to find East's beta as it should be the same as Nelson's.

0.95 = 2/3 β $_{East}$ + 1/3 β $_{West}$
β $_{West}$ = 1.5 β $_{East}$
0.95 = 2/3 β $_{East}$ + (1/3 × 1.5 β $_{East}$)
0.95 = 1.167 β $_{East}$
β $_{East}$ = 0.814

(b) Nelson's beta, when calculated from its share price movements may differ from the values calculated in (a) for the following reasons.

BPP Publishing

(i) To calculate an accurate beta share movements will have to be observed over an extended period. During this time the operating practices of all four companies might have changed.

(ii) We are not told whether the four companies are of a similar size. If one is markedly smaller, its beta will be higher, since small firms are assumed to be riskier than larger ones.

(iii) We have assumed that the debt finance in the capital structure of Oak and Pine is risk-free. If it is not, then the use of the formula in (a) (i) and (iii) would be invalid.

(iv) The beta factor calculated may be distorted by severe fluctuations in share prices for various reasons. It is important to note that Nelson plc has only been quoted for two months. It will take some time before the share price settles down. Initially the company may be considered risky by the market until more is known about it.

(v) The mathematical techniques used to calculate the beta, such as linear regression, will only provide an approximation to the actual beta factor.

(c) The reason why a risky company may have a lower beta factor than an equivalent company considered less risky is as follows. The total risk of a security comprises systematic risk and unsystematic risk. Unsystematic risk is unique to each security and so can be reduced by having a well-diversified portfolio. Systematic risk depends on such things as changes in the economy and cannot be diversified away.

The beta factor measures a security's systematic risk, its connection with the general market. Therefore it is possible for a security to possess a high level of unsystematic risk (because of its own activities) but a low level of systematic risk (because of a weak relationship with the market). An example would be a dealer in commodities: the nature of its operations is inherently risky, but on the other hand its results will only be influenced slightly by general economic factors.

22 UNIVO

> *Tutorial note*. The first part of the question asks for a simple description of two of the theories of share price determination and was well answered except when candidates confused technical analysis and fundamental analysis.
>
> In part (b), the equity beta can be estimated using the WACC based on market values. This beta can then be used to estimate the cost of equity capital to be used in the dividend growth model to calculate the share price. This should be based on the PV of expected dividends at the start of 19X4 when the growth rate becomes constant. To this price must then be added the PV of expected dividends for 19X2 and 19X3 when the growth rate is different.

(a) The fundamental theory of share values is based on the premise that there is an intrinsic market price of a share which is dependent upon the valuation of expected future dividends. The share price equals the present value of all future dividends, discounted at the investors' cost of capital. Thus the price of a share is predictable provided that investors all have the same information and agree on expectations of future profits and dividends, and that investors all have a known cost of capital.

In general terms, fundamental analysis does seem to be valid. However in practice, share prices fluctuate from day to day depending on variations in other factors such as the relative strength of supply and demand and market interest rates. These fluctuations cannot be predicted using fundamental analysis.

To deal with this situation, analysts may use charting or technical analysis to predict price movements. Technical analysis is based on the premise that previous patterns in share prices will be repeated. It is a purely empirical approach with no underlying economic rationale, but it does seem to have some value in predicting price changes.

Random walk theory was developed in an attempt to disprove chartism and to account for the fluctuations around the share price predicted by fundamental analysis in a more rational way.

(b) (i) The dividend growth model may be formulated as follows.

$$MV = \frac{d(1 + g)}{(r - g)}$$

where: MV = market price of the share (ex div)
      d   = current net dividend
      r   = cost of equity capital
      g   = expected annual rate of dividend growth

In this example, the first step is to calculate the cost of equity capital. This may be done using the CAPM, assuming that debt and equity betas are weighted using market values. The CAPM takes the form:

$$r = \beta(R_m - R_f) + R_f$$

where: r   = cost of capital
      β = beta factor relating to the type of capital in question
      R_m = market rate of return
      R_f = risk free rate of return

The current market price of the shares (cum div) is 217 pence. There are 40,000,000 shares in issue, and thus the estimated 19X1 dividend per share is 7 pence. The market price ex div is therefore 210 pence per share. The market capitalisation is £84m (40m × 210p).

The current market price of the debentures ex interest is £89.50. The total market value of the debentures is therefore £13.425m (15m × £0.895).

The beta of the equity can be estimated as follows:

$$Wa = \frac{E\beta_e}{E + D(1 - t)} + \frac{D(1 - t)\beta_d}{E + D(1 - t)}$$

where: β_a = asset beta   (0.763)
      β_e = equity beta
      β_d = debt beta   (0.2)
      E   = market value of equity   (£84m)
      D   = market value of debt   (£13.425m)
      t   = corporate tax rate   (35%)

$$0.763 = \frac{84\beta_e}{84 + (13.425 \times 0.65)} + \frac{13.425 \times 0.2 \times 0.65}{84 + (13.425 \times 0.65)}$$

β_e = 0.82

This can now be substituted into the CAPM expression to find the cost of equity.

      r $= \beta(R_m - R_f) + R_f$
      r $= 0.82(17\% - 12\%) + 12\% = 16.1\%$

Dividend growth between 19W9 and 19X1 has been 9.5% per year. It is estimated that growth in 19X2 and 19X3 will be 25%, thereafter reverting to 9.5%. Dividends for the next three years can be estimated as follows.

BPP Publishing

	Total dividend	Dividend per share	Discount factor 16%	PV Pence
19X1	2,800,000	7.00p		
19X2	3,500,000	8.75p	0.862	7.54
19X3	4,375,000	10.94p	0.743	8.13
19X4	4,790,625	11.98p		
				15.67

The dividend growth model can now be applied from 19X4 onwards when growth in dividends will be constant. The current net dividend to be used will be 11.98p as at the start of the year. This should therefore be discounted using 0.743 as a discount factor, giving a PV of 8.9p.

$$MV = \frac{d(1+g)}{(r-g)}$$

where: MV = market price of the share (ex div)
d = current net dividend (8.9p)
r = cost of equity capital (16.1%)
g = expected annual rate of dividend growth (9.5%)

$$MV = \frac{8.9 \times (1 + 9.5\%)}{(16.1\% - 9.5\%)}$$

MV = 147.66p

To this must be added the PV of the dividend for 19X2 and 19X3.

Estimated intrinsic value = 147.66 + 15.67 = 163.33p

The actual market price of the shares (ex div) is 210 pence per share. A fundamental analyst would therefore regard the shares as being overpriced and would recommend their sale.

(ii) If the interest rate increased by 2%, the return required on equity is likely to increase by a similar amount to approximately 18%. The PV of dividends to be used in calculations will therefore fall.

	Total dividend	Dividend per share	Discount factor 18%	PV Pence
19X1	2,800,000	7.00p		
19X2	3,500,000	8.75p	0.847	7.41
19X3	4,375,000	10.94p	0.718	7.85
19X4	4,790,625	11.98p		
				15.26

The PV of the expected dividend from 19X4 onwards will fall to 8.6p (11.98p × 0.718).

$$MV = \frac{d(1+g)}{(r-g)}$$

where: MV = market price of the share (ex div)
d = current net dividend (8.6p)
r = cost of equity capital (18%)
g = expected annual rate of dividend growth (9.5%)

$$MV = \frac{8.6 \times (1 + 9.5\%)}{(18\% - 9.5\%)}$$

MV = 110.79p

To this must be added the PV of the dividend for 19X2 and 19X3:

Estimated intrinsic value = 110.79 + 15.26 = 126.05p

(c) The efficient markets hypothesis was developed in an attempt to explain share price behaviour in the major stock markets. It is assumed that in these markets prices of securities

101

change quickly to reflect all new information, transaction costs are insignificant and no single individual of group is able to dominate the market. In its semi-strong form, it is assumed that share prices reflect all publicly available information which is of relevance to the shares; the strong form contends that, in addition, share prices will reflect information only available to specialists and insiders.

In an efficient market, it would be expected that the price of a share will reflect its intrinsic value. However in this case, the actual market price is not consistent with the hypothesis. The difference could be due to a number of non-quantifiable factors such as investor confidence and might possibly be predicted by random walk analysis. If the market is efficient, the difference in price will not necessarily mean that the share is overpriced and therefore it should not necessarily be sold.

Empirical research suggests that investment analysts are not able to 'beat the market' consistently, which is as would be expected if a semi-strong form of efficiency exists. However, analysts in trading shares do form one of the mechanisms by which market prices adjust to new information and thus from the point of view of the market do serve a useful purpose. They will also be able to help investors to build a balanced portfolio of securities with regard to risk, ethical status and other criteria.

23   ABC

(a) *Factors influencing a company's choice of dividend policy*

Despite the views of some theoreticians, notably Modigliani and Miller, that maximising shareholder wealth is independent of dividend policy, empirical evidence shows that dividend policy is a major preoccupation of senior management. The discrepancy between theory and practice is mostly due to the impact of costs and market imperfections which were assumed to be absent in the theoretical analysis.

In the first instance, a company must be sufficiently profitable to generate the necessary after tax income out of which dividends might be paid. Although a company can pay dividends out of past rather than current profits, this can clearly be at most a short term policy. In the UK, there is a legal prohibition on making dividends without having realised profits out of which to pay them.

Besides needing to be profitable, a company must also have sufficient cash resources to pay dividends. This is the most important single factor in determining a company's dividend policy. Paying out a high proportion of the company's earnings as dividends is likely to leave it short of the cash needed for further investment in its business. Accordingly, it will need to raise further equity capital. In financial theory, choosing to distribute profits as dividends and then raising further capital is a perfectly valid approach. In practice, however, it is not.

Ease of access to the capital markets depends on the size and trading record of the company; large multinationals can raise fresh capital with very little difficulty but small, privately owned companies have to rely on the personal resources of their owners. In fact, both sets of circumstances tend to make retaining profits a more attractive course than paying dividends. In the case of the large, publicly owned company, the directors will have to convince the market that their investment plans are sound before fresh capital can be raised. This involves some loss of commercial secrecy, heavy investment of senior management's time, and possibly significant issue costs. Retaining earnings does not require the market to make a fresh decision, which relieves the company's management of the burden of persuasion. The small privately owned company faces different problems. Communication between the company's managers (directors) and owners (shareholders) is not the problem, since the two groups are often the same people. Instead, taxation is the principal reason for retaining profits to fund new investment rather than paying dividends and then calling for fresh capital. Shareholders will normally be subject to income tax if they receive dividends but no tax allowance for introducing fresh capital to the company (unless the investment is made under the new Enterprise Investment Scheme).

The cost of using the capital markets and the impact of taxation are perfectly sensible reasons for directors to choose retained earnings as their principal source of investment

102

funds, with the consequence that dividends are much lower than they might otherwise be. Much less easy to understand, however, is the influence of habit on the choice of dividend policy. Empirical research has shown that directors want to control two aspects of dividend policy in particular. First, they try to ensure dividends do not fall, and certainly that they are never suspended altogether. Second, they attempt to make certain that dividend payments increase in size smoothly and predictably. When earnings rise significantly, dividends frequently do not reflect the rise fully for fear of having to fall if the earnings growth turns out to be temporary. Stability of dividend payments thus becomes the most important determinant of dividend policy. As a result, a company with stable earnings is likely to be able to distribute more profits as dividends than one with volatile earnings.

In conclusion, choice of dividend policy appears to be little influenced by financial theory which postulates that it does not affect shareholders' wealth and so can be ignored in setting financial objectives. Setting dividend levels is a major management decision in practice. The level of future investment and the stability of a company's earnings are the principal influences on dividend policy, since retained earnings are the most favoured source of investment capital and directors believe, probably correctly, that financial markets place a high value on stability and predictability.

(b) Company A, which has deliberately avoided paying any dividends in the last five years, is pursuing a sensible policy for a rapidly growing company. All its post-tax profits are being reinvested in the company's business. By adopting this strategy, Company A reduces to a minimum its need to raise new capital from the market. Issue costs are reduced or eliminated and the company has greater flexibility in its investment programme since decision taking is not dependent on gaining market approval. Furthermore, since the company is probably investing heavily its taxation liability may well be small. Paying dividends would mean a UK company had to pay ACT too, which might not be recovered against the main company tax bill and so could cause a net cash outflow.

At first sight the policy pursued by Company B, of distributing 50% of post-tax profits, appears to offer the shareholders predictability. In fact, however, with changes in the company's operating profits and in the tax regime, the post-tax earnings may fluctuate considerably. Reducing the dividend of a quoted company normally causes its share price to fall sharply, since the market takes this as casting considerable doubt on its future earnings potential. But, the more mature and predictable that Company B's business is, the greater the merit in its dividend policy. A mature business usually needs less new capital investment than a growing one and so a higher level of dividend is justified. Distributing profits allows shareholders to make some adjustment to the risk and return profile of their portfolios without incurring the transaction costs of buying and selling.

Company C's policy falls between those of A and B in that a dividend is paid, albeit a small one. The predictability of the dividend will be welcomed by shareholders, since it allows them to make their financial plans with more certainty than would otherwise be possible. It also gives C part of A's advantage; retained earnings can be used as the principal source of investment capital. To the extent that they are relevant at all, scrip issues are likely to increase a company's market value, since they are often made to increase the marketability of the shares. Shareholder concessions are simply a means of attracting the 'small' shareholder who can benefit from them personally, and have no impact on dividend policy.

In addition to looking at the cash flows of each company, we must also consider the impact of these dividend policies on the after tax wealth of shareholders. Shareholders can be divided into groups or 'clienteles'. Different clienteles may be attracted to invest in each of the three firms, depending on their tax situation. It is worth noting that one clientele is as good as another in terms of the valuation it implies for the firm.

Company A would be particularly attractive to individuals who do not require an income stream from their investment and prefer to obtain a return through capital growth. Company B's clientele prefer a much higher proportion of their return to be in the form of income, although it would not be income on which they rely since it may be very variable from year to year. Tax exempt funds, such as pension funds, are indifferent between returns in the form of income or capital and might well invest in B since they need a flow of income to meet their day to day obligations. A large, diversified portfolio would reduce the effect of

103

variability in the dividend. Company C is more likely to appeal to the private investor since most of the return is in the form of capital growth and there are shareholder concessions too.

So, each company may maximise the wealth of its shareholders. If the theorists are right, A, B and C all maximise shareholder wealth because the value of the companies is unaffected by dividend policy. Alternatively, each company's group of shareholders may favour their company's policy (and so their wealth is maximised) because the dividend policy is appropriate to their tax position and so maximises their post-tax returns.

24 TUTORIAL QUESTION: DIVIDEND VALUATION MODEL AND DIVIDEND POLICY

(a) The dividend valuation model can be expressed as:

$$MV = \frac{d(1 + g)}{(r - g)}$$

where: MV = market price of shares
d = dividend at end of year 0
g = expected rate of dividend growth
r = cost of capital

In this case the rate of dividend growth changes at the end of year 2. The approach will therefore be to evaluate the dividend for each of the first three years at the cost of capital and then to apply the above formula for year 4 onwards.

Year	Growth %	EPS p	Payout %	DPS p	Discount factor at 18%	Disc DPS
19Y2	25	77.5	40.3	31.3	0.847	26.5
19Y3	25	96.9	40.3	39.1	0.718	28.1
19Y4	10	106.6	50.0	53.3	0.609	32.5

Thereafter: $MV = \dfrac{(53.3 \times 0.609)(1 + 0.1)}{(0.18 - 0.1)}$

MV $= 446.3$

Expected MV = 446.3 + 26.5 + 28.1 + 32.5 = 533.4 pence

The P/E ratio $= \dfrac{\text{Market price per share}}{\text{Earnings per share}} = 533.4/62 = 8.6$

The dividend valuation model includes a number of assumptions:

(1) Future dividends will be of the same risk class as existing dividends.

(2) Shareholders can be viewed as a homogenous group, ie there are no variations in their information, attitude to risk etc.

(3) Transaction costs can be ignored.

Its major weakness relates to the assumption that the level of business risk will not change as the firm develops. If this assumption cannot be met then it might be more appropriate to use a different approach to valuation such as the capital asset pricing model.

(b) The policy being put forward is consistent with the basic accounting concept that dividends should only be paid if there are sufficient distributable profits available to cover the payout. However, profits vary from one accounting period to the next, and companies face the conflicting demands of maintaining a constant payout ratio and level of dividend cover against maintaining a consistent level of actual dividend payments. This conflict has been brought to public attention in the recent recession where some firms have adopted a conservative policy and severely cut the dividend, while others have maintained the level of payments in line with their view of longer term future prospects rather than short term current performance. ICI is an example of a company which has recently paid an uncovered dividend.

(i)   Financial institutions tend to prefer dividend income to capital growth for two reasons.

    (1) They can reclaim the ACT imputed to the dividend payments.

    (2) Cash flows are required to meet their liabilities, and if these cash flows are in the form of dividend payments they can avoid the transaction costs involved in realising capital gains.

    It is therefore likely that institutional shareholders would prefer the increased payout ratio in the period of reduced growth. There has been pressure on companies recently from institutions such as the Prudential to ensure that dividend levels are maintained during periods of reduced profit performance.

(ii)   The position of small private investors will vary. Where they are investing through a Personal Equity Plan (PEP) or fall below the income tax threshold then they too are likely to express a preference for an increased payout ratio. However these tax advantages are not available to other investors. They are likely to prefer capital gains since they are able to take advantage of the indexation allowances and the additional annual exemption for capital gains tax. They will also be able to time their realisation of capital gains in order to minimise their tax liability.

(c)   There are a number of other options available to RG. These include the following.

(i)   The company could decide not to set a defined long term payout ratio but could instead make a review of its shareholders each year to decide what would be most appropriate and to follow the trends being set by other firms.

(ii)   Instead of managing the payout ratio, the company could decide to try to maintain a constant real level of dividends regardless of the profit performance in an individual year.

(iii)   RG could decide not to make any distributions at all but to aim for investors interested in capital growth, and to use retained earnings as a major source of finance.

25 DEERWOOD PLC

Director A

A is correct to say that the use of internally generated funds as the main source of finance cuts down on incidental expenses. However, the significance of such expenses depends on the amount of finance required and the external sources which might be used. It may be that external sources will be needed in any case, and that some incidental expenses are therefore irrelevant to the decision on profit retention because they will be incurred in any case.

There are, however, other arguments which might support A's position. The company may be able to make better immediate use of funds than shareholders; individual shareholders may prefer to receive their returns as capital gains rather than as income, so as to make use of their annual capital gains tax exemptions; and the company can, by not paying dividends, avoid the cash flow disadvantage of paying advance corporation tax and only later setting it off against its corporation tax liability.

On the other hand, excessive retention of earnings may lead to a high cost of equity, because shareholders will be unhappy with a company which gives little income in the short term, and the company's capital structure may become non-optimal. If the dividend paid is merely the residue after investment needs are met, a stable dividend (which investors generally appreciate) will be very hard to maintain.

A's point about the fall in the share price when the shares go ex dividend has no merit. Shareholders and the market well understand that the fall in price is compensated for by the impending dividend.

BPP Publishing

Director B

The research cited by B states the obvious: that if your income is taxed highly, income is an undesirable form in which to receive your returns, and that some companies manage to take account of this. Beyond that, caution is required in drawing specific lessons for the company. The research was done in another country with a different tax system, and it may well be out of date by now. Furthermore, the company's shareholders are of many different sorts, including both individuals and institutions, some of which pay tax and some of which do not. There are also substantial nominee holdings, and the tax position of the beneficial owners is unknown. A dividend policy formulated on the basis of B's views could end up satisfying a few, and upsetting many. Indeed, it may be that the company has the shareholders it currently does because they have been attracted by its current dividend policy.

Director C

C is right to say that many investors prefer cash now to possible future capital gains, either because they have an immediate need for income or simply because they prefer certainty. Small amounts of income cannot be economically replaced by regular sales of shares, because of transaction costs.

Having said that, dividends do not themselves increase shareholders' wealth: only good management can do that. In an efficient market, the returns on shares will be high enough to compensate for the risks involved.

Director D

The equation cited by D contains no term for dividends, and this reflects the view of Modigliani and Miller that dividend policy is irrelevant to shareholders' wealth. However, their theory makes several unrealistic assumptions, including perfect capital markets and the absence of taxes. Although others have argued that even when corporate and personal taxes are introduced, dividend policy remains irrelevant, great caution is needed when basing actual business decisions on such theories. Furthermore, D's views by themselves leave the board with no guidance on the appropriate decision.

Conclusion

Probably the most appropriate policy for a public company with a wide variety of shareholders is to pay dividends at a level which can be steadily increased, at least in line with inflation, over the years, without leading to liquidity crises. Shareholders than know where they stand, and the company need not seek external finance except for major projects.

26 CORPORATE PLANNING

Financial planning forms one part of the corporate planning process, but strategic planning takes into account more than the access to and control of financial resources. The period to be covered by a corporate plan will depend on the nature of the business. However, in general the minimum period will be that necessary for the implementation of decisions on the development of new products, services and facilities, and entry into a new market area for existing products.

The stages that a company is likely to go through are as follows.

(a) *Business review and assessment*. This includes the appraisal of corporate strengths and weaknesses. Two approaches are possible.

    (i) *Functional approach*. The strengths and weaknesses of each function are reviewed with the aim of determining which strengths may be best exploited in long-term plans.

    (ii) *Total entity approach*. This attempts to re-appraise and express in simple terms the basic nature of the company's activities. To what class of products do the existing products relate? What basic needs do these products satisfy? To what markets could the products and skills be relevant?

The review will enable a forecast to be made of likely changes in sales, profitability and capital requirements. Comparison of this with the results of the restatement of the company's objectives will identify the 'gap' which must be overcome by new strategies.

(b) *Establishment of objectives.* Corporate objectives must be stated in a way which is precise and quantifiable, for example a defined rate of growth in EPS.

(c) *Choice of alternative strategies.* Objectives may be achieved by either intensive or extensive development.

  (i) *Intensive development* involves increasing the penetration of existing markets, exploiting new markets with the existing product range, or improving existing products with the aim of increasing demand.

  (ii) *Extensive development* involves some form of diversification, for example by vertical integration with adjacent links in the product chain.

  The product/marketing strategies selected will give rise to strategic decisions on the facilities and finance required to meet the requirements.

(d) *Detailed evaluation of the plan.* This should be undertaken in terms of the effect on profits, cash flow and the business position. The level of risk inherent in the plan should be evaluated using techniques such as sensitivity analysis and financial modelling.

(e) *Establishment of short-term budgets.* The original forecast can now be amended to reflect the results of the different strategic options which have been identified, and to evaluate these against the corporate objectives. The validity of the final plan must be checked and it must be formulated in such a way as to define management responsibilities for its achievement. The final result will be a series of annual plans with detailed supporting schedules analysed by responsibility.

(f) *Implementation and monitoring.* Once the plan is implemented, actual performance should be monitored and reviewed through the budgetary control process. Planning is in fact a continuous process, and future plans must be re-evaluated in the light of actual performance and changes in the operating environment, and amended where necessary.

27 AGGRESSIVE, MODERATE OR CONSERVATIVE

Tutorial note. This question requires a broad discussion of the conflicting objectives that must be held in balance when determining working capital policy. It might be helpful to structure the discussion by considering the different elements of working capital and their financing separately. It is important to define how you are interpreting the terms 'aggressive' and 'conservative' since these can be used in different ways.

It is assumed that the degree of aggression or conservatism in the management and financing of current assets relates to the degree of risk which the company is prepared to accept. This can be assessed by taking each element of the current asset base in turn.

(a) *Cash and marketable securities.* All companies will require a certain amount of cash to be available for their day to day operations - to pay suppliers, wages, expenses etc. The precise amounts required will be determined by means of a regularly updated short term cash flow forecast which will highlight peaks and troughs in cash demands. A company with a conservative cash policy will probably maintain a bank balance which is sufficient to cover the normal peaks in demand. The cash forecast will be updated less often - perhaps twice a month - and the company will accept that there is likely to be some idle cash in the account.

A company with an aggressive policy will monitor the cash position throughout the day and will seek to minimise the amount held in the bank account. Wherever possible surplus funds will be transferred to other accounts and investments, or alternatively placed on overnight deposit to ensure that interest is maximised. The downside of such a policy is that there will be an overhead incurred in monitoring the situation and moving the funds around. There is also the risk that if forecasts are inaccurate the company may need to call on other reserves at short notice and so incur a loss of interest. It may even face the embarrassment and loss of confidence of its suppliers if mistakes result in some of its cheques being bounced.

(b) *Stock and work in progress.* The first decision to be faced by a company is whether to manufacture to order or to supply from stock. If it chooses the latter option then it must then decide on the level of stock it should carry, and to do this it will need to make demand forecasts. The key problem is that all such forecasts are subject to some degree of error and the company must decide what level of buffer stock is appropriate to minimise the risk of a stock out occurring. Although models are available which attempt to quantify the relative costs of carrying excess stocks as against a stock out, it is very difficult to estimate what the effect of a stock out will be on future business. A company which chooses an aggressive policy in the sense of being prepared to accept a higher level of risk will probably choose to stock at a lower level than one which adopts a more conservative policy.

(c) *Debtors*. An aggressive policy in respect of debtors could be one of two things. If aggression is to be defined in terms of attitude to risk, then a company with an aggressive policy is likely to have a high level of debtors, being generous in allowing credit in order to achieve the maximum level of sales. A more conservative company would be more cautious in both granting credit to a customer and in the size of the credit limit applied and this may mean that some sales are sacrificed as a result.

Alternatively, an aggressive approach to the level of debtors might mean that the company seeks to minimise the amount of capital tied up by debtors. In this situation the aggressive policy would be to allow the minimum amount of credit to customers, to chase up payments as soon as they become due and to place 'on stop' customers who exceed their credit limit or who are late with their payment.

The traditional view is that short-term assets should be financed from short-term sources of capital such as the bank overdraft. However it is commonly accepted that in practice working capital is unlikely to fall below a certain amount and that this level can be regarded as semi-permanent requiring a longer term more secure source of finance. The more aggressive company is likely to try to minimise interest costs by using a source of finance which can be varied in amount to match the fluctuations in requirements, rather than committing itself to a longer term loan. It is also likely to try maintain a high level of trade creditors and to use this as a source of finance, although such a policy obviously carries a risk of interruption of supply or litigation if creditors' terms are not complied with.

28 TUTORIAL QUESTION: IMPROVING CASH FLOW

It would seem that B Ltd relies entirely on A plc for finance, and so cannot raise money from a bank loan or overdraft. The maximum loan from A plc is £50,000, but the cash budget projects an 'overdraft' of up to £262,000 (month 10).

B Ltd would appear to be profitable and growing. A very rough estimate of profits in the year could be made by preparing a funds flow statement in reverse.

	£'000
Increase in bank balance (35 – 30)	5
Increase in finished goods stock	114
Net increase in debtors and raw materials stocks less creditors	x
Purchases of fixed assets (70 + 10 + 15 + 5)	100
Dividend paid	80
Tax paid	120
	419 + x
Less depreciation	y
Profit before tax	419 + x – y

A combination of seasonal business, growth in trading and fixed asset purchases would appear to be the reason why B Ltd is only expected to increase its cash balance by £5,000 over the whole year, in spite of these profits.

Possible measures to reduce the requirement for cash include the following.

(a) Do not pay the dividend to A plc in month 3. However, A plc is short of cash, and is probably relying on the dividend income. It would therefore seem unlikely that A plc would agree either to cancel the dividend or to lend more than £50,000.

(b) Delay the payment of corporation tax from month 9 (presumably, this is the statutory payment date, 9 months after the year end). The Inland Revenue might allow B Ltd to do this, although there would be an interest charge for the delay.

(c) Improve stock control. We do not know the total of finished goods, but stock levels will rise by £114,000 in the year. Clearly, the increase in stock is expected because of the company's sales growth. However, some reductions in the investment in stocks might be possible without prejudice to sales, in which case the cash flow position would be eased by the value of the stocks reduction. ✓

(d) Improve creditors control. Three months credit is taken from suppliers, but raw material purchases are every 2 months. The credit period already seems generous, and some suppliers are probably making a second delivery of materials before they are paid for the first. Taking longer credit would be difficult to negotiate. However, if B Ltd is on very good terms with its suppliers, and is a valued customer of those suppliers, it might be possible to defer by a further month payments due in months 6, 8 and 10, which cover the cash crisis period. ✓

(e) Improve debtors control. Two months' credit is allowed to customers. If all sales are on credit, customers are likely to be commercial or industrial buyers, who would expect reasonable credit terms. A shortening of the credit period is probably not possible, without damaging goodwill and sales prospects, unless an incentive is offered for early payments, in the form of a discount. The discount would have to be sufficiently large to persuade customers to take it. Suppose, for example, that from month 5 sales onwards, a 10% discount were offered for payments inside a month. (10% would be very generous and unrealistic perhaps, but is used here for illustration). If all customers accepted the offer, this would affect cash flows from month 6 on, as follows. ✓

Month	Original budget £'000		Revised budget £'000	Net change £'000
6	75	+ (90% of 80)	147	+72
7	80	−80 + (90% of 90)	81	+1
8	90	−90 + (90% of 110)	99	+9
9	110	−110 + (90% of 150)	135	+25
10	150	−150 + (90% of 220)	198	+48
11	220	−220 + (90% of 320)	288	+68
12	320	?	?	?

The effects on cash flow would then be substantial, although the cost of the discounts would reduce profits by a substantial amount too.

(f) Postpone capital expenditure. Since the company is growing, the option to postpone capital expenditure on new equipment, building extensions and office furniture is probably unrealistic. The routine replacement of motor vehicles should be deferred, but this would only ease the cash situation by £10,000. ✓

(g) B Ltd has an investment which will pay a dividend of £45,000 in month 7. This is obviously a fairly large investment. If B Ltd's cash flow problems cannot be solved in any other way, the company's directors might have to consider whether this investment could be sold to raise funds.

Summary

B Ltd is a profitable company, but is faced with serious cash flow problems which would seem to be hard to overcome without drastic measures being taken. Because B Ltd is profitable, closure of the company is unthinkable, and it would be against the company's long term interests to abandon its plans for growth. A plc is acting as a serious constraining influence on B Ltd.

However, the sort of radical action and response outlined above for debtors, coupled with a postponement of the tax payment by 3 months or so and a deferral of £10,000 in motor vehicle purchases until next year, would be virtually sufficient to overcome the firm's cash flow problems in the year, with a slight problem still in month 8: see workings below.

				Month				
	5	6	7	8	9	10	11	12
Postpone purchase of vehicles	10							
Defer tax payment					120			(120)
Discounts for early payment								
by debtors - possible effect	—	72	1	9	25	48	68	?
Change	10	72	1	9	145	48	68	?
Cumulative change	10	82	83	92	237	285	353	?
Original cash budget	1	(71)	(66)	(144)	(216)	(262)	(130)	35
Revised cash budget balances	11	11	17	(52)	21	23	223	?

If B Ltd is to overcome its problems within the constraints set by A plc's financial policy, it is likely that action on debtors is the key to a practical solution.

29 OXOLD

(a) The MM valuation formula referred to in the question is:

$$V = V_e + tD$$

where   V is the total value of the company
   V_e is the total value of the company if it was all-equity financed
   t is the marginal rate of corporation taxation (35% for Oxold)
   D is the value of debt in the company's capital structure

Suppose that the company invests £n in projects with an IRR of 15%. Annual cash flows generated will then be £0.15n. Because the stock market capitalise these cash flows at 17%, the value of the company will fall by the following amount:

$$-n + \frac{0.15n}{0.17} = -0.1176n$$

If equity finance were to be used, the projects would therefore be rejected. But if debt finance is used, the fall in value calculated above may be more than compensated.

Suppose that the company raises £d in new debt to finance the investment. The value of the company would then be:

$$V = V_e + 0.35D - 0.1176n + 0.35d$$

V_e and D (the existing equity and debt) are constant, and therefore the objective function is to maximise $-0.1176n + 0.35d$.

The constraints are as follows.

   $n \le £2,000,000$

   $n \le d + £1,500,000$

   $d \le 0.4n$

(b) If no new funds are borrowed, the investment opportunities would not be pursued because of their negative net present value.

If borrowing is undertaken, the taxation benefits of debt finance may make the project worthwhile. In fact, the maximum increase in the company's value is achieved by undertaking the full £2,000,000 worth of investment, and financing £800,000 by debt.

30 ADSUM

> *Tutorial note*. The information provided can be used to produce two funds flow statements. There is no point in calculating expected values since this appears to be an 'either/or' situation. Explain the implications of the forecasts for Adsum's financing over the next three years and consider both external and internal sources of funds. In part (c) it is helpful to outline the financial planning process and then to evaluate how far Adsum has progressed towards producing a complete financial plan.

(a) Projected funds flow statements have been prepared for the two growth scenarios (see below). The expected value would be of little value in this context.

In both growth situations, taxable profits are expected to increase over the three year period. However, Adsum is likely to experience severe cash flow problems in years 2 and 3. Even if the overdraft facility is fully used, there will be a cash shortfall of £1.908m by the end of year 3 with slow growth, and £1.616m with rapid growth. This is mainly due to the large fixed asset purchases planned for the period, since working capital and dividend payments are not expected to increase beyond the rate of growth in the level of trading.

However, by the end of year 3 there will also be a significant increase in reserves - to £4.026m with slow growth and to £4.178m with rapid growth. This should result in a large fall in the gearing from its current level of 118% ((420 + 3,000)/(500 + 2,400)). The new figure will depend on how the cash deficit is financed. There should be similar improvements in the level of interest cover.

PROJECTED FUNDS FLOW - SLOW GROWTH

	Year 1 £'000	Year 2 £'000	Year 3 £'000
Source of funds:			
Sales	5,936	6,899	8,149
Profit before tax (12% sales)	712	828	978
Asset disposals	224		
	936	828	978
Applications of funds:			
Taxation	92	104	125
Purchase of assets	0	2,132	1,124
Dividend	168	188	215
Changes in working capital:			
Increase in stock	319	318	401
Increase in debtors	492	498	637
Increase in creditors	(571)	(583)	(751)
	500	2,657	1,751
Increase/(decrease) in funds	436	(1,829)	(773)
Opening cash balance	80	516	(1,313)
Closing cash balance	516	(1,313)	(2,086)

PROJECTED FUNDS FLOW - RAPID GROWTH

	Year 1 £'000	Year 2 £'000	Year 3 £'000
Source of funds:			
Sales	6,300	7,828	9,493
Profit before tax (12% sales)	756	939	1,139
Asset disposals	210		
	966	939	1,139
Applications of funds:			
Taxation	107	143	182
Purchase of assets	0	1,874	926
Dividend	166	207	251
Changes in working capital:			
Increase in stock	443	499	523
Increase in debtors	683	786	840
Increase in creditors	(793)	(922)	(995)
	606	2,587	1,727
Increase/(decrease) in funds	360	(1,648)	(588)
Opening cash balance	80	440	(1,208)
Closing cash balance	440	(1,208)	(1,796)

Workings

	Year 1 £'000	Year 2 £'000	Year 3 £'000
Sales			
Slow growth:			
At current prices	5,300	5,500	5,800
Add 12% inflation	5,936	6,899	8,149
Rapid growth:			
At current prices	6,000	7,100	8,200
Add 5% inflation	6,300	7,828	9,493
Taxation			
Slow growth:			
Profit before tax	712	828	978
Less capital allowances	(450)	(530)	(620)
Taxable profit	262	298	358
Tax at 35%	92	104	125
Rapid growth:			
Profit before tax	756	939	1,139
Less capital allowances	(450)	(530)	(620)
Taxable profit	306	409	519
Tax at 35%	107	143	182
Purchase of assets			
Slow growth:			
At current prices	0	1,700	800
Add 12% inflation	0	2,132	1,124

112

	Year 0 £'000	Year 1 £'000	Year 2 £'000	Year 3 £'000
Rapid growth:				
At current prices		0	1,700	800
Add 5% inflation		0	1,874	926
Dividend				
Slow growth (+ 12% pa):		168	188	211
Dividend as percentage pre-tax profit		23.58%	22.73%	21.55%
Adjust dividend to required range		168	188	215
Rapid growth (+ 5% pa):		158	165	174
Dividend as percentage pre-tax profit		20.83%	17.61%	15.24%
Adjust dividend to required range		166	207	251
Stock				
Slow growth:				
Sales	5,000	5,936	6,899	8,149
Percentage increase		18.72%	16.23%	18.11%
80% × percentage increase		14.98%	12.98%	14.49%
Stock level	2,130	2,449	2,767	3,168
Stock increase		319	318	401
Rapid growth:				
Sales	5,000	6,300	7,828	9,493
Percentage increase		26.00%	24.25%	21.27%
80% × percentage increase		20.80%	19.40%	17.01%
Stock level	2,130	2,573	3,072	3,595
Stock increase		443	499	523
Debtors				
Slow growth:				
Sales	5,000	5,936	6,899	8,149
Percentage increase		18.72%	16.23%	18.11%
90% × percentage increase		16.85%	14.60%	16.30%
Debtor level	2,920	3,412	3,910	4,548
Increase		492	498	637
Rapid growth:				
Sales	5,000	6,300	7,828	9,493
Percentage increase		26.00%	24.25%	21.27%
90% × percentage increase		23.40%	21.83%	19.14%
Debtor level	2,920	3,603	4,390	5,230
Increase		683	786	840
Creditors				
Slow growth:				
Sales	5,000	5,936	6,899	8,149
Percentage increase		18.72%	16.23%	18.11%
95% × percentage increase		17.78%	15.42%	17.20%
Creditor level	3,210	3,781	4,364	5,114
Increase		571	583	751
Rapid growth:				
Sales	5,000	6,300	7,828	9,493
Percentage increase		26.00%	24.25%	21.27%
95% × percentage increase		24.70%	23.04%	20.20%
Creditor level	3,210	4,003	4,925	5,920
Increase		793	922	995

(b) The main problem that Adsum will face in the next three years is financing the cash deficit. Due to the current high level of gearing, it will not be possible to finance this solely through

113

debt: at least some element of additional equity will be needed. Adsum could also consider the following options.

(i) Reduce the level of dividends, at least in the short term.

(ii) Delay or modify its capital expenditure plans. Adsum could also consider the possibility of leasing some of the additional assets, and possibly converting any existing freeholds to leaseholds.

(iii) Improve the stock turnover ratio. The current stockholding period is 155 days, which is high. If this could be reduced, then funds would be released for other purposes.

(iv) Improve the debtor collection period. The current collection period is 213 days, which is high. An improvement in the collection period would have a similar effect to a reduction in the stockholding period.

(v) Improve profits through better return on sales, increased volumes and reduced overheads.

(c) Financial objectives cannot be achieved unless the company has a clear idea of what it is trying to achieve and plans how to achieve these objectives. The medium term (three to five year) financial plan should be consistent with the long term strategic goals of the organisation.

The steps in the planning process will include the following.

(i) Produce forecasts based on assumptions about demand, inflation, macroeconomic factors and the likely situation of competitors.

(ii) Draw up contingency plans to be used in the event of targets failing to be met and actual events not being as predicted, for example interest rates increasing faster than forecast.

(iii) Secure the finance necessary to carry through the plan.

(iv) Monitor actual against planned performance.

So far, Adsum has started to produce forecasts for two economic scenarios. However, these need to be converted into full financial and functional statements to fulfil step (i) of the planning process. It has not yet moved on to the other stages of the process.

The main problem in the planning process is dealing with uncertainty, and this too has not been dealt with by Adsum. This can be addressed in a number of ways.

(i) Investigate the sensitivities of the forecasts to changes in the key variables such as sales volumes.

(ii) Prepare a probability distribution of the possible outcomes under different scenarios.

(iii) Evaluate the best and worst case situations.

(iv) Use computer modelling techniques. These may be deterministic (a single situation forecast), probabilistic (where probabilities are applied to different variables), or optimising (whereby the model develops a plan to optimise the achievement of the financial objectives).

The quality of the plan cannot be superior to the accuracy of the assumptions used in its preparation. It is not clear how Adsum has arrived at some of the figures used in its forecast. For example, on what basis have the two inflation rates of 5% and 12% been arrived at, and is it too simplistic to assume a single inflation rate for the entire three year period? Business levels and operating costs do not appear to have been adjusted to reflect improvements generated by the additional investment in fixed assets. The amount by which the asset base is expected to increase seems very high for the straightforward replacement of existing assets.

Thus it appears that the directors of Adsum have made a start on the financial planning process, but still have a way to go in producing a fully developed financial plan.

BPP Publishing

31 TUTORIAL QUESTION: REPORT ON A SUBSIDIARY

(a) Appropriate ratios include the following.

(i) *Return on capital employed.* This provides a measure of the rate of return being earned on the investment in XYZ and can be calculated as:

Earnings before int erest and tax
      Capital employed

Book values of the assets will be used as there is insufficient information available to adjust the figures for both years (for instance to adjust stock to the lower of cost and net realisable value).

	19X2	19X1
	£'000	£'000
Earnings before interest and tax	22	(98)
Total assets	5,760	4,552
Less current liabilities	(715)	(644)
Capital employed	5,045	3,908
Return on capital employed (%)	0.44	(2.51)

(ii) *Return on sales.* This measures profitability. It can be calculated as:

Operating profit
    Sales

It is assumed that the 'Other income' shown in the profit and loss extracts arises from the normal activities of the business.

	19X2	19X1
Operating profit (£'000)	22	(98)
Sales (£'000)	6,575	5,918
Return on sales (%)	0.33	(1.66)

(iii) *Quick ratio.* This measures liquidity. It can be calculated as:

Current assets excluding stock
    Current liabilities

	19X2	19X1
Total current assets (£'000)	2,360	1,622
Less stock & WIP	(1,250)	(893)
Current assets excluding stock	1,110	729
Current liabilities	715	644
Quick ratio	0.64	0.88

(iv) *Interest cover.* This shows whether a company is earning enough profits to pay its interest comfortably. It can be calculated as:

Earnings before int erest and tax
    Interest ch arges

BPP Publishing

	19X2	19X1
Earnings before interest & tax (£'000)	22	(98)
Interest charges (£'000)	395	339
Interest cover	0.06	(0.29)

(v) *Debtor days*. This provides a measure of the average length of time taken for the company's customers to settle their accounts. It can be calculated as:

$$\frac{\text{Trade debtors}}{\text{Sales}} \times 365 \text{ days}$$

The effects of VAT will be ignored since it is not known what if any proportion of the sales is zero rated.

	19X2	19X1
Debtors (£'000)	765	476
Turnover (£'000)	6,575	5,918
Debtor days	42.5	29.4

(b)

To: ABC plc MANAGEMENT BOARD
From: MANAGEMENT ACCOUNTANT
Date: 18 October 19X3

Subject: XYZ Ltd Performance review - 19X1/19X2

INTRODUCTION

This report will consider the financial performance of XYZ Ltd over the last two years. Alternative strategies as to the future of XYZ within the group will be set forward, together with suggestions as to the basis on which it would be appropriate to value the subsidiary.

RECENT FINANCIAL PERFORMANCE

Profit performance in recent years has been poor. However there was a small improvement in 19X2 when the company returned to profit showing a small positive return on sales of 0.33%. This is almost entirely due to an improvement in gross margin from 8.0% to 10.0%. There was a similar small improvement in the return on capital employed, although the level of return at 0.44% is well below the cost of funds employed in the business.

While profits have improved over the last year, management of working capital has deteriorated. The payment period of trade debtors has increased from 29.4 days in 19X1 to 42.5 days in 19X2. This movement should be investigated to determine whether there has been a slackening in credit control and debt collection procedures or whether there is a potential large doubtful debt against which provision should be made. The average stockholding period has also increased from 60 to 77 days. This suggests a decline in the quality of stock management, although it could also be due to a change in stocking policy aimed at improving the level of customer service.

The quick ratio measures the ability of a company to repay its creditors. It is generally the case that a level of at least 1.0 is necessary to protect against insolvency through insufficient liquidity. Although the ratio for XYZ has declined from 0.88 to 0.64, this may not necessarily be a cause for concern since the debtor payment period is relatively short compared with other firms.

Although the historical analysis of the accounting data for XYZ provides only limited encouragements, it must be remembered that such an analysis by itself is inadequate to provide a basis for decisions about the future of the company. Historical analysis is by definition backward looking and cannot take into account current changes in the market and operating environment, or of the results of ongoing long term investment projects in areas such as research and development or new production facilities. Any judgements made about the future are essentially subjective and financial analysis is but one tool that can be used in the decision making process.

BPP Publishing

STRATEGIC OPTIONS

Any review of strategic options for XYZ must take account of the high level of investment that has been made in the company during the last year. £1.047m of new share capital has been injected (shareholders' funds increased from £1.726m to £2.520m after a post tax loss of £0.253m) and net borrowings have also been increased by £0.241m. Of this, £0.645m has been invested in plant and equipment and other long-term assets (an increase of 22% in the fixed asset base). It is probably too soon to consider a change of strategy or a divestment until there has been time for the results of the new investment to be evaluated.

POSSIBLE VALUATION BASES

Probably the most appropriate approach to valuing XYZ would be to discount the future cash flows. The first step in such a process is to produce a cash flow projection assuming a continuation of the existing strategic direction. This should be set in the context of the external environment taking into account the market situation, the likely introduction of new products, the competitive structure of the industry and of the industries into which the products are sold, the supply position, and the likely effect of any forthcoming legislation. Internal group operating factors should also be taken into account, for instance transfer pricing and operating synergies. It may be appropriate to produce alternative cash flow projections based on different environmental scenarios. The cash flows can then be discounted at the cost of capital to arrive at the net present value of the business.

When valuing the business, account should be taken of the position of likely buyers. For instance, if other companies are keen to break into the market this may inflate the value of XYZ. Alternatively, it may be possible to gain more from a piecemeal disposal or from closure of some parts of the business. In the latter case it will also be necessary to estimate the likely exit costs, such as redundancies.

CONCLUSION

Historical financial analysis of XYZ shows a mixed picture. While performance has improved in some areas it appears to have declined in others. This may be because it is too early for the full benefits of the recent large investments to be realised. It is unlikely that a major change in strategy is appropriate at the moment, but performance should be kept under close review in the short to medium term. If significant improvements are not achieved, then some form of disposal or closure may be the only option remaining.

32 **XQ PLC**

(a) We can derive figures for the share price at the time of the calculation of the price-earnings (PE) ratio immediately after the preliminary announcement of the annual results as follows.

Share price = earnings per share (EPS) × PE ratio

where EPS = profit after taxation ÷ 30,000 shares in issue.

The calculations are set out below.

	EPS pence	PE ratio	Share price pence
19X6	90.8	5.7	518
19X7	101.5	5.3	538
19X8	95.5	6.0	573
19X9	102.0	5.5	561
19Y0	107.3	6.5	697

This shows that the share price increased progressively over the period, and there was therefore 'incrementation of equity value' if we view the share price as the best indicator of equity value.

We are not given information on whether 'undue risks' have been taken. However, we can say the following.

BPP Publishing

(i)   Interest cover (profits before interest and tax + interest charges) would appear to be relatively high (a figure of at least 3 would be considered acceptable) and therefore gearing does not appear to be unacceptably high, even though interest charged increased by 50% in 19X9.

(ii)   The improvement in the PE ratio suggests that investors do not perceive risks known to them to be unacceptable.

(iii)   Dividends have been increased over the period to represent a rising proportion of earnings and indicating that less profits are being retained to expand the business.

(b) The figures presented show that the company's record has indeed not followed the strategy professed by the Works Council. Profits after taxation and turnover have increased in money terms, but taking into account inflation over the period they have not increased significantly in real terms. Over the period 19X6 to 19Y0 the number of employees has fallen to stand at the 19Y0 year end at about 60% of their level four years earlier. This trend indicates substantial gains in productivity without significant gains in the real level of profit.

One wonders where the cost savings from the reduction in employee numbers have gone! Some may have gone in increasing the real wages of employees, in which case the employee representatives of the Works Council should presumably be more pleased than they appear to be. Some may reflect the costs associated with capital equipment installed to replace the losses in the workforce, or there may have been an increase in the amount of subcontracting. To the extent that the employee representatives are concerned about the plight of those who have lost their jobs and may find it difficult to find new jobs, the representatives have good reason to be displeased. It may be that cost savings from reduced employee numbers have been 'absorbed' by lower prices to customers, which may have been necessitated by greater competition in the industry in which the business operates.

Although the past record of the business shows that the directors' objectives appear to have been met while employee representatives' preferred objectives have not, it is more important in any 'reconciliation' of views to take matters from where they now are, and to look to the future. It seems unlikely that employee numbers will be cut much below their current much reduced levels if the business maintains its current level of activity.

Whether there is room for future volume growth of the business will depend partly upon market conditions. An expansion of the business is likely to require either higher gearing or a higher level of retention of earnings, and these considerations should be explained to the Works Council. The figures presented show that the directors have adopted a policy of increasing the level of dividend payouts per share year by year. Shareholders may be happy for their growth in dividends to cease if they have the prospect of increased future earnings from future expansion of the business. Increasing the dividend year by year is not a prerequisite to 'incrementing' the equity value (ie the share price). Higher gearing would increase the level of risk perceived to attach to the holding of the equity capital, and shareholders may expect higher rewards as a result.

The management accountant may have a key role to play in outlining the various different 'scenarios' which could be envisaged so that these can be discussed by representatives and directors. Different aspects of the current position of the business need to be clarified, and the implications of alternative future strategies need to be explained.

(c) Employees considering the purchase of shares in the company which employs them will be interested in whether the investment is appropriate for them. If an investment carries a high level of risk, then it would be unwise for an employee to invest a lot of their savings in it. An investment which is perceived to be a long-term investment with short-term risks attached will be inappropriate for an investor who may need to realise their investment in the near future. For employees, there is the additional consideration that by investing in the employer company, the employee risks losing both savings and job at the same time if the company goes into liquidation. As a general rule someone should not invest money in shares which they cannot afford to lose.

The annual report and accounts will show the track record of the company to date. A five year summary of results will give an idea of the consistency of performance under different economic conditions: it must be remembered that some companies survive conditions of recession more easily than others. Various ratios can be calculated from figures given in the accounts, including for example the gross profit margin, sales/asset ratios, value added per employee and the gearing ratio. Employees may also be interested in the company's commitment to employees as gauged from pension contribution information. Figures of sales per employee may help to clarify the reasons behind the dramatic reduction in the workforce. Information given in notes to the account, for example on extraordinary or exceptional items, may add more commentary on the progress of the business.

Directors' reports tend to adopt a standardised presentation and wording and are sometimes rather uninformative, but there are sometimes exceptions to this tendency. The annual report and accounts provides information on what has already happened rather than on the future prospects of the business. The employees will therefore need to look to the directors for more information about future plans. Working capital forecasts and profit forecasts will help to show whether these plans appear to be achievable. In practice, it is unlikely and perhaps too much to expect that the directors should make more information available to employees than they make available to other potential investors.

As well as information about the operations of the company itself, potential investors, including employees, will want to make some assessment of the prospects for the markets within which the company sells its products. The particular company's position within the market and any foreseeable future events (eg a possible change in legislation) which could affect that position also need to be assessed. This kind of information might be gleaned from trade associations or press articles.

(d) The agency theory of the firm sees the company as a team whose members act in their own self interest but who at the same time accept that their individual success is dependent on the survival of the company in competition with other firms. Traditional theory holds that the main objective of a company is to maximise the wealth of the ordinary shareholders, and thus much attention has been directed to the attitudes and desires of the shareholders.

The return to the shareholders will be maximised through some combination of dividend payments and capital growth. In general, a shareholder will prefer a certain current income to an uncertain future income, in other words will demonstrate risk aversion. In practical terms, this means that shareholders will prefer to see a satisfactory level of dividends in the short term rather than sacrifice these in the expectation of a higher level of payments in the future, but with a greater level of risk attached. The effect of this on policy making within the firm is that there will be some tendency towards short-termism and risk avoidance; however at the same time there will be a concern to secure the survival and growth of the firm in the long term which tempers this tendency. It is also true that a shareholder can spread his risk by investing in a number of different companies and therefore he may well be prepared to accept a degree of risk in an individual company in anticipation of higher returns.

Managers on the other hand are in a significantly different position. Their financial security is primarily determined by the fortunes of the employing company. In practice this means that they are likely to be more risk averse in their decision making. The difference is that managers are interested in the total risk position of the company, while a diversified shareholder is only interested in the systematic risk of the company.

Due to the separation of ownership and control these factors mean that in practice organisations often behave differently from the manner predicted by traditional theory. The agency theory of the firm seeks to provide a behavioural explanation for some of these divergences.

33 CITY CODE

(a) The City Code refers to the principles and rules of behaviour which companies are expected to follow during the course of a takeover or merger. The Code is not enforceable by law, but is administered by the Takeover Panel. Its nature and purpose are described within the Code as follows.

BPP Publishing

'The code represents the collective opinion of those professionally involved in the field of takeovers on a range of business standards. It is not concerned with the financial or commercial advantages of a takeover, which are matters for the company and its shareholders, or with those wider questions which are the responsibility of the government, advised by the Monopolies and Mergers Commission.

'The code has not, and does not seek to have, the force of law, but those who wish to take advantage of the facilities of the securities markets in the UK should conduct themselves in matters relating to takeovers according to the code. Those who do not so conduct themselves cannot expect to enjoy those facilities and may find that they are withheld.'

(b) General principles which must guide the financial manager in defending an unwelcome bid are as follows.

(i) Any information provided to shareholders must be provided to all shareholders and not be restricted to those of a particular class or group.

(ii) Shareholders must be given sufficient information, advice and time to enable them to make a properly informed decision. No relevant information may be withheld from them.

(iii) Once the offer has been made the board of the target company must not take any action to frustrate the bid without first securing the consent of the shareholders in general meeting.

(iv) The interests of minority shareholders must be taken into account fully and they must be fairly treated. This is relevant in the case of an offer being made for the partly owned subsidiary of a holding company.

The financial manager must also be governed by a number of specific detailed rules laid down in the Code.

(i) The shareholders must be notified as to the identity of the bidder and the terms and conditions of the bid.

(ii) The board of the target company must seek independent financial advice from eg a merchant bank.

(iii) New shares can be issued and major assets acquired or disposed of only with the consent of the general meeting.

(iv) The company may not support the market price of its shares by providing financial guarantees or finance for the purchase of its own shares.

The Code also provides clear rules for when and under what circumstances a company may use defensive tactics such as 'golden parachutes' and 'white knights'.

34 MANAGEMENT BUYOUTS

(a) A management buyout is the purchase of all or part of a business from its owners by one or more of its executive managers. For example, the directors of a subsidiary company in a group might buy the company from the holding company, with the intention of running it as proprietors of a separate business entity.

(b) Management's purposes in a management buyout are to set up as the owners of the business themselves and perhaps to avoid redundancy if their company is threatened with closure.

The selling company's purposes in a management buyout may be:

(i) to dispose of an ailing subsidiary to willing purchasers;

(ii) to raise capital for other aspects of the group's operations;

(iii) to divest its assets in one area of business operations in order to concentrate on other markets and industries;

(iv) to rearrange the asset portfolio of a non-trading holding company.

BPP Publishing

(c) The usual problem with management buyouts is that the managers involved believe that they can run their business profitability, but they have little or no experience in financial management or financial accounting. They may therefore be unaware of the possible sources of finance noted in (d).

Other problems are:

(i) tax and legal complications can occur;

(ii) difficulty in deciding on a fair price to be paid;

(iii) convincing employees of the need to change working practices;

(iv) inadequate cash flow as a smaller company to finance the maintenance and replacement of tangible fixed assets;

(v) maintenance of previous employees' pension rights;

(vi) accepting the board representation requirement that many sources of funds will insist upon;

(vii) loss of key employees if the company moves geographically, or wage rates are decreased too far, or the perceived risk of the new company is unacceptable.

(d) Possible sources of finance are:

(i) banks - through loans or overdrafts;

(ii) second mortgages on the directors' houses;

(iii) 3i group, or other venture capital specialist organisation;

(iv) the Enterprise Investment Scheme announced in the November 1993 Budget;

(v) the previous employees' redundancy payments;

(vi) organisations such as the Welsh Development Agency or Scottish Development Agency;

(vii) deferral of payment to the vendor company for the company transferred;

(viii) loans from friends or relatives.

35 M AND C

> *Tutorial note.* This question requires appraisal of a particular proposal. It is essential to consider the interests of both sets of shareholders.

(a) *M plc and C plc*

The earnings per share of the two companies and of the group are, or are expected to be, as follows (assuming, for the group, that all shareholders in C plc accept the share offer, the cash offer being below the market price of C plc shares, so that the number of shares in issue becomes $20 + 42.6 \times 2/5 = 37.04$ million).

	M plc pence	C plc pence	Group pence
The current year			
M: $4.8 \times 0.65/20$	15.6		
C: $6.6 \times 0.65/42.6$		10.1	
Group: $(4.8 + 6.6) \times 0.65/37.04$			20.0
Group per old C share: $20.0 \times 2/5$			8.0

	M plc	C plc	Group
Four years hence			
M: $4.8 \times 1.2^4 \times 0.65/20$	32.3		
C: $6.6 \times 1.05^4 \times 0.65/42.6$		12.2	
Group: $(4.8 \times 1.2^4 + 6.6 \times 1.05^4) \times$ $0.65/37.04$			31.5
Group per old C share: $31.5 \times 2/5$			12.6

These calculations suggest that in the short term shareholders in M plc will be better off with the merger than without it, whereas shareholders in C plc would be worse off. This is to be expected, because although M plc's earnings per share are higher than C plc's, the ratio between them is only $15.6:10.1 = 1.545:1$, while the terms of the offer are 5 C shares for 2 M shares or $5:2 = 2.5:1$. In the longer term, however, the position is reversed, with M plc shareholders being marginally worse off with the merger than without it, and C plc shareholders being marginally better off. This is because M plc's earnings are expected to grow much faster than C plc's. The shareholders in C plc have the opportunity to buy into a rapidly growing business, and the M plc shareholders will, if the merger goes ahead, have their interest in that rapidly growing business diluted.

The above calculations make significant assumptions. In particular, earnings forecasts have been relied upon, and it has been assumed that the earnings of the two separate companies can be simply added together, without either business impinging on the other. As both businesses involve retailing food, this seems to be a dangerous assumption. On the other hand, the information given about other companies suggests that both M plc and C plc are average companies in their sector (except that C plc's P/E ratio is a little low), so there is no reason to suppose that there are special temporary factors affecting either company.

As to capital values, it is impossible to predict values in four years time, but the post-announcement prices do seem to make the offer a poor one for shareholders in C plc. Five shares in C plc are worth £1.50 × 5 = £7.50, whereas two shares in M plc are worth £2.60 × 2 = £5.20. These prices could of course change, depending on the progress of the bid.

(b) Dilution of earnings per share will only be acceptable in exchange for some other benefit. Such benefits could include improved long-term earnings prospects (as in the example above), protection from a hostile bid, improved asset backing and increased stability of earnings.

36   JUSTIFICATIONS

Tutorial note. This question requires you to discuss the validity of three reasons for expansion by takeover. Cases can be made both for and against the validity of these reasons, and a good answer will recognise this and be reasonably even-handed.

(a) *Economies of scale*

It is often thought that larger companies have lower unit costs, because fixed costs are spread more thinly. While there are almost certainly some savings to be made, particularly where the companies concerned are in the same industry, it should be remembered that diseconomies of scale are possible. A business may become too large, or a group of businesses too diverse, to be managed effectively. It may also be difficult to bring together two companies in such a way as to obtain all potential economies of scale.

122

(b) *Diversification and risk*

A group with interests in several different businesses will be less vulnerable to fluctuations in the fortunes of one business than a company which has only one business. Acquisition of existing businesses, which can be left under their existing management so long as performance remains satisfactory, may be the best way to diversify. On the other hand, shareholders can diversify their portfolios themselves, by investing in a wide range of companies each of which has a single business. It is therefore arguable that managers should concentrate on the success of their own businesses, rather than seeking to do the shareholders' work for them.

(c) *Undervalued shares*

If a company is really worth more than the price it can be bought at, its purchase would seem to be justified. However, a prospective purchaser should enquire carefully into the true value of the company. Its share price may be low because of justified doubts about its prospects. The reliability of information suggesting that a company is undervalued should be investigated, and one should ask why the market has not taken account of it. If it is because the information is not in the public domain, the risk of prosecution for insider dealing should not be ignored. On the other hand, if the information is public, it is possible that others have not realised its significance, and that the company is indeed undervalued.

37   TUTORIAL QUESTION: BID CALCULATIONS

(a) The first step is to calculate the theoretical market capitalisation of the two companies once the reorganisation has taken place.

National plc	£'000
Existing market capitalisation (45m × 166p)	74,700.0

P/E ratio 74,700 / 9,337.5 = 8.0

Existing equity earnings	9,337.5
Less: earnings lost on sale of division	(1,500.0)
	7,837.5
Add: 20% efficiency savings	1,567.4
New annual equity earnings	9,404.9
Theoretical new capitalisation assuming P/E of 8.0 (9,404.9 × 0.8)	75,239.2
Add: proceeds from sale of division	10,200.0
Total capitalisation	85,439.2

Provincial plc	
Existing market capitalisation (14m × 840p)	117,600.0
Add: proceeds from property sale	16,000.0
Less: reorganisation costs	(4,500.0)
Total capitalisation	129,100.0

The total combined market capitalisation after reorganisation is:

£85,439,200 + £129,100,000 = £214,539,200

The total number of shares in issue in National plc is 45 million. A two for nine offer means that Provincial plc will need to issue a further 10 million shares, bringing the total number of Provincial shares in issue to 24 million.

The theoretical price of a Provincial share is therefore 214,539.2 / 24,000 = 894 pence.

The theoretical price of a National share is 2/9 times the Provincial share price = 198.7 pence.

(b) The shares in National plc will not only be valued on the basis of market estimates of the potential merger synergy. In practice, the price will depend on the expectations of buyers and sellers of the likely success and ultimate format of the bid, as well as the amount of competition for the company from other bidders. If competition for the acquisition is strong, then it is likely that the shares in National plc will rise to a higher level as the market anticipates a premium having to be paid by the final buyer in order to secure the company. On the other hand, if there is little interest in the company from other bidders, Provincial may not need to offer much above the current market price of the shares in order to secure the acquisition, and National's shares will therefore be valued at a lower figure.

(c) Since investors are risk-averse, a cash alternative will normally be more attractive than a share offer. This is supported by the fact that many mergers fail to achieve the forecast synergies as quickly as expected, and therefore earnings in the early years post-merger are often lower than anticipated. Thus a cash alternative is likely to be lower than the current value of the share exchange.

However, Provincial plc must also take into account the tax situation of the National shareholders and the reason why they are holding National shares. Thus although a cash offer will avoid the investors incurring transaction costs when they wish to sell their new shares, they will immediately become liable to capital gains tax and this may make a cash offer less attractive. Provincial should ascertain the ownership structure of the National equity, for example the proportion of institutional investors, and seek to ascertain the preferences of the major shareholders.

(d) The existing price of a National share is 166p. For the shareholders in National to achieve a 10% gain in the value of their shares, the price would have to be $166 \times 1.1 = 182.6$ p.

A share price of 182.6 pence implies a market capitalisation for National of 45m $\times$ 182.6p = £82.17m. The total market capitalisation of the new group is £214.5392m (as calculated above). With a share price of 182.6 pence, the National shareholders would therefore hold 38.3% of the group.

The number of new shares to be issued by Provincial plc to achieve this can be calculated as follows.

Let n = additional number of shares to be issued.

$$\frac{n}{14m + n} = \frac{38.3}{100}$$

$$100n = 38.3n + 536.2m$$

$$61.7n = 536.2m$$

$$n = 8.69m$$

Thus Provincial plc will have to offer 8.69m shares in exchange for the 45m existing National plc shares. This represents an offer of one for 5.18.

38 TUTORIAL QUESTION: BASES OF VALUATION

(a) (i) Balance sheet value = £454,100.

(ii) Replacement cost value = £454,100 + £(725,000 – 651,600) + £(550,000 – 515,900) = £561,600.

(iii) Realisable value = £454,100 + £(450,000 – 651,600) + £(570,000 – 515,900) – £14,900 = £291,700.

Bad debts are 2% × £745,000 = £14,900. Bad debts are assumed not to be relevant to balance sheet and replacement cost values.

(iv) The Gordon dividend growth model value depends on an estimate of growth, which is far from clear given the wide variations in earnings over the five years.

BPP Publishing

(1)   The lowest possible value, assuming zero growth, is as follows.

Value cum div $= \dfrac{£25,000}{0.12} + £25,000 = £233,333$.

It is not likely that this will be the basis taken.

(2)   Looking at dividend growth over the past five years we have:

19X4 dividend = £25,000
19X0 dividend = £20,500

If the annual growth rate in dividends is g:

$$(1 + g)^4 \quad = \quad \left(\dfrac{25,000}{20,500}\right) = 1.2195$$

$$1 + g \quad = \quad 1.0508$$

$$g \quad = \quad 0.0508, \text{ say } 5\%$$

$$\text{Then, MV cum div} \quad = \quad \dfrac{\text{Dividend in 1 year}}{0.12 - g} + \text{current div}$$

$$= \quad \dfrac{25,000(1.05)}{0.07} + £25,000$$

$$= \quad £400,000$$

(3)   Using the rb model, we have:

Average proportion retained =

$$\dfrac{12,800 + 44,200 + 18,300 + 13,400 + 27,200}{33,300 + 66,800 + 43,300 + 38,400 + 52,200} = 0.495 \text{ (say b = 0.5)}$$

$$\text{Return on investment this year} \quad = \quad \dfrac{53,200}{\text{average investment}}$$

$$= \quad \dfrac{53,200}{(454,100 - 27,200/2)}$$

$$= \quad 0.1208 \text{ (say r = 12\%)}.$$

Then g = 0.5 × 12% = 6%

so MV cum div $= \dfrac{£25,000(1.06)}{0.06} + £25,000 = £466,667$.

(v)   *P/E ratio model*
Comparable quoted companies to Manon Ltd have P/E ratios of about 10. Manon is much smaller and being unquoted its P/E ratio would be less than 10, but how much less?

With a P/E ratio of 5, MV = £53,200 × 5 = £266,000.
With a P/E ratio of 10 × 2/3, MV = £53,200 × 10 × 2/3 = £354,667.
With a P/E ratio of 10, MV = £532,000.

(b) (i)   The *balance sheet value* should not play a part in the negotiation process. Historical costs are not relevant to a decision on the future value of the company.

(ii)   The *replacement cost* gives the cost of setting up a similar business. Since this gives a higher figure than any other valuation in this case, it could show the maximum price for Carmen to offer. There is clearly no goodwill to value.

(iii)   The *realisable value* shows the cash which the shareholders in Manon could get by liquidating the business. It is therefore the minimum price which they would accept.

BPP Publishing

All the methods (i) to (iii) suffer from the limitation that they do not look at the going concern value of the business as a whole. Methods (iv) and (v) below do consider this value. However, the realisable value is of use in assessing the risk attached to the business as a going concern, as it gives the base value if things go wrong and the business has to be abandoned.

(iv)   The *dividend model*. The figures have been calculated using Manon's K_e (12%). If (2) or (3) were followed, the value would be the minimum that Manon's shareholders would accept, as the value in use exceeds scrap value in (iii). The relevance of a dividend valuation to Carmen will depend on whether the current retention and reinvestment policies would be continued. Certainly the value to Carmen should be based on 9% rather than 12%. Both companies are ungeared and in the same risk class so the different required returns must be due to their relative sizes and the fact that Carmen's shares are more marketable.

One of the main limitations on the dividend growth model is the problem of estimating the future value of g.

(v)   The *P/E ratio model* is an attempt to get at the value which the market would put on a company like Manon. It does provide an external yardstick, but is a very crude measure. As already stated, the P/E ratio which applies to larger quoted companies must be lowered to allow for the size of Manon and the non-marketability of its shares. Another limitation of P/E ratios is that the ratio is very dependent on the expected future growth of the firm. It is therefore not easy to find a P/E ratio of a 'similar firm'. However, in practice the P/E model may well feature in the negotiations over price simply because it is an easily understood yardstick.

(c)   The range within which the purchase price is likely to be agreed will be the minimum price which the shareholder of Manon will accept and the maximum price which the directors of Carmen will pay. Examining the figures in part (a), the range is £291,700 (realisable value) to £561,600 (replacement cost).

39   TAKEOVER

> *Tutorial note.* In part (a) it is helpful to calculate key ratios for the two companies pre-acquisition, such as the trading margin and the price/earnings ratio. These can help to explain why the effect on EPS is so marked.
>
> In part (c) take into account the role of mezzanine finance in structuring a takeover bid. When considering the factors to be taken into account when deciding the form of payment, it may be helpful to view these in three categories - financial factors, legal constraints (eg Articles of Association) and the needs of the shareholders in the target company.

(a)   Relevant ratios for the two companies, and for the new group assuming that the bid is successful, are as follows. These figures assume that the combined earnings of the new group can be found additively.

	Rayswood	*Pondhill*	*Combined*
Turnover	56.0	42.0	98.0
Profit before tax	12.0	10.0	22.0
Margin	21.4%	23.8%	22.4%
Available to shareholders	7.8	6.5	14.3
Shares in issue	20.0	15.0	22.5
Earnings per share	39p	43.3p	63.6p
Group EPS per old Pondhill share (64p × $^1/_6$)			10.7p
Market price of shares	320p	45p	314.4p
P/E ratio	8.21	1.04	4.94

It is assumed that the financial structure of the two companies is similar.

An offer of one Rayswood share for six Pondhill shares values the Pondhill shares at 53.3 pence (320p/6). This implies a premium of 8.3 pence per share (18.4%) over the current market price of 45 pence. However, earnings per share would be enhanced from the point of view of the Rayswood shareholders, rising from 39 pence to 63.6 pence per share. This would be at the expense of the Pondhill shareholders who would see a dilution in their effective earnings per share from 43.3 pence to 10.7 pence per share.

It can be seen that the shareholders in Pondhill would not be receiving a particularly good deal in terms of earnings. The Pondhill shares are currently trading on a very low price/earnings ratio of 1.04, compared with the Rayswood P/E of 8.21. This is in spite of the fact that Pondhill has better trading results with a margin before tax of 23.8% compared with Rayswood's margin of 21.4%. Given also that the share price of a potential acquisition target is likely to rise in anticipation of a bid, the P/E ratio appears to be abnormally low. This suggests either that the current level of earnings is expected to diminish significantly, or that the market is aware of other adverse conditions threatening the company and is discounting the shares accordingly.

The above figures imply an increase in earnings per share of 63%. In his statement, the chairman only anticipates a 13% increase in EPS. Assuming that this figure is not depressed due to exceptional reorganisation costs following the merger, this means that the chairman is actually assuming performance post merger to be as follows.

	Rayswood	Pondhill	Combined
Available to shareholders	7.8	2.1	9.9
Shares in issue	20.0	15.0	22.5
Earnings per share	39p	14p	44.1p
Group EPS per old Pondhill share (44.1p × ¹/₆)			7.4p
Market price of shares	320p	45p	314.4p
P/E ratio	8.21	3.21	7.13

Provided that the chairman's estimate of Pondhill's post merger performance is realistic, then the deal would seem to be beneficial to the Rayswood shareholders due to the abnormally low P/E ratio at which the Pondhill shares are trading. However, Rayswood must be confident both that it will be able to cope with the problems that it appears Pondhill is facing, and that it will be able to manage the diversification effectively. The risk of this will increase with the degree of diversification represented by the acquisition.

It would be helpful to know more about Pondhill and the reasons for its low P/E ratio. Details of its financial structure and its borrowing commitments as well as its trading outlook would be useful.

(b) The current market capitalisation of the two companies is as follows.

	Shares in issue million	Market price Pence	Market capitalisation £'000
Rayswood	20	320	64,000
Pondhill	15	45	6,750
			70,750

If the bid is successful, one Rayswood share will be issued for every six Pondhill shares. This means that the 15m Pondhill shares will be replaced by 2.5m new Rayswood shares. The total number of shares in issue will therefore be 22.5m (20m + 2.5m).

Assuming that the acquisition does not alter the market's view of the appropriate capitalisation figure for the new group, the theoretical share price will be 314.4 pence (£70.75m/22.5m).

(c) The alternative forms of payment available in a bid include any combination of the following methods.

BPP Publishing

(i) *Cash*. In this case, a price is agreed for the shares in the target company and the shareholders receive this amount in cash.

Recently, there has been a tendency for the cash to be raised not by a rights issue or using medium-term secured loans, but from 'mezzanine finance'. In this situation a loan is arranged which is short to medium-term and unsecured, but which often gives the lender the option to exchange the loan for shares after the takeover. The rate of interest charged on these loans is much higher than on traditional loans because they are unsecured.

(ii) *Shares*. The bidding company issues new shares to pay for the acquisition. These are exchanged for the old shares in the target company in an agreed ratio eg two for one. Paper offers are often accompanied by a cash option.

Alternatively, the bidding company may issue new shares on the stock market in order to raise cash to pay for the acquisition. This will appear as a cash offer to the target company - however the effect on the bidding company will be to increase the number of shares in issue.

A further variation occurs when a company acquires another in a share exchange but the shares are then immediately sold on the stock market to raise cash for the seller. The sale is arranged by the stockbroker acting for the buying company and is known as a vendor placing.

(iii) *Loan stock*. This is similar to a purchase with shares, but loan stock is issued instead of shares.

When deciding on the form of consideration to be offered, the bidder must take the following factors into account.

Legal constraints

(i) *Borrowing limits*. The company must ensure that it does not exceed its powers to borrow as laid down in the Articles of Association.

(ii) *Increase in authorised capital*. The company must ensure that it does not exceed its authorised share capital as laid down in the Articles, or alternatively it must pass the necessary resolutions to amend this in a general meeting of shareholders.

(iii) *Pre-emptive rights*. The existing shareholders frequently have pre-emptive rights to any new issue of shares. If the company wishes to issue further shares for the purpose of a share exchange, then it must gain permission to waive pre-emptive rights in a general meeting. Such a waiver can normally be obtained for a period of one year at a time.

(iv) *Restrictive covenants on debentures*. The company should examine the covenants on any debentures or loan stock to ensure that the proposed new financing and control structure does not contravene these.

Financial factors

(i) *Dilution of earnings per share*. This is likely to occur when the consideration takes the form of equity shares, and the effect on the existing shareholders must be taken into account.

(ii) *Control structure*. Purchase by means of a new share issue may significantly change the structure of ownership and control. The company must take into account the likely reaction of its existing shareholders.

(iii) *Cost to the company*. The company should evaluate the relative cost of different forms of finance. A loan stock issue is likely to be cheaper than issuing new equity due to the tax benefits.

(iv) *Gearing*. The company must take into account the effect of the new finance on the gearing and decide whether any increase is both safe and acceptable to existing providers of finance.

BPP Publishing

Attractiveness to shareholders in the target firm

A share offer may be more acceptable than cash since it will not give rise to an immediate tax liability. The new shares can be disposed of if cash is required in such a way as to minimise liability to capital gains tax. Further, the shareholders may want to maintain a degree of control after the takeover, and this too may make a paper offer more attractive.

40 WOPPIT

> *Tutorial note*. The first part of this question was very specific. A general essay on traded options was *not* required, and your answer should have stuck very closely to the precise point. The examiner remarked that 'some answers were excellent, others merely discussed economic events.' The second part of the question required you to make two calculations, and then to discuss them and other matters. In such questions each piece of discussion, however short, should be carefully planned.

(a) A company's traded option price will fluctuate when its share price does so (unless the options are already 'out of the money'), because of the change in the difference between the share price and the exercise price. A volatile option price can therefore indicate a volatile share price, and that may in turn be a sign of financial weakness.

However, one certainly cannot deduce financial weakness from a volatile traded option price. Even if the volatility reflects a volatile share price, the share price's fluctuations may be due to factors other than the company's weakness. There are also several other factors which affect the price of traded options. The value of an option depends on the price of the underlying share at the exercise date, which may be several months away. Estimates of share prices so far ahead must be made on the basis of unreliable hunches, and participants in the market are liable to change their minds about such estimates frequently, either because of rumours about the company concerned or because of general market sentiment.

It should also be noted that option values are inherently more volatile than the underlying shares. A call option at 320p is worth about 20p if the share price is 340p, but if the share price falls by only 3% to 330p the value of the option falls by 50% to 10p.

(b) (i) *The net assets plus future profits basis*

	£m
Net assets per accounts excluding freehold property (620 – 150)	470
Freehold property (150×1.25^4)	366
Profits 1.51×7.115 (Note 1)	1,074
Valuation	1,910

Note 1

$$7.115 = \sum_{n=1}^{5}(1.12)^n$$

The valuation arrived at is $1,910/400 = 477.5$ pence per share, 7.5p above the current share price.

The dividend valuation model

According to the dividend valuation model, the market value of a share is given by:

$$MV = \frac{D_0(1+g)}{r-g}$$

In this formula, g is the rate of growth in Grapper's dividends, 12%.

We can use the dividend valuation formula for Grapper, with r derived from the CAPM $10\% + 1.05(16\% - 10\%) = 16.3\%$.

$$MV = \frac{£76,000,000(1.12)}{0.163 - 0.12} = £1,980 \text{ million}$$

BPP Publishing

This represents a value of 495 pence per share, 25 pence above the current share price.

The selection of a bid price

The two valuation methods both produce values reasonably close to the current share price. The net assets part of the first valuation has the merit of being reasonably objective, subject to any uncertainty attaching to the revaluation of freehold property, but the inclusion of future profits makes the valuation as a whole highly subjective. It is assumed that the past growth rate will be maintained, which it may well not be. The valuation of 477.5p a share may well be a significant overvaluation.

The dividend valuation model produces a higher value in this case. The main general criticism of this model is again that it relies on predictions which may not be borne out. Growth rates may easily change. A specific criticism in this case is that the conduct of Grapper's trade could change drastically following a takeover, leading to a substantial change in the rate of growth of earnings. Furthermore, a company's past dividend policy becomes irrelevant following a takeover, as dividends paid by a subsidiary do not amount to funds leaving the group (except to the extent that there are minority interests).

It seems that neither valuation is appropriate. There is no point in bidding at below the market price, but there seems to be no justification for bidding much above it. Some premium will, however, be needed to attract shareholders who had not previously intended to sell.

(ii) Whether growth by acquisition will deter a bid depends on both the size and the quality of the acquisitions. If a company becomes very large, only the largest companies will be able to make takeover bids. On the other hand, a series of high quality acquisitions will make a group attractive to other companies, both because of the existing group members and because a management team able to make good acquisitions is itself valuable.

In this case, the proposed takeover seems unlikely to be large enough to eliminate all possible bidders for Woppit, so to that extent the risk of a bid remains.

(iii) Woppit is more profitably managed than Grapper (20% compared to 16.6% operating profit to sales). If Woppit's management practices are extended to Grapper, this may improve operating efficiency. For example, Woppit turns over both its stock and its debtors faster than Grapper (stock turnover (based on sales value) 10.3 times against 6.4 times; debtors turnover 31 days against 50 days).

There may also be economies of scale. Only one central administrative organisation will be needed for the whole group. It may be that the activities of the companies can be usefully co-ordinated, with any surplus stocks of raw materials or finished goods in one company being transferred to meet shortages in the other.

Finally, Grapper may have confidential know-how which Woppit could use to improve its operational efficiency.

41 APCON

Tutorial note. When considering reasons for divestment in part (a), give examples from the financial press if you can. The question does not ask for possible methods of divestment and these can be ignored. Although the question asks for DCF analysis, do not neglect to consider a straightforward sale of assets. It is necessary to make a number of assumptions, for example concerning the taxable status of the amount that would be realised in the event of a sale. These should be clearly stated, possibly as notes to your answer.

(a) The divestment decision can be evaluated in two ways: (i) would the relevant cash flows arising if the division is to be retained exceed the offer price? (ii) would the funds realised if the division ceased production and the assets sold exceed the offer price?

130

(i) In view of the information available, the discounted cash flow that would arise if the division is retained will be calculated over a five year period.

The first step is to calculate the tax charge for each of the five years in question.

	19X3 £'000	19X4 £'000	19X5 £'000	19X6 £'000	19X7 £'000
Turnover (Note 1)	13,416	13,953	14,511	15,091	15,695
Direct costs (Note 2)	(10,368)	(11,197)	(12,093)	(13,061)	(14,106)
O'head (Note 3)	(1,716)	(1,888)	(2,076)	(2,284)	(2,512)
Depreciation (Note 4)	(500)	(500)	(500)	(500)	(500)
Taxable profit	832	368	(158)	(754)	(1,423)
Tax @ 35%	291	129	(55)	(264)	(498)

It is now possible to calculate the relevant annual cash flows.

	19X3 £'000	19X4 £'000	19X5 £'000	19X6 £'000	19X7 £'000
Turnover	13,416	13,953	14,511	15,091	15,695
Direct costs	(10,368)	(11,197)	(12,093)	(13,061)	(14,106)
Overhead	(1,716)	(1,888)	(2,076)	(2,284)	(2,512)
Taxation	(291)	(129)	55	264	498
Redundancy costs		(500)			
Land/buildings (Note 5)					5,554
Other income (Note 6)					1,000
Cash flow	1,041	239	397	10	6,129
Discount factor (Note 7)	0.855	0.731	0.624	0.534	0.456
Discounted cash flow	890	175	248	5	2,795

The expected discounted cash flow from the division over a five year period is £4,112,000. The offer price, after deducting redundancy payments, is £4,500,000. The offer should therefore be accepted on financial grounds.

Notes

1   Turnover and direct costs are calculated assuming an annual growth rate of 4% based on the 19X2 figure.

2   It is assumed that the 8% annual increase in direct costs includes both the volume effect of increased prices and the money effect of increased prices.

3   Relevant overhead is calculated on the basis of 65% of the 19X2 figure, increasing at 10% per year.

4   Depreciation is assumed constant at £500,000 per year.

5   The 19X7 market value of the land and buildings is (£2,100,000 × 1.8), plus 8% per year for 5 years.

6   This is the further amount of £1 million that would be receivable at the end of five years. This is assumed to be net of tax.

7   Since it is the cash flows that are being evaluated, the money rate WACC with a 3% risk premium should be used. This rate takes into account the cost of finance, and the central finance charge can therefore be ignored.

(ii) Calculate the realisable value of the division if production ceases and the assets are sold.

	£'000
Market value of land and buildings (2,100 × 1.8)	3,780
Market value of plant (3,650 × 0.75)	2,738
Net current assets at book value	120
	6,638

131

These calculations suggest that the division is worth more than the £6m offer price, and that therefore the bid should be rejected and the assets sold, or a higher price negotiated. However it assumes that the book value of the net current assets is fully realisable, which is often not the case in practice. Further, redundancy costs in the event of a closure could be very high, and in excess of the £1.5m suggested, unless it is possible to transfer staff to a different location.

(b) Possible reasons for divestment include the following.

(i) The division being sold is loss making and the company does not have the time and resources available to improve its performance.

(ii) The company may have undertaken a strategic review and decided to concentrate its attention on what it considers to be its core businesses. Other activities will then be disposed of.

(iii) Divestment may be undertaken for cash flow reasons. This might be because the company has limited cash resources and needs to sell in order to continue with its main activities. Alternatively it might be seeking to reduce its overall level of business risk by disposing of those divisions which have highly geared operating cash flows.

(iv) Divestment might be a means of financing a recent takeover. Some groups eg Hanson Trust specialise in taking over firms and then breaking them up into smaller parts, some of which are then sold in order to make a profit on the purchase.

(v) Similarly to (iv) above, a company may realise that if it splits into two or more parts, the market values resulting may be more than the market value of the company as a whole. This is particularly likely at times when the stock market is depressed. A current example is the proposed demerger of ICI into two separate firms.

(vi) Sometimes, a profitable area might be disposed of to protect the remainder of the company from an unwelcome takeover bid.

42 DIVESTMENT PLC

> *Tutorial notes.* The answer is required in the form of a report, but the question does not specify to whom this is to be addressed. It is reasonable to assume that it is to other members of the management team, and the figures should accordingly be made accessible to people who do not have a detailed financial knowledge.
>
> It is necessary to calculate the effect of the buyout upon the cash flows to the company, and then to capitalise the relevant incremental revenues. A net assets basis can also be demonstrated.

(a) A Company Ltd

To: Management team
From: Company Secretary
Date: 21 March 1994

Subject: Management buyout - financial implications

Introduction

Following the feasibility study recently carried out it has been possible to prepare financial projections for the first year of trading following buyout. These figures are included as Appendix 1 to this report. As a result it is now possible to consider the price that could be considered for the buyout, together with means of raising the necessary finance.

Pricing of buyout

The figures show that the projected net profit before tax for the first year of trading is £1.36m. However this includes a one-off item of £2m in respect of advertising costs. The profits thereafter would be in the region of £3.36m per annum. As agreed, we require a return of 30% on our investment, and therefore it is possible to capitalise the projected revenue figure to arrive at the maximum price that could be paid for the assets of the company as follows:

$$\text{Price} = 3.36\text{m} / 0.30 = \pounds11.2\text{m}$$

An alternative method of valuation is to calculate the fair value of the net assets of the firm as follows.

	£'000
Land and buildings at valuation	6,000
Plant and machinery at valuation	1,000
Stock at valuation	1,000
Debtors (assumed to be collectable)	3,000
Overdraft	(2,000)
	9,000

On this basis, the highest price that the team should be prepared to pay is £11.2m, based on the accounting rate of return method of valuation. Alternatively, it could be argued that the £2m advertising costs needed to achieve this should be deducted from the valuation, giving a top price of £9.2m.

It would also be worth establishing P/E ratios for other similar firms in this sector in order to look at an earnings based valuation.

Financing of buyout

Funding is required initially to finance the purchase price together with £2m to pay for the advertising costs. By the end of the first year of trading, the net assets (excluding the overdraft) should be in the region of £10.98m. Thus in round figures, we are looking for finance in the region of £11m, plus a further amount to cover week to week variations in the level of working capital.

It is conventional and prudent to match long term assets to long term funding, only using cheaper short term finance to fund short term assets and working capital fluctuations. In this case, long term assets consist of the fixed assets (£7m) plus a semi-permanent level of working capital (approx £4m). The following sources should be considered for this long term funding.

(i)   Specialist venture capital organisations who will provide medium to long term equity finance. However it must be recognised that they are likely to require a seat on the management board in return for their investment.

(ii)   Personal funds raised and loans secured by the new directors. A venture capitalist is likely to want to see some personal commitment on behalf of the management team.

(iii)   Grants from the local Enterprise Agency.

(iv)   When the price is being negotiated with Divestment plc, it would be beneficial if payment can be staged in order to allow other financing to be negotiated without a tight deadline, and so that part of the payment can be made out of future profits.

(v)   Consideration should be given to possible sale and leaseback of some of the fixed assets. If the current premises are not being fully utilised, then it may be possible to sell or lease a part of the land and buildings to another firm. Short term funding will be required to finance working capital fluctuations and the immediate costs of advertising. A combination of medium term loans and overdraft facilities from the bank are probably most appropriate for this.

Conclusions

The feasibility study figures now provide a basis for negotiations with Divestment plc on price, and also allow us to start to put together a financing package. It will also be necessary to give some consideration to other associated issues, such as the effect of the buyout on employees service contracts, and the setting up of acceptable alternative pension arrangements. These could well impact further upon the price negotiations.

BPP Publishing

APPENDIX 1

FORECAST PROFIT AND LOSS ACCOUNT FOLLOWING BUYOUT - YEAR 1

	£'000	£'000
Sales		12,000
Cost of sales:		
Purchases	(3,840)	
Wages	(3,600)	
Other expenses	(1,200)	
Advertising	(2,000)	
		(10,640)
Net profit		1,360

FORECAST BALANCE SHEET FOLLOWING BUYOUT (END OF YEAR 1)

	£'000	£'000
Fixed assets:		
Land and buildings at valuation	6,000	
Plant and machinery at valuation	1,000	
		7,000
Current assets:		
Stock	1,440	
Debtors	3,500	
		4,940
Current liabilities:		
Bank overdraft	(620)	
Creditors	(960)	
		(1,580)
Net assets		10,360
Represented by:		
Ordinary shares		1,000
Reserves		9,360
		10,360

Notes

Purchases:
Current cost is 40% of sales. If materials were bought from a competitor, this would reduce to 32% (40/1.25).
Expected cost = 12,000 × 0.32 = 3,840

Wages:
Current cost is 30% of sales. This level would be maintained.
Expected cost = 12,000 × 0.30 = 3,600

Depreciation:
Plant and machinery have been written down to scrap value.
Since it is stated that they will not require replacement in the immediate future, no depreciation has been charged.

Other expenses should be adjusted as follows:

	£'000
Current level	1,500
Less head office charge	(500)
Effect of increased turnover	200
	1,200

Stock:
Write off over-valuation of stocks of 1,000 against reserves.
Stock level is currently 50% of purchases. This could be reduced by 25%.
Expected stock level = 3,840 × 0.50 × 0.75 = 1,440

Debtors:
It is assumed that the level of sales to the parent company would remain unchanged.

	£'000
Parent company debt = 10,000 × 0.2 × 0.5 =	1,000
Other debt = ((10,000 × 0.8) + 2,000) × 0.25 =	2,500
	3,500

Creditors:
It is assumed that only purchases of materials are made on credit.
Expected creditors = 3,840 × 0.25 = £ 960,000.

Reserves:	£'000
Retained profits	7,000
Add retained profit for year	1,360
Less stock write off	(1,000)
Add revaluation of land & buildings	4,000
Less plant & machinery write off	(2,000)
	9,360

Cash:	
Opening overdraft	(2,000)
Add net profit	1,360
Add reduction in stock	560
Less stock write off	(1,000)
Less increase in debtors	(500)
Add increase in creditors	960
	(620)

(b) A company may decide to make a takeover bid for one or a combination of reasons.

Market factors

Acquisition of competing products. The company may see the opportunity, particularly in a static or declining market, to reduce competition by acquiring the products of its competitors. One way to do this is to make a bid for the competing company. This will only be possible if the acquisition satisfies the Monopolies and Mergers Commission.

Entry to a new market. Where a company is seeking to enter a new market which is dissimilar to its own, the fastest and lowest cost method of achieving this may be to acquire an existing firm. The dangers of this are that the company may lack the expertise to value it accurately, or to integrate it effectively following takeover.

Operational factors

The opportunity to make economies of scale. One company may bid for another firm in a similar line of business to its own in the belief that in doing so it will be able to achieve economies of scale in one or more areas of its operations. For example, it may be able to concentrate production on key sites which can then work to capacity to supply the regional market. Alternatively, the two firms may be able to share and rationalise their transport and distribution systems or their sales operations. Where the same customer base is served with similar products, further economies of scale may be possible in administrative and research functions eg debt collection and product development.

However, it should be remembered that diseconomies of scale are also possible due to problems of management and the effective integration of operations.

Management acquisition. Cases arise where it becomes apparent that the management team is not of the calibre needed to take the company through a period of continued growth. In

BPP Publishing

this situation, one option is to acquire a company with a competent team of managers already in place.

Access to innovation. A company which lacks its own research and development facilities and which is falling behind the market technically may see an acquisition as the best way to return to the forefront of innovation in its particular field.

Diversification

The directors may decide that it is in the best interests of the shareholders in the long term to reduce risk by conglomerate diversification. One of the most effective ways to achieve this is to take over an existing profitable firm in a different market sector - ideally one in which systematic risk is negatively correlated with that of the existing company. The new company can then be allowed to continue to operate under its existing management, provided that its performance is satisfactory.

Financial factors

Access to liquid funds. A company which needs a large amount of working capital may seek to improve this situation by the acquisition of a firm which is a cash generator. An example of this latter type of firm would be a chain of petrol stations, where goods are obtained by the company on credit and sold to its customers for cash.

Improved asset backing. Firms in a risky sector with high but volatile earnings levels in relation to the net assets may acquire companies with a high asset backing in order to attempt to improve the risk profile and assist in raising further funds through borrowing.

Growth in earnings per share. It may be cheaper for a company to achieve growth in earnings per share (or sales, dividends and market share) by acquisition than by organic growth. The bidding company may also perceive that due to poor management or lack of resources, the assets are not being used to their fullest capacity to generate earnings, and believe that it could use those assets more effectively itself.

Undervalued shares in the target company. The shares in the target company may appear to be undervalued, and the predator may see an opportunity to acquire the company at a discount. In this situation, the bidding company must make sure that the shares are truly undervalued due to the market having failed to take account of a publicly available piece of information, and not discounted due to expectations of poor performance in the future.

43   TUTORIAL QUESTION: FINANCIAL RECONSTRUCTION

(a)   NEMESIS HOLDINGS plc: BALANCE SHEET POST-RECONSTRUCTION

	£'000	£'000
Fixed assets		
Property (90,000 × 60%)		54,000
Plant ((70,000 × 60%) + 25,000)		67,000
		121,000
Current assets		
Stock	50,000	
Debtors (40,000 × 90%)	36,000	
		86,000
		207,000
Ordinary shares (See below)	48,000	
14% Unsecured debentures 19 × 5 (100,000 × 50%)		50,000
		98,000
Trade creditors (60,000 × 50%)	30,000	
Bank overdraft (70,000 + 9,000)	79,000	
		109,000
		207,000

Ordinary shares are made up as follows:

	£'000
Original balance × 10%	10,000
Preference shares × 10%	2,000
Issue to debenture holders	20,000
	32,000
Rights issue (32,000 × 50%)	16,000
Total	48,000

(b) *Note.* It is assumed that the additional investment in plant that would be required in order to earn the additional £6m per annum is represented by the investment of an additional £25m in plant and machinery referred to in point (x), and that the interest charges on this would be included in those referred to as permitting break-even after the reconstruction.

Ordinary shareholders. In the event of a forced sale, the ordinary shareholders would receive nothing, since the value of the assets is less than the total owed to trade creditors, the bank and the debenture holders. If the reconstruction is undertaken, the shareholders will have to subscribe a further £5m to take up the rights issue (£100m × 10% × 50%).

It is assumed that the new investment would be made out of the cash released in the reconstruction, and that therefore there would be no further interest charges associated with the investment. On this basis, 31.25% (15/48) of the incremental earnings of £6m would be attributable to the existing shareholders. This amounts to a return of £1.875m on the incremental investment of £5m – 37.5%. Thus the shareholders are likely to feel that this is worthwhile and in their best interests if they are confident that the profit forecasts are realistic and achievable. If there is doubt as to their validity, then they run the risk of losing further on the investment, and may prefer to cut their losses. They also need to take into account the fact that there is a substantial shift in the balance of ownership and control since they would now only own 31.25% of the equity and would not have a controlling vote.

Preference shareholders. In the event of a forced sale, the preference shareholders are in an equally bad position as the ordinary shareholders and would receive nothing. If the reconstruction is undertaken, they will have to make a proportionately similar investment to the ordinary shareholders in order to take up their rights. The sum involved in this case is £1m (£20m × 10% × 50%).

In return for this further investment, they would receive earnings of £0.375m (£6m × 3/48), which amounts to a return of 37.5% on their incremental investment. They would sacrifice the opportunity to receive a fixed annual income, being now dependent upon the dividend payments. However, in return they would receive a stake in the control of the company, albeit only 6.25%. Again, their confidence in the profit forecasts is also important. If they feel that these are realistic, then they might well believe that it is worth making the additional investment.

Debenture holders. In the event of a forced sale, the debenture holders rank alongside the other creditors in order of priority for the repayment of funds. It is not apparent from the figures provided what if anything is owed to the preferential creditors (PAYE, VAT, NIC, wages, salaries and pension scheme arrears). However, assuming the best position ie that there are no preferential creditors, the assets amount to £120m, and the creditors (bank overdraft, trade creditors and debenture holders) amount to £230m. This represents a maximum potential settlement of 52.18 pence in the pound. Thus if the debentures are written down by 50%, the holders are in only a slightly worse position than if the company was to be wound up. In addition, they would receive equity in compensation, and would therefore in the future be able to participate in the decision making and earnings of the company, as well as continuing to receive some fixed income from the remaining debentures. Although they would have to make a further investment of £10m to subscribe to the rights issue, they would now have the controlling stake in the equity of the company (62.5%).

They would earn a return on their equity of £3.75m. Their effective investment amounts to cash foregone of £52.18m, plus a further £10m in taking up the rights issue. Their total new returns would be 14% of £50m plus £3.75m, ie £10.75m. This amounts to an overall rate of return of 17.29%.

BPP Publishing

It therefore seems that the debenture holders have nothing to lose by accepting the scheme, and have the potential to gain through participating in the equity in the future, provided that they have confidence in the company's forecasts.

Trade creditors. As shown above in the discussion of the debenture holders' position, the maximum that would be received in the event of a break up would be 52.18%. In reality, the amount received is likely to be smaller after preferential creditors have been paid. If the reconstruction is undertaken, they would receive only 50%, and the opportunity to continue to supply the company should they wish to do so.

Thus the offer appears reasonable from the point of view of the creditors; however there is little incentive for them to opt for the reconstruction.

Bank. If the company went into liquidation, the bank would be owed £70m and would rank with the other creditors for repayment. As has been shown above, the maximum which it could expect to receive would be 52.18 pence in the pound. If it were to accept the reconstruction, the overdraft would be increased and the risk to the bank would therefore be greater. However, it would be obtaining what appears to be a very high rate of return on the increase in the overdraft, when compared with current interest rates and the rates the company has been paying to preference share and debenture holders.

Again, the bank will want to have good evidence with which to substantiate the profit forecasts made by the directors, and it is also likely to want to see a cash budget which has not yet been provided. If these are satisfactory, then accepting the reconstruction would mean that the bank avoids incurring a large loss on its lending, and it would also be able to earn a good return on the incremental funds provided.

(c) (i) If the bank had a fixed charge on the property, then it would be able to realise £35m on the sale of the property in the event of a break up. It would then rank alongside the other creditors in seeking payment of the balance owing. In this case the assets available for the unsecured creditors would amount to £85m, and the creditors would hold debts amounting to £195m. Therefore the maximum which they could expect to receive would be 43.59 pence in the pound.

In the event of break up therefore, the bank could expect to receive £50.26m (£35m + (£35m × 43.59%)). This is considerably more than would be obtained if the overdraft was unsecured, and thus the bank would stand to lose more by agreeing to the reconstruction, depending on the reliability of the company's profit forecast.

The ordinary and preference shareholders' position would be unaffected since they would still stand to lose everything in the event of the company being wound up.

The debenture holders would also receive less in the event of winding up - £43.59m instead of £52.18m - and therefore it would be likely to increase the attractiveness of the reconstruction. The yield on the new investment would now amount to 20.06% (£10.75m return on £53.59m).

Similarly the trade creditors would also receive less if the company went into liquidation, and this would therefore enhance the attractiveness of the reconstruction.

(ii) If the bank held a floating charge on the assets, it would receive payment in full in the event of a liquidation. It would therefore not be in its best interests to accept the reconstruction since it would be lending further funds with no guarantee that the new project would yield the projected returns. If things went wrong, the asset base might be further diminished and in the event of a later liquidation, the floating charge might no longer be adequate to ensure repayment of the overdraft in full.

The ordinary and preference shareholders' position would be unaffected since they would still stand to lose everything in the event of the company being wound up.

The debenture holders would now receive even less in the event of the company being wound up, with only £50m being available for the debenture holders and the trade creditors. Each party would receive only 31.25 pence in the pound, and thus the attractiveness of the reconstruction for both groups would be further enhanced. In the case of the debenture holders, the effective rate of return on the new investment would increase to 26.06% (a return of £10.75m on an investment of £41.25m).

44 GOODSLEEP PLC

REPORT

To: The Board
From: A N Accountant
Date: 4 July 19X0
Subject: Proposed scheme of reconstruction

Introduction
This report considers the proposed scheme, looking at the need for a scheme, its likely acceptability to creditors and to shareholders, and whether the scheme will achieve its objectives.

The need for a scheme
If nothing is done, the company will be unable to meet all its liabilities when the 10% debenture has to be redeemed later this year. Liquidation, at the instance of debenture holders or (if debenture holders are paid) other creditors is the likely result.

Acceptability of the scheme to creditors
If the company goes into liquidation, the net realisable values of the assets would be:

	£'000
Land and buildings	6,400
Plant and machinery	2,600
Stock	2,200
Debtors	3,000
Cash	200
	14,400

The secured liabilities (debentures and bank loan) total £10,500,000, so they could all be paid, but unsecured creditors could only expect a dividend of:

$$\frac{14,400 - 10,500}{5,900} \times 100 = 66.1p \text{ in the pound.}$$

As one of the unsecured creditors is the bank, substantial opposition to liquidation may be expected.

Under the scheme, all debenture holders would receive par value, which should be acceptable to them. The loss of a few months' interest would be compensated for by the receipt of the redemption money (which is in excess of current market value) a few months early.

The bank, while lending nearly as much after the reconstruction as before, would have a greater proportion of its lending secured, and would have the opportunity to switch to the current interest rate on the term loan. It is therefore likely to support the scheme.

Other creditors' prospects would depend on the trading success of the reconstructed company. If good cash returns are achieved soon, they may expect repayment in full. If not, they might even get less than the dividend they would have got on a liquidation now.

Acceptability of the scheme to shareholders
Preference shareholders would receive more than the current market value for their shares, though presumably the two years' arrears of dividend would never be received. Thus, although these shareholders might feel hard done by, they would be better off than in a liquidation, when they would receive nothing.

Ordinary shareholders would also receive nothing in a liquidation. Under the scheme, they are being asked to risk new money, though if they choose not to do so the scheme can go ahead because the issue will be underwritten. Ordinary shareholders' main concern is likely to be control of the company. Even if they take up all their rights and convert all their debentures, their total shareholding will be only $8,000,000 + 6,000,000/5 = 9,200,000$ shares, out of a total of $9,200,000 + 5,000,000 + 2,000,000 = 16,200,000$ shares. Growall Capital plc's stake in the total share capital would be $5,000,000/16,200,000 = 31\%$, and that could give Growall Capital plc effective control, particularly if there are no other substantial shareholders apart from the overseas private investor. Existing shareholders may well be concerned about Growall Capital plc's objectives.

Achievement of objectives
The immediate problem, payment of the debenture holders, will be solved.

A further objective is to raise the funds needed for a new product. Total funds raised will be as follows.

	£'000
Shares (15,000 × 50p – 3,500 × 40p)	6,100
Debentures (2,000 – 6,000)	(4,000)
Bank (5,500 + 1,000 – (4,500 + 2,100))	(100)
Surplus property	1,600
Improved working capital management	150
	3,750

The funds raised thus fall short of the £4,000,000 required, and some amendment to the scheme and/or to the proposed investment will be needed.

The scheme would be unacceptable if it would lead to similar problems recurring in the near future. We should therefore consider the worst possible outcome (low returns on the new investment and no conversion of debentures into shares).

	£'000	£'000
Earnings before interest and tax		1,200
Less interest:		
Convertible debentures (5% × 6,000/5)	60	
13% debentures	260	
Bank loan	660	
Overdraft	110	
		1,090
		110
Less tax (assuming there are no losses brought forward)		39
		71

Earnings per new ordinary share = 0.47p

Earnings per share would be very low, and interest cover would be only 1,200/1,090 = 1.1 times, which is worryingly low, especially for a company which has already got into difficulties. The scheme will not give shareholders and creditors long-term security unless the company's management are very skilled. Growall Capital plc could use its influence in this respect.

Conclusion
The scheme is not ideal, but it may be the best which can be achieved in the circumstances. Growall Capital plc and the overseas private investor in particular are taking a considerable risk.

45 ROCK BOTTOM PLC

(a)

	£
Ordinary shares	
Previous ordinary shareholders	200,000
Previous preference shareholders	150,000
Previous debenture holders	650,000
	1,000,000
Rights issue (for cash)	2,000,000
	3,000,000

140

ROCK BOTTOM PLC
BALANCE SHEET AFTER REORGANISATION

	£		£
Ordinary shares of £1	3,000,000	Fixed assets	2,250,000
Capital reserve		Stock	600,000
(balancing figure)	200,000	Debtors	450,000
	3,200,000	Cash	
10% debentures	350,000	(2,000,000 − 750,000)	1,250,000
Trade creditors	1,000,000		
	4,550,000		4,550,000

(b) (i) If the capital reorganisation took place, the expected profits of the company would be as follows.

	£
Profits before interest	400,000
Interest (10% of £350,000)	35,000
Profit after interest	365,000

It is assumed that we can ignore taxation. The earnings per share will be 12.17 pence.

(ii) If the company went into liquidation, the money raised from the assets would be distributed as follows.

	£
Secured creditors with fixed charge (bank overdraft)	750,000
Liquidation expenses - assumed to be nil	0
Unsecured creditors (balance)	1,500,000
	2,250,000

Since unsecured creditors, who are the 15% debenture holders and the trade creditors, amount to £2,000,000 these would receive 75p in the £1.

(iii) *Existing ordinary shareholders*

These have the choice of allowing the company to go into liquidation (and receiving nothing) or injecting £400,000 of new cash into the company and holding 600,000 ordinary shares. Earnings on these shares would be (× 12.17p) £73,000 per annum, which represents a return of 18.25% on the extra £400,000 investment.

This might seem a worthwhile return, although the shareholders should be advised to consider alternative, possibly less risky, investments for their £400,000 which would yield more than 18.25%.

If any major shareholder is also an employee of the company, perhaps a director, he or she might wish to invest in the company in order to retain his/her job.

(iv) *Existing preference shareholders*

These also have the choice of allowing the company to go into liquidation (and receiving nothing) or injecting £300,000 of new cash into the company and holding 450,000 shares. Earnings on these shares would be (× 12.17p) £54,750 per annum, which represents an 18.25% return on the £300,000 investment.

The choice is therefore similar to the one facing existing ordinary shareholders, although investors in preference shares might be more reluctant to invest in high-risk equity. The advice to these shareholders should be the same as for the ordinary shareholders - ie consider the prospective return, the risk and alternative investment options before reaching a decision.

(v) *Existing debenture holders*

If the company went into liquidation, these would receive £750,000. If they agreed to the reorganisation, their annual earnings would be:

BPP Publishing

	£
From 1,950,000 shares (× 12.17p)	237,250
Interest on new debentures	35,000
	272,250

To earn this annual return they would have to invest £1,300,000 in new capital, for the rights issue of shares. Thus, in order to earn £272,250 per year, the debenture holders must forgo £750,000 in cash receipts and pay out £1,300,000 - a total capital investment of £2,050,000. The return on this investment would be (£272,250 + £2,050,000) = 13.3%.

This is a low return, especially in view of the risky nature of the investment. It seems probable that more suitable alternative investments could be found for their capital.

(vi) *Trade creditors*

If the company went into liquidation, these would receive £750,000 'now'. If they agreed to the moratorium on debt payments they could expect their full £1,000,000 in six months' time, plus the prospects of continuing to trade profitably with Rock Bottom and receive cash on delivery for new supplies.

Although there is some risk involved, the trade creditors would seem to have sufficient justification for encouraging the company to continue in existence.

However, if any trade creditor is owed a large amount of money and is in urgent need of cash, settling for a payment of 75p in the pound 'now' might seem a more desirable option.

46 COMMON MARKET

> *Tutorial note.* This is a question on the different types of international trade agreement and the benefits from engaging in free trade and economic co-operation. Bear in mind that a common market such as the EC is a localised free trade area which may (as the EC does) adopt protectionist measures which militate against freedom of trade with countries outside the common market area.

(a) A free trade area exists when there is no restriction on the movement of goods and services between countries. This may be extended into a customs union when there is a free trade area between all member countries of the union, and in addition there are common external tariffs applying to imports from non-member countries into any part of the union. In other words, the union promotes free trade among its members but acts as a protectionist bloc against the rest of the world.

A common market encompasses the idea of a customs union but has a number of additional features. In addition to free trade among member countries there is also complete mobility of the factors of production. A British citizen has the freedom to work in any other country of the European community, for example. A common market will also aim to achieve stronger links between member countries, for example by harmonising government economic policies and by establishing a closer political confederation.

(b) The most obvious benefits which countries might gain from forming a common market are associated with free trade between them. The benefits of free trade are illustrated by the law of comparative advantage which states that countries should specialise in producing those goods where they have a comparative advantage. Specialisation, together with free trade, will result in an increase in total output and all countries will be able, to a great or lesser extent, to share in the benefits.

In particular, different countries have different factor endowments and, as the international mobility of these factors tends to be severely limited, trade increases the range of goods and services available in a particular country. By becoming part of a common market, imports from other member countries are available more cheaply and easily. Imports of certain raw materials or types of capital equipment not otherwise available in a particular country will improve its productive potential, enabling a faster rate of economic growth to be achieved.

BPP Publishing

Similarly, improvements in the range and quality of consumer goods available will tend to enhance a country's standard of living.

In addition, there is a larger market for domestic output and firms may be able to benefit from economies of scale by engaging in export activities. Economies of scale improve efficiency in the use of resources and enable output to be produced at lower cost. This also raises the possibility of benefits to consumers if these cost savings are passed on in the form of lower prices. In addition, the extension of the market in which firms operate increases the amount of competition they face and hence should improve efficiency.

Establishment of a common market is often accompanied by some form of exchange rate agreement between members and this in turn is likely to encourage further trade as it reduces uncertainty for both exporters and importers. Stability of exchange rates is also beneficial to a government in formulating its domestic economic policies.

Membership of a common market may be particularly beneficial to smaller or weaker economies as, in addition to increasing the availability of essential factors of production and the range of goods and services available to domestic consumers, it also enables them to benefit from any economic growth experienced by their fellow members. Spin-offs may be in the form of larger markets for their exports, lower import prices, improved employment opportunities and so on.

In addition to fostering economic ties between countries, common markets provide the basis for stronger political links. Again, this may be particularly important for smaller countries enabling them to benefit from an enhanced position in the world economy. It may also encourage further international economic co-operation, in turn providing an additional stimulus to growth.

47   EUROCURRENCIES

> *Tutorial note.* Part (a) of the question can be answered quite briefly. Part (b) attempts to test your knowledge of the factors which led to the slow-down in the growth in the eurocurrency markets from the early 1980s.

(a)   A eurocurrency is a bank deposit of currency which has been deposited outside the currency's country of origin. For example, US dollars deposited with a UK bank are eurocurrency (eurodollars). Banks make wholesale loans in eurocurrencies that have been deposited with them, and these loans are referred to as eurocurrency loans.

Eurocurrency loans are sometimes made by syndicates of banks, rather than an individual bank.

(b)   (i)   The debts of the developing countries consist mainly of outstanding eurocurrency loans from international banks. The rapid growth of the eurocurrency lending market in the 1970s and until 1982 was caused largely by the rapidly-increasing loans to developing countries. When the debt problem became apparent from 1982, the impact on the eurocurrency bank lending market was dramatic.

(1)   The developing countries were unable to service their outstanding debt. In many cases, they were unable to meet the interest payments due on the debt.

(2)   International banks were asked to re-schedule existing debts, and to provide new loans to allow developing countries to meet the payments on their existing debts.

(3)   The banks have been very reluctant to agree to new lending, unless the borrowing country also arranges a loan from the IMF and agrees to accept IMF loan conditions.

(4)   New lending has been much less frequent, with the consequence that growth in the eurocurrency markets has slowed down dramatically since 1982, in spite of the 'alliance' between the banks and the IMF.

(5)   The debt problem has remained unresolved. The international banks have made substantial provisions for bad debts on their loans, in their financial accounts.

The difficulties of countries in South America have not been resolved, and the countries face a debt burden that they find hard to bear. Thus, in 1987 Brazil declared a moratorium on its foreign debt; in 1989 Venezuela declared a moratorium on the repayment on principal on its outstanding debts.

(ii) Securitisation is assumed to refer to the development of the markets in eurobonds, euronotes and eurocommercial paper, whereby large international companies and other large international organisations are able to borrow by issuing debt `paper' - ie as a security - direct to investors.

The impact of securitisation on the eurocurrency lending market has been to reduce the demand for eurocurrency loans from `creditworthy' borrowers. This is because eurobonds, commercial paper and so on provide an alternative to eurocurrency borrowing as a method of raising funds on the domestic and international financial markets. Thus, securitisation was a contributory factor to the decline in syndicated eurocurrency lending after the early 1980s.

It should be added that securitisation has also begun to emerge as a method of dealing with outstanding debts from developing countries. Some lending banks have experimented with issuing and selling securities that are secured against a package of outstanding eurocurrency loans. The lending bank obtains some immediate payment from selling the securities, and the security holders are entitled to the proceeds from the packaged loans (but only if the loans are eventually repaid).

(iii) Liberalisation in the domestic financial markets refers to the removal of restrictions on domestic financial transactions. In the USA for example, restrictions on inter-state banking were removed. The consequence of liberalisation in domestic banking markets is that domestic bank lending is able to develop more freely, and to compete more strongly with eurocurrency bank lending (eg by offering more competitive interest rates on loans and to depositors).

The continuing liberalisation of domestic markets in various countries during the 1980s therefore contributed to the decline in the eurocurrency markets.

48   NEW EXPORT MARKETS

> *Tutorial note.* The question asks what advice, as well as practical help, a local branch of the bank can give to a small business about exports. Advice might well include introducing or referring the business managers to other organisations, such as Overseas Trade Services which might be able to help them.

(a) A local branch of a bank can obtain information from a branch of the bank's international division, and pass it on to the small business customer. The type of information which might be provided by the bank is:

(i) whether the product is likely to find a profitable market in any particular overseas country;

(ii) whether this country has exchange control regulations, and if so, what they are;

(iii) whether the country has economic problems which might create exchange control problems in the future.

(b) If the small business already knows of foreign buyers who might wish to purchase its products, the bank might be able to provide a general status report about the creditworthiness of the buyers.

(c) The small business might not be aware of any potential buyers in a particular country, and the bank might then be able to provide the names of potential customers. (If the small business wanted to find an agent abroad, the bank might be able to suggest the names of any overseas firms which might be potential agents).

BPP Publishing

(d) The bank can also suggest the names of reliable forwarding agents or export packers in the UK whose services can be used to prepare goods for overseas shipment and to arrange for shipment.

(e) The small business might well be interested in finding out more about terms of settlement in overseas trade. The bank should be able to provide advice and assistance in this matter, by advising on:

(i) the method of settlement (open account, collections etc);
(ii) the terms of payment (credit allowed etc)

which might be appropriate for customers in a particular country.

In addition, the bank should provide the firm with details of its export finance scheme and details of export credit insurance available from NCM UK and other private sector firms (for short-term deals) or ECGD (longer-term deals).

(f) The small business might be concerned about its ability to finance export sales on credit. The bank should advise the customer whether it might be prepared to make advances to the business against the security of a bill of exchange drawn on a foreign buyer (and accepted by the buyer) or else to negotiate bills of exchange with the customer.

(g) The bank should also advise the exporter on methods by which the bank can help to obtain payments from overseas buyers (documentary collections, documentary credits etc).

(h) The management of the small business might be advised to send representatives to an overseas market to meet potential customers. The bank might be able to arrange letters of introduction to potential customers itself. Otherwise, it can provide the firm with letters of introduction to correspondent banks in those countries. The correspondent banks will then arrange introductions to local businesses.

(i) The bank should refer (or introduce) the firm to other organisations which exist to help exporters. These include Overseas Trade Services, but also the local Chamber of Commerce, as well as the Small Business Club and Export Club themselves.

Overseas Trade Services can provide a wide range of help and assistance, such as:

(i) advice about the likely success of the firm's product in an overseas market;

(ii) general status reports about the creditworthiness of potential buyers;

(iii) advice about the methods of settlement and terms of payment in an overseas country;

(iv) advice about the practical problems which might be experienced by exporters in any particular foreign country;

(v) sponsorship of trade missions to an overseas country, whereby the costs of an overseas visit by a firm can be sponsored.

(j) If the small firm decides to go ahead and enter a new export market, the bank should continue to offer its assistance to the firm (eg advice on export documentation).

49 TINTINNABULUM LTD

(a) The only alternative to payment in advance which may be considered secure from the exporter's point of view is an irrevocable letter of credit. The exporter may want the irrevocable letter of credit (L/C) to be confirmed by a bank in Germany.

(b) To know with a reasonable degree of certainty what its costs will be, Tintinnabulum Ltd will need to know its bank's and the German bank's charges, as well as to establish the exchange rate by means of a forward contract, forward option contract, or pure option contract.

(i) Under a forward contract, the bank would agree to sell Tintinnabulum a specified amount of DM on a specified date at a rate agreed now.

(ii) Under a forward option contract, the bank would agree to sell Tintinnabulum a specified amount of DM between two specified dates at a rate agreed now.

BPP Publishing

(iii) Under a pure option contract, the bank would agree to sell Tintinnabulum a specified amount of DM at an agreed rate ('the strike price') agreed now, should Tintinnabulum wish to exercise its option. This could be at expiry only in the case of an European option, or at any time up to the expiry date in the case of an American option.

Bank charges will include L/C charges, any payment/acceptance and discounting charges, and the German bank's charges. Various banks charge commissions for forward contracts. For pure options, the premium is almost always payable up front.

(c) Forward contracts and forward option contracts are immediately firm and binding on both the customer and the bank, as stated in the following definition:

'An immediately firm and binding contract between a bank and its customer for the purchase or sale of a stated quantity of a specified foreign currency at a rate of exchange fixed at the time of entering the contract, for performance by, and delivery of, the specified currency on or between two specific dates.'

Thus, in the case of a forward option contract, the customer has the option as to when to deliver (or call for delivery), but it is bound to fulfil the contract by the expiry date at the latest. The contract has to be fulfilled either by delivery or by way of extension or close out.

A pure option contract, in contrast, is an obligation on the bank only, and not on the customer as well: ie the customer can walk away from the contract but the bank must fulfil it if the customer so requires. A pure option contract can be defined as:

'an agreement by which the purchaser buys the right but not the obligation, upon payment of a premium, to call (ie purchase) or put (ie sell) up to a stated amount of base currency against delivery of a counter contract, at a strike price agreed with the writer ... upon entering the contract.'

50 FRAME-UP LTD

> *Tutorial notes.*
>
> 1. We are told that it is a buyer's market, so we should focus on financing methods related to open account trading, rather than documentary collections or documentary credit.
>
> 2. For consumer goods, appropriate financing should be short-term.
>
> 3. The methods below are (largely) without recourse to Frame-Up Ltd.

(a) *Export credit insurance facilities*

Some banks in the UK offer smaller exporter schemes. For a fixed charge which covers administration and a predetermined interest rate, the bank finances up to 90% or 100% (depending on the bank) of an export order of £100,000 or less (more, under exceptional circumstances) on evidence of shipment, without recourse to the exporter. The cost of lending is usually less than overdraft finance.

This would be secured by an export credit insurance policy, with the exporter covered under the umbrella of the bank's policy or one managed by a reputable policy manager.

Alternatively, if Frame-up Limited has its own export credit insurance policy, the bank could lend between 70% and 100% against it, in sterling or another major currency. The bank would only have recourse to Frame-up Ltd if it breached the terms of its commercial contract.

Costs would include the insurance premiums, the policy manager's fee, bank collection charges (where relevant), interest on advances and an acceptance fee.

(b) *Factoring and invoice discounting*

Frame-up Ltd could sell its trade debts (documentary bills or invoices) to a factoring company.

Payment is without recourse (unless Frame-up Ltd specifically requests 'with recourse finance'): 70% to 85% (or whatever figure is agreed between the factor and exporter) of the invoice value is paid to Frame-up Ltd immediately. The balance (less charges) is credited to Frame-up Ltd on the due date, regardless of whether the importer has since become unable or unwilling to pay. The factor will refuse to finance sales to buyers whose creditworthiness appears questionable from its researches. Its credit searches are normally available to the customer at the negotiation stage so that orders are not accepted from bad credit risks.

The handling charge is usually in the range 0.25 to 2% depending on the type of debt and the work expected and interest is calculated on the basis of a margin, say 3%, over the factor's base rate. Exchange risk is allowed for in the cost and so covered by the factor.

Normally, a factor insists that the importer knows of its purchase of the debt. If, however, Frame-up Ltd does not wish the importer to know that the debt has been sold, the undisclosed non-recourse factoring is arranged (unbeknown to the importer) as follows:

(i)   Frame-up Ltd sells the goods, not to the importer on credit, but to the factor for cash;

(ii)   the factor, in turn, appoints Frame-up Ltd as its agent for the delivery of the goods to the importer, and for the collection of the debt at maturity.

Factoring normally includes the financing service discussed above plus the accounting and debt collection functions (and occasionally shipping and forwarding); whereas invoice discounting limits itself to the financing (ie Frame-up Ltd acts as agent for the factor, collecting the debt, and paying the cash over to the factor on receipt). Factoring tends to be used by exporters with a steady annual turnover of at least £100,000, and invoice discounting by smaller and/or less frequent exporters.

51   BLANC ET BLANC

> *Tutorial note.* The expressions 'traditional' and 'non-traditional' are used by many bankers, so it is useful to know what is intended by them. Traditional is generally synonymous with 'bank finance', whereas *non-traditional* includes some types of bank finance and so called non-bank finance, although this latter is often provided by specialist divisions or subsidiaries of banks. This answer is considerably longer than what would be expected given the marks allocated.

Short-term traditional export finance

(a)   *Bank loans and bank overdrafts*

This form of borrowing can be very convenient but, as business increases, it is unlikely that Blanc et Blanc can finance their exports entirely from a general purpose loan or overdraft, particularly since borrowing in either of these ways may be more expensive than other forms of borrowing specifically designed for exporters.

Bank loans and overdrafts may be provided in sterling or another currency (probably that of the majority of Blanc & Blanc's outward invoices), and will be on either a secured or an unsecured basis, depending on the bank's assessment of the risk.

Security could be provided by UK assets, parent company guarantee, or a standby letter of credit issued by the parent company's bankers. Alternatively, security may be provided by the assignment of an export credit insurance policy but, by borrowing through a general loan or overdraft, Blanc et Blanc will not be able to pay at the preferential *consensus rate* (a rate subsidised by the government, where applicable).

(b)   *Export finance schemes*

Some banks in the UK offer smaller exporter schemes. If Blanc et Blanc has its own export credit insurance policy, the bank could lend between 70% and 100% against it, in sterling or another major currency. The bank would only have recourse to Blanc et Blanc if they committed some failure under the commercial contract.

BPP Publishing

(c) *Using documentary credits procedures*

> *Tutorial note.* Documentary credits available by term drafts drawn on the advising or issuing bank are known as documentary acceptance credits. They should not be confused with acceptance credit facilities to be discussed under (d) below.

If Blanc et Blanc give credit to the buyer by way of a term draft drawn under a documentary credit, Blanc et Blanc may seek to obtain finance by arranging for the term draft to be:

(i) negotiated by the negotiating bank, with recourse, where the draft is drawn on the applicant or the issuing bank (without recourse if the credit is confirmed); or

(ii) discounted without recourse by the advising bank or discount house if the draft is drawn on and accepted by the advising bank; or

(iii) discounted without recourse by the issuing bank if it is drawn on and accepted by it. (UK accepting houses provide this service if the draft is drawn in marketable currency.)

(d) *Using bills of exchange*

Bills of exchange can be used to obtain export finance in the four 'traditional' ways described below. In each of these four cases, the bank normally retains right of recourse to the exporter in the event of non-acceptance and/or non-payment of the bill. Of course, as well as the risk of non-payment, Blanc et Blanc might also be short of funds. The bank will have the right to sell the goods without reference to the customer. This is vital if the goods are perishable and/or incurring expensive charges awaiting customs clearance. If the bill is denominated in a foreign currency and is dishonoured, Blanc et Blanc will have to bear the exchange loss (if the rate has gone against them) of replacing the funds due to us.

The four traditional ways of using bills of exchange for export finance are now discussed individually.

(i) *Negotiation*

Here the word 'negotiation' is used to mean the purchase of an outward collection, whether a bill of exchange or a cheque sent by the importer to Blanc et Blanc. Some people confine the use of the word 'negotiation' to bills (and 'purchase' to cheques). If a bill rather than a cheque is used, the negotiation is made by a bank before the bill has been sent abroad for collection. Negotiation might be ad hoc or, once Blanc et Blanc sells regularly, they may request a revolving negotiation line of credit (also known as a negotiation facility) up to a specified maximum.

In effect, the bank is giving finance to Blanc et Blanc against the security of either the goods or the standing of the drawee.

(ii) *Discount*

Whereas sight bills as well as term bills can be negotiated, only term bills can be discounted, and they must have been accepted beforehand. Blanc et Blanc should be party to the bill, preferably as the drawer or perhaps as an endorser.

(iii) *Advances against collections ('bill advances')*

An alternative to negotiating or discounting is for us to make an advance (normally with recourse) of about 80 to 90% of the face value of the bill. Where large amounts are involved, Blanc et Blanc would be well advised to consider using factoring (described later), or arranging a revolving London acceptance credit, described next.

(iv) *London acceptance credit*

This method has a variety of interchangeable names including accepting house credit, acceptance credit lines and accommodation finance. It must not be confused with a documentary acceptance credit which was discussed above. London acceptance credit facilities are usually for amounts exceeding £250,000. They are granted by members of the Accepting Houses Associations and, increasingly, by clearing banks, and by the UK offices of those foreign banks whose acceptances are eligible for re-discount at

148

the Bank of England. It is often cheaper to borrow in this way because the so-called eligible banks are obliged to keep a given percentage of their eligible liabilities in the form of call money at relatively low rates with discount houses, which are, in turn, able to offer discount rates which are lower than other rates of interest. The procedure is as follows.

(1) Blanc et Blanc draws documentary drafts on the importer in the normal way.

(2) The bills are pledged to the accepting house, which handles them as documentary collections.

(3) Blanc et Blanc draws another draft (known as a 'clean' or 'accommodation' draft) for an agreed percentage (often 85%) of the face value of the documentary bill, with a maturity date a few days after that of the documentary bill.

(4) The accommodation draft, once accepted, is discounted, and the proceeds paid to Blanc et Blanc.

(5) Then, at maturity, if the documentary bill is paid at or within a few days of the due date, all well and good; the accommodation bill is, in turn, paid, and the balance is credited to the Blanc et Blanc. However, if the documentary bill is not paid, the bank must notwithstanding pay the discounted accommodation bill which bears its acceptance, and it must obtain reimbursement from Blanc et Blanc.

Short-term non-traditional export finance

(a) *Factoring and invoice discounting*

The firm could sell its trade debts in the form of documentary bills or invoices to a factoring company ('a factor'). The factor normally obtains/ renews status enquiries (via its overseas associates) and gets them updated periodically.

Payment may be with or without recourse. 70% to 85% (or whatever figure is agreed between the factor and exporter) of the invoices' value is paid to B&B immediately. The balance (less charges) is credited to B&B on the due date (regardless of whether the importer has since become unable or unwilling to pay). The handling charge is usually in the range of 0.25 to 2% depending on the type of debt and the work expected, and interest is calculated on the basis of a margin, say 3%, over the factor's base rate.

Factoring normally includes the financing service discussed above plus the accounting and debt collection functions (and occasionally shipping and forwarding) whereas *invoice discounting* is purely a financing method.

(b) *Export houses*

Most export houses specialise in particular goods and/or territories. Some have their own retail outlets overseas.

An export house does not extend credit to an exporter. It does, however, provide one or other of the following services which effectively reduce the time which Blanc et Blanc would otherwise have to wait for payment:

(i) as an *export merchant* it assumes the position of principal vis a vis the importer: it buys goods outright from Blanc et Blanc (paying cash, usually within seven days), to sell them abroad on its own account; or

(ii) as an *export agent* (the name *export manager* is sometimes used) it pays Blanc et Blanc on evidence of shipment (and, if it sees fit, arranges or grants credit to the overseas buyer).

The export house can promote the supplier's goods overseas, hold stocks at home or overseas, and, in effect, act as the supplier's export sales department, arranging packing, shipping and insurance, if requested. But, even though the supplier receives cash on shipment, he remains in contractual relationship with the importer as far as performance of the contract is concerned. This should be contrasted with the first situation described in (i) where, as export merchant, the export house assumes the position of principal vis-a-vis the importer.

BPP Publishing

52   HEAVY ENGINEERING PLC

> *Tutorial note.* Countertrade arrangements are generally made to suit the potential importer, because the importer is looking for some means to pay for the purchase of the principal goods, rather than the exporter, in this case Heavy Engineering plc (HE), wanting to receive some merchandise which it is going to have to dispose of somehow. As well as the possible disadvantages (part (b)), there are also potential benefits (part (c)). The answers to parts (b) and (c) and for that matter part (d) need to be tailored to HE.

(a) Countertrade means payment (wholly or partly) in kind rather than entirely in money. A countertrade can be said to be a trading transaction where sales to a given country are conditional on some form of agreement to accept imports (usually from the country in question, but occasionally from a third country). Countertrade deals can take various forms.

   (i) *Counter purchase*, the most common form of countertrade involves two parallel but legally separate contracts; one for the delivery, the other for the counterdelivery. The agreement may be either a declaration of intent, or a binding contract, specifying amongst other things the goods and/or services to be supplied, the markets in which they may be sold, and the penalties for non-performance. The value of the undertaking is usually set between 10% and 100% (or occasionally more) of the principal export order.

   (ii) *Linked purchases:* two UK companies make separate contracts, one to sell goods to the foreign country, the other to buy other goods for the same amount from the same foreign country for cash.

   (iii) *Barter* involves the direct exchange of goods and/or services for goods/services, a single contract covering both flows. In many cases, it is agreed that the principal export is not delivered until a stated amount of revenue is realised from selling the bartered goods. Types of barter include:

      (1) *Balanced barter* (rarely encountered): the value put on the goods/services flowing in each direction is the same.

      (2) *Unbalanced barter*: the value of each side of the deal is different, and the difference (in one direction or the other) is paid in cash.

      (3) *Switch trading* sometimes called triangular barter: the purchase from one country is matched by a sale to a third country, which makes payment to the original exporting country. Sometimes, there are imbalances in long-term bilateral trading, and these lead to large credit balances. Suppose Country B has a large credit surplus with Country P. These surpluses might be tapped by third parties, so that (for example) UK exports to B might be financed from the sale of P's goods to the UK or elsewhere. Such transactions are known as switch or swap deals because they typically involve switching the documentation and the destination of the goods while on the high seas. This can be very complex, involving a chain of sellers, brokers and buyers in different markets.

   (iv) *Buyback agreements*: the exporter supplies a process/plant, eg mining equipment, and agrees to buy certain percentages of the goods produced over a period from start-up. Such agreements tend to be for a longer term and for much larger amounts than simple barter or counterpurchase deals.

   (v) *Offset agreements*: the term 'offset' is applied to agreements where the importer insists that some components and/or a certain percentage of the input to the products or processes are procured in the host country. Such a condition is quite common with advanced technology products. It might sound odd that the host country, which is not so advanced in a particular technology, should be supplying part of its own needs. The explanation is that its desire to enhance its base of knowledge and skills is the very reason for insisting on being made part of the supply of specified components. Offset is particularly long established in aircraft and defence systems acquisition and installation; and is becoming more common in other industries where the host country wants to develop its capabilities. In some cases, the host country demands that the

BPP Publishing

foreign investor establish full production facilities locally, and not just a 'screwdriver' assembly plant.

(vi) *Evidence accounts agreements*: firms with a significant volume of continuing business in a country may be required to purchase from that country. For example, a multinational firm with a manufacturing subsidiary in country X may be required to export from that country at least as much as it imports in materials and even machinery. It is impractical to handle matters item by item, the firm should negotiate the right to handle matters by way of so-called evidence accounts, debiting what it brings into country X, and crediting what it exports from country X. The firm is likely to need a period when the account can initially stay in debit before and just after start-up. Beyond that, however, host country X will expect the account to be maintained more or less in balance year by year; or even (if so agreed) in credit.

(b) *Possible disadvantages of countertrading to Heavy Engineering plc (HE)*

(i) Negotiations between the parties are typically long and complex.

(ii) The Eastern European government is likely to have much more experience of such negotiations than HE.

(iii) HE needs to take care that it will not fall foul of any import restrictions on the offtake goods (whether they finish up in the UK or a third country).

(iv) Also to be taken into the calculations are commissions/fees for any escrow agency arrangements (ie the bank acting as trustee holding one party's money on account until the other part of the agreement is fulfilled), as well as any performance and/or repayment bonds.

(v) The costs (eg brokers' and bank fees, and insurance premiums) might exceed HE's estimates, and the 'disagio' (ie discount) may prove to be insufficient.

(vi) If there has to be a long chain of buyers and sellers, there is an increased chance of the whole deal coming to grief.

(vii) The merchandise may prove to be unsaleable.

(viii) Penalty payments may have to be made if the offtake goods are not taken within the specified time.

(c) *Potential benefits of countertrading to HE*

(i) Countertrade may be the only option open to HE, if it wants to penetrate the markets in question.

(ii) Countertrade might give HE a decisive edge over competitors unwilling to enter such agreements.

(iii) Countertrade can establish an on-going relationship between HE and its customers, possibly improving HE's chances of future business.

(iv) With a countertrade arrangement, the arrival of the offtake goods may prove to be more reliable, compared with the receipt of hard currency with a cash or credit deal.

(d) If HE cannot get paid in a freely convertible currency, but nonetheless wishes to do business, then it is usually preferable to agree to receive payment in the form of a widely traded, stably priced commodity (preferably raw materials used by HE) rather than, at the other extreme, shoddy goods which have no relevance to HE, or indeed for which there is no market at all. In between these two extremes will be semi-specialised chemicals, pharmaceuticals, and good quality consumer products. Thus, most arrangements will be counterpurchase deals. Where, however, as in this case, the principal contract involves major industrial equipment (and its installation) some combination of buyback agreements and perhaps barter or offset might be possible.

53 FOREIGN EXCHANGE RATE FORECASTS

(a) (i) Purchasing power parity theory attempts to explain changes in exchange rates exclusively by the rate of inflation in different countries. The theory states that the exchange value of a currency depends on the purchasing power of the currency in its own country, as compared with the purchasing power of another currency in its own country.

For example, if the rate of exchange between sterling and the US dollar is $1.50 = £1, and inflation is running at 4% pa in the USA and at 6% pa in the UK, the US dollar would strengthen in value against sterling by a factor of (1.06/1.04) pa, so that after 1 year, say, the exchange rate would be (1.50 × 1.04/1.06) = $1.47 = £1.

(ii) The monetary theory of exchange rates attempts to explain changes in exchange rates by the movement of money between one country and another. The movement of money arises from:

(1) the balance of payments between a country and other countries;
(2) movements of capital;
(3) to a lesser extent, use of a country's official reserves.

This means that exchange rates are determined by supply and demand.

(b) *Purchasing power parity theory*

Forecasts would first of all have to be made for the rate of inflation in the countries whose currencies are under review.

Having established estimates of inflation rates, estimates of exchange rates could then be made as illustrated in solution (a)(i).

Problems and weaknesses in doing this are as follows.

(i) Purchasing power parity theory might be valid in the longer term, but it cannot account for short-term fluctuations in exchange rates. It could not have predicted, for example, the very high US dollar value in 1984/85, nor its sharp collapse in value in 1987, nor its recovery in 1988 and 1989.

(ii) Even if the method is reliable over the longer term, it would be difficult to predict the long-term rate of inflation in various countries. Econometrics experts attempt to do this, but their forecasts are based on numerous assumptions, covering economic policies in various countries, the growth in demand and output, wages and productivity, and so on.

Monetary theory

In order to make exchange rate forecasts, forecasts would have to be made of the likely movements of money between various countries. This would mean having to forecast:

(i) the balance of payments on current account for various countries;

(ii) the likely movement of capital, which will depend in turn on interest rates in different countries.

Having made these estimates, forecasts of changes in the exchange rate could be made, probably using an econometric model for the country's economy.

The major problem with exchange rate forecasting by this method is uncertainty about the economic conditions which cause the movements of money into and out of a country. For example, interest rate levels can be influenced by government policy towards the exchange rate itself, and a country's balance of payments position will depend on factors such as the state of world trade and domestic inflation.

Long-term exchange rate forecasts, whatever prediction model is used, will therefore be very uncertain, and this uncertainty ought to be recognised when strategic plans are made and strategic decisions are taken.

BPP Publishing

(c) Technical analysis is a term more commonly applied to share price analysis. This is a technique which seeks to predict future share price movements from price movements in the past, and from recognising typical patterns or cycles of price behaviour.

In the same way, future exchange rate movements could be predicted, over the long term, medium term or short term, from an analysis of exchange rate movements in the past.

The potential strength of technical analysis, for share price forecasts or exchange rate forecasts, would be that it might be as good a forecasting method as anything else. If it works, it is worth using. The weakness of technical analysis is that it has no theoretical justification or rationale. In theory, it is just as likely to be incorrect as correct.

54 TUTORIAL QUESTION: FINANCING STRATEGIES

(a) One of the key determinants of the return required by an investor is the level of risk attached to the investment. The return required by investors from a company represents the cost of finance to the company. The cost of debt finance to a company is usually cheaper than equity because the risk borne by the providers of debt is less than the risk borne by the equity shareholders. This is apparent in two respects.

   (i)   In the event of the company going into liquidation the providers of debt will rank above the equity shareholders for repayment of capital.

   (ii) No dividend can be paid to the shareholders until the providers of debt finance have received their interest payments.

(b) In order to assess to feasibility of Mr Axelot's proposal it is necessary to calculate the effect of 100% debt finance on some of the key financial performance indicators. In particular, attention should be directed to earnings per share, interest cover and gearing since these represent the effect on the financial risk of the company, and therefore the likely effect on the ordinary shareholders and the market valuation of the shares.

The effect on these indicators on financing expansion using a 13% debenture is calculated below. It can be seen that the growth in earnings is sufficient to support 100% debt financing and still produce an improvement in interest cover and earnings per share, as well as a reduction in the level of gearing. Thus, contrary to expectations, the policy does appear to be feasible.

Year	0	1	2	3	4	5
	£'000	£'000	£'000	£'000	£'000	£'000
EBIT (+20% pa)	13,750	16,500	19,800	23,760	28,512	34,214
Interest	(3,000)	(3,650)	(4,300)	(4,950)	(5,600)	(6,250)
	10,750	12,850	15,500	18,810	22,912	27,964
Tax (@ 35%)	(3,762)	(4,497)	(5,425)	(6,583)	(8,019)	(9,788)
	6,988	8,353	10,075	12,227	14,893	18,177
Dividend (@ 40%)	(2,795)	(3,341)	(4,030)	(4,891)	(5,957)	(7,271)
Retained profit	4,193	5,012	6,045	7,336	8,936	10,906
EPS (p) (Note 1)	43.7	52.2	63.0	76.4	93.1	113.6
Interest cover (Note 2)	4.6	4.5	4.6	4.8	5.1	5.5
Total debt	24,000	29,000	34,000	39,000	44,000	49,000
Equity	24,600	29,612	35,657	42,993	51,929	62,835
Gearing (Note 3)	97.6%	97.9%	95.4%	90.7%	84.7%	78.0%

Notes

1   Earnings per share is calculated as earnings available to equity ie profit after tax but before dividend, divided by the number of shares in issue (4,000 / 0.25 = 16,000).

2   Interest cover is calculated as earnings before interest and tax divided by interest.

3   Gearing is calculated as total debt over equity. Included in the total debt figure are short term loans, overdrafts, debentures and loan stock and unsecured bank loans.

When assessing these figures however, it should be borne in mind that they are likely to be sensitive both to earnings growth being lower than predicted, and to the actual interest rate being higher than predicted. Either of these circumstances could produce an outcome significantly worse than the scenario evaluated, and a consequent increase in the level of risk borne by the ordinary shareholders.

(c)   The effect on performance of financing using the 13% debenture has been calculated in (b) above. For the debenture to be attractive to investors there needs to be an expectation that the share price will have increased to at least 450p per share in year 5 so that it will be worth exercising the warrants and achieving some capital gain. Assuming that the rate of return required by investors does not change over the period, it is possible to calculate the theoretical share price in year 5 using the dividend valuation model, as follows:

$$MV = d / i$$

where: MV = market price of shares
         d = dividend per share
         i = rate of return required by investors

Currently: 250   = 17.47 / i
              i   = 7%

At the end of year 5:

    MV = 45.44 / 7%
    MV = 650p

On this basis, the warrants priced at 450p should be very attractive to investors with a potential capital gain of 200p per share at the exercise date. In practice, the gain may be less than this since exercise of the warrants may cause some dilution of earnings, and hence dividends, per share.

The effect of financing using the Swiss Franc bond will depend on the effective interest rate incurred. This in turn will depend on the relative rates of interest and inflation in the UK and Switzerland, and the movements in the exchange rate over the period. The likely movement in the exchange rate can be calculated using the purchasing power parity theory which relates movements in exchange rates to inflation. Since inflation in the UK is higher than in Switzerland, the pound is likely to fall in value against the Swiss franc. By the end of the first year, the pound is likely to have fallen as follows:

$$\% \text{ fall} = \frac{\text{UK inflation rate} - \text{Swiss inflation rate}}{1 + \text{UK inflation rate}}$$

$$\% \text{ fall} = \frac{0.08 - 0.02}{1.08}$$

$$\% \text{ fall} = 5.56\%$$

The exchange rate should therefore be SF2.3091 - 2.3138/£.

The actual amount of interest payable at the end of year 1 will be:

$$\frac{12.25m \times 8\%}{2.3091} = £424,408$$

This represents an effective rate of interest of 8.5%. The amount to be repaid at the end of the period will also increase if the pound continues to fall by 5.56% per year. This means that although the annual interest cost of the Swiss Franc bond is less, it could actually prove to be a more expensive financing option than the 13% debenture. The precise effect will depend on the relative movements in exchange rates over the ten year period. A further factor which should be considered is the currency structure of IXT's receipts and payments. If IXT earns revenues denominated in Swiss Francs, then it may be able to match these receipts with the payments of interest and capital due under the bond, and in this situation

154

the bond is likely to be more attractive than the debenture since losses on exchange can be avoided.

The effect of using a placing can be calculated in a similar manner to the effect of using a debenture. It can be seen that due to dilution, the effect on earnings per share is not quite as good as that achieved through using the debenture. However, there is a significant improvement in both interest cover and the level of gearing, the latter being reduced from 97.6% to 33.5% by year 5. Thus the placing would provide a less risky offer than using debt finance. It is also likely however that the use of a placing, possibly with institutional investors, would significantly alter the ownership structure of IXT, and this may not be popular with existing shareholders, including Mr Axelot who currently has the controlling interest.

To summarise, provided that the financial sensitivities are acceptable, the use of debt finance is likely to prove more attractive to the existing shareholders. This also has the benefit of providing the best improvement in earnings per share.

(d) Mezzanine finance is a form of borrowing, so called because it lies part way between debt and equity financing. Typically the loans are short to medium term junior debt (ie loans that are unsecured and rank low in priority for repayment in the event of a liquidation). They carry a correspondingly high rate of interest (typically 4-5% over LIBOR), and they often have warrants attached for share purchase. Such loans have frequently been used to finance takeover bids with a cash purchase option and management buyouts.

This form of finance could prove useful to IXT if it wishes to raise more money than is possible using conventional debt or equity financing.

55 BOLAR

> *Tutorial note.* The calculations required are quite lengthy, but can be broken down. Each security can be tackled separately, reducing the number of details to keep track of. If you tackled the securities in the order in which they were set out in the question, you should have found that the easier ones came first. The examiner commented that this question should not have been attempted by candidates with only superficial skills in this area.

(a) For each security, we will first try a discount rate of 10%. If that produces a positive net present value, 15% will be tried. If it produces a negative net present value, 5% will be tried. The yield will then be estimated by interpolation or extrapolation.

(i) *The unsecured bonds*

		10%		15%	
Year	Cash flow £	Factor	PV £	Factor	PV £
0	(95)	1.000	(95.0)	1.000	(95.0)
1 - 3	14	2.487	34.8	2.283	32.0
3.5	107	0.716	76.6	0.613	65.6
			16.4		(2.6)

$$\text{Approximate redemption yield} = 10 + \frac{16.4}{16.4 + 2.6} \times (15 - 10) = 14.3\%.$$

(ii) *The secured debentures*

6 month period	Cash flow £	10% Factor	PV £	15% Factor	PV £
0	(91.5)	1.000	(91.5)	1.000	(91.5)
1 - 9	5	7.146	35.7	6.449	32.2
10	105	0.621	65.2	0.497	52.2
			9.4		(7.1)

Approximate redemption yield = $10 + \dfrac{9.4}{9.4 + 7.1} \times (15 - 10) = 12.9\%$.

As the nominal interest rate is well below the rate on the unsecured bonds, it has been assumed that the company will retain this source of finance for as long as possible, and redeem at the latest possible date.

Annuity factors are calculated using the annuity formula $\dfrac{1}{r}\left[1 - \dfrac{1}{(1 + r)^n}\right]$

The interest rates (r) per six months are as follows.

For 10% a year, $(1 + 0.1)^{1/2} - 1 = 0.0488$.

For 15% a year, $(1 + 0.15)^{1/2} - 1 = 0.0724$.

(iii) *The unsecured convertible debentures*

(1) *5% annual growth in the share price*

With 5% annual growth, the share price would be $190 \times (1.05)^2 = 209.5$ pence on the first conversion date and $190 \times (1.05)^4 = 230.9$ pence on the second conversion date.

The conversion price on 1 January 19X3 is £88.50 ÷ 40 = 221 pence, and on 1 January 19X5 it is £92 ÷ 30 = 307. Conversion is therefore unlikely if the market price increases by 5% per year.

Retention to maturity

Year	Cash flow £	10% Factor	PV £	5% Factor	PV £
0	(85)	1.000	(85.0)	1.000	(85.0)
1 - 9	8	5.759	46.1	4.772	38.2
10	108	0.386	41.7	0.247	26.7
			(2.8)		(20.1)

Approximate yield = $10 + \dfrac{2.8}{2.8 + 20.1} \times (15 - 10) = 10.6\%$.

(2) *10% annual growth in the share price*

The share price at the first conversion date will be $190 \times (1.10)^2 = 229.9$ pence, and at the second conversion date it will be $190 \times (1.10)^4 = 278.2$ pence.

Conversion into 40 shares could take place on 1 January 19X3 at 230 pence per share. Ignoring transaction costs, the total value on disposal is £92, which is greater than the expected market value of £88.50. Therefore, conversion is likely on 1 January 19X3.

Year	Cash flow £	10% Factor £	PV £	15% Factor £	PV £
0	(85)	1.000	(85.0)	1.000	(85.0)
1 - 2	8	1.736	13.9	1.626	13.0
2	92	0.826	76.0	0.756	69.6
			4.9		(2.4)

The approximate yield from conversion at the first date is

$10 + \dfrac{4.9}{4.9 + 2.4} \times (15 - 10) = 134.4\%$

(iv) *The unsecured Eurobonds*

Cash flows need to be converted into sterling. The effect of the 3% per year depreciation of sterling can be shown as follows.

Year	Exchange rate ($/£)	Interest £	PV 10%	PV 15%
1	1.552	38.66	35.1	33.6
2	1.505	39.87	32.9	30.1
3	1.460	41.10	30.9	27.0
4	1.416	42.37	28.9	24.3
5	1.374	43.67	27.1	21.7
Redemption value (£)		727.80	452.0	361.7
			606.9	498.4
Market value in sterling			531.2	531.2
NPV			75.7	(32.8)

Ignoring transaction costs: approximate redemption yield =

$$10 + \frac{75.7}{75.7 + 32.8} \times (15 - 10) = 13.5\%$$

(b) The redemption yields found are as follows.

Security	Yield %
Unsecured bonds	14.3
Secured debentures	12.9
Unsecured convertible debentures	10.6 or 13.4
Unsecured Eurobonds	13.5

It is not surprising that the unsecured bonds should have a higher yield than the secured debentures. This is to compensate for the higher risk of lending without security.

The convertible debentures' yield is affected both by the interest and by the possibility of conversion. The yield on such securities depends very much on the company's future share price. The yields computed are based on arbitrarily selected growth rates, which may not be realised.

The yield on the unsecured Eurobonds is subject to exchange rate risk. If sterling were to rise or maintain its value against the dollar, the actual yield would be higher.

(c) *Advantages of using Eurobonds*

(i) Large amounts can be raised quickly if the company is regarded as sound.

(ii) Interest rates may be lower than would be charged in the UK, reflecting other countries' lower inflation rates.

(iii) The securities are actively traded, facilitating early redemption if appropriate.

Disadvantages of using Eurobonds

(i) The issuer is exposed to substantial foreign exchange risk. If his domestic currency falls in value against the currency of the bonds, interest payments and the eventual capital repayment can become much more costly than anticipated.

(ii) If a company's standing declines, further Eurobond issues (perhaps to replace maturing issues) may not be possible.

(iii) Eurobond issues are not suitable for small amounts of capital. A company may find it has to raise more capital than it needs immediately, and may then be unable to find suitable investment opportunities for the surplus.

BPP Publishing

56   INTERNATIONAL GROUP

> *Tutorial note:* It is helpful to relate the policies that are available in part (b) to the categories of exposure identified in part (a).

(a) Foreign exchange exposure can be defined as the vulnerability of the group to risk arising from its transactions denominated in more than one currency. For an international company, exposure may arise in three ways.

   (i)   *Transaction exposure*. This arises as a result of the time taken to complete normal trading transactions. For example, there is normally a time delay between invoicing and receipt of payment. During this time the exchange rate may move against the supplier causing a loss to be made in the settlement of the account and its conversion into a different currency.

   (ii)   *Translation exposure*. This arises when the group holds assets and liabilities which are denominated in different currencies. The value of these items will fluctuate with the exchange rate and this may influence lenders and investors in their dealings with the group.

   (iii) *Economic exposure*. This relates to the longer term competitiveness of the group and arises from the economic performance of the countries in which the group operates and with which it trades. For example, the group might decide to serve the european market from a facility in France. If the franc strengthens, then the competitiveness of the operation will be eroded.

(b) The precise policy to be adopted will depend on the group's attitude to risk. Different approaches and techniques are available to handle the different types of exposure described above.

   (i)   *Transaction exposure*

      (1) Forward exchange contracts can be used to arrange to buy or sell currency at a predetermined future date and rate. Such contracts can be matched to known future operational transactions to reduce the uncertainties associated with exposure. However, the group may miss the opportunity to make a profit on the exchange rate.

      (2) Matching receipts and payments in a given currency, generally using a bank account denominated in that currency, is another means of minimising exposure to risk.

      (3) Using the currency markets to borrow or lend amounts in local currency immediately which will subsequently be offset against the payment or receipt which has to be made in the future.

      (4) Currency options can be useful in situations where the actual date and amount of the transaction are uncertain, for example where the company issues a price list in a local currency. The company buys an option to buy or sell currency at an agreed rate and date in the future. If exchange rate movements are unfavourable, the option can be abandoned. Options are expensive, but they do allow the company to take advantage of any favourable movements in rates as well as avoiding any losses.

      (5) Currency swaps may be made directly with another company or through a bank.

      (6) The futures market can be used to hedge against possible gains or losses on exchange.

   (ii)   *Translation exposure* can best be minimised by ensuring that as far as possible assets and liabilities denominated in given currencies are held in balanced amounts. However if the group is willing to tolerate a higher level of risk then it may try to arrange its financial structure to take advantage of the relative strengthening or weakening of the different economies.

BPP Publishing

(iii)   *Economic exposure* is harder to avoid since much longer term decisions are involved, such as where to locate production facilities. However it can be reduced by diversifying the trading base across different countries. Capital structure decisions will also be important.

57   FOREIGN EXCHANGE RISK STRATEGIES

> *Tutorial note.* This question is testing your understanding of how exchange rates can affect companies both directly through gains and losses on exchange, and indirectly through their effect on the competitive position of the company. It provides an opportunity to show your knowledge of the current situation of the ERM.

(a)   The manager in company A is making two important assumptions:

(i)   Foreign exchange markets are efficient.

(ii)   Gains and losses in efficient markets will balance out.

It will be helpful to look at these two assumptions in more detail.

(i)   For a foreign exchange market to operate efficiently it is necessary for all the currencies involved to be floating freely against one another. Although this is true for some of the currencies in which the company trades, very few of the currencies will be allowed to respond directly to economic forces without some form of government intervention or management (ie where the government buys or sells currency to manipulate the rate).

(ii)   Even if the market is efficient, gains and losses on exchange will be experienced in the short term as sterling weakens and strengthens against other currencies. The company is spreading its risk in that it is trading with a global spread of companies. However it is possible that sterling could strengthen against a number of currencies simultaneously and the firm's losses on exchange could then exceed its gains. The manager must be confident that the firm has sufficient resources to cover these losses until such a time as gains begin to balance them out.

The views of the manager in this company are not consistent with a risk averse strategy. Even given efficient currency markets, it would be safer to hedge to minimise the risk of exchange losses building up to a point where the company's liquidity could be threatened.

(b)   Although company B does not engage in foreign trade, exchange rate movements are not irrelevant. Some of the ways in which they can influence the company include the following.

(i)   If sterling strengthens against other currencies then foreign competitors' products may become relatively cheaper. The company will therefore face stiffer competition in its home markets.

(ii)   If sterling weakens, then imports will become more expensive. If some of the company's suppliers use components manufactured abroad then material prices may rise.

(iii)   If the government manipulates interest rates as a means of controlling the exchange rate this could affect the cost of capital to the company.

(c)   The manager of company C is presumably assuming that the home country is a member of the ERM. He is also assuming that all the European companies with which he trades are similarly members. If this is the case, then the member countries' currencies will be trading within a given percentage of their central parity value. The existence of the ERM does not eliminate exchange rate losses. It limits them to a potentially smaller percentage than with freely floating currencies, although since the ERM margins were raised to 15% in August 1993, the mechanism has become less significant. Larger losses can occur in the event of a realignment of currencies within the system.

While the UK continues to be outside the ERM, then the existence of the system does nothing to help prevent currency losses. The relationship of sterling with ERM currencies is no different from its relationship with other currencies and potential gains and losses on exchange are unrestricted.

58 FOREIGN CURRENCY OPTIONS

> *Tutorial note.* This question requires an understanding of the purpose and operation of foreign exchange options. In the calculations, make it clear which figures you have selected to use and why.

(a) A foreign currency option gives to its buyer the right but not the obligation to buy or to sell a specified amount of a currency at a specified rate of exchange at any time up to a specified date.

The advantages are as follows.

(i) They can be used as a hedge against exchange risk when a company is uncertain as to whether a particular risk will actually occur eg when tendering for a contract or when issuing a foreign currency price list.

(ii) Where a company is trading regularly in a foreign currency and when markets are volatile, options provide a hedge against general exchange rate exposure.

(iii) They allow companies to use the market to take advantage of favourable exchange rate movements.

The disadvantages are as follows.

(i) Costs may be significant: a premium is payable whether or not the option is exercised.

(ii) Currencies may not move in the manner envisaged when the option was taken out.

(iii) Exchange-traded options are only available in a limited number of currencies with specific expiry dates, although it may be possible to arrange more flexible 'over-the-counter' options.

(b) (i) The relevant rate for selling sterling for dollars in this case is $1.8950. If this is the rate obtaining in three months time, when the company will receive $3,079,375 if it uses the spot market. However, option prices are available for September (ie three months time) at $1.90, $1.95 and $2.00. The company would need to buy 130 put option contracts on sterling. The amount receivable at each of these option prices can be calculated as follows.

Exercise price	Receipts in $ (Ex price × 1.625m)	Option cost (Put × 1.625m)	Net receivable $
1.90	3,087,500	(6,825)	3,080,675
1.95	3,168,750	(67,438)	3,101,312
2.00	3,250,000	(152,750)	3,097,250

In each case, the amount received will be greater than if the company used the spot market. The option price of $1.95 will give the company the highest expected receipts.

(ii) If the spot rate for buying dollars in three months time is $2.0240, the company will receive $3,289,000. This is greater than the amount that could be received by taking out an option contract (see calculations above). The company should therefore rely on the spot market. However, in so doing it exposes itself to the risk that the dollar will not strengthen in the way in which the financial manager anticipates, and that it will not therefore receive the amount anticipated.

The decision will depend on the extent to which the company is prepared to expose itself to foreign exchange risk. If this risk is not acceptable, then the company should hedge using a contract at $1.95.

59   TUTORIAL QUESTION: SALES TO THE USA

(a)   (i)   The following are advantages of forward exchange contracts for the exporter.

(1)   He can guarantee his profit margin on a sale by fixing in advance his sterling income.

(2)   He knows precisely what his cash flow will be in the future. This could be important for budgeting.

(ii)   Assuming the merchant entered into forward contracts to sell dollars to his bank at 1.690 in one month and 1.684 in three months he would receive the following amounts in sterling.

	£
$60,000 at 1.692	35,461
$45,000 at 1.690	26,627
$45,000 at 1.684	26,722
	88,810

(iii)   Without hedging the merchant would have received the following amounts in sterling.

	£
$60,000 at 1.692	35,461
$45,000 at 1.696	26,533
$45,000 at 1.704	26,408
	88,402

Clearly the decision to hedge has proved to be beneficial.

(b)   (i)   Transactions in financial futures on the London International Financial Futures and Options Exchange (LIFFE) are very similar to forward exchange contracts, the main difference being that on the LIFFE the contracts are not individually tailored. Instead, dealings are in standard contracts for specific future dates.

There are also some administrative differences between the two forms of contract. On the LIFFE participants must lodge a deposit to cover possible losses. The open competition leads to low transaction costs.

(ii)   Other contracts available include certain currencies (sterling, deutschmark, Swiss franc and yen) against the US dollar, and interest rate contracts. They are advantageous for financial managers because transaction costs are low, competition ensures that the best price is obtained and contracts can be concluded very quickly.

These advantages are in addition to the usual advantages of all forward contracts given in (a)(i) above.

60   FREIMARKS

> *Tutorial note.* This question covers not only methods of reducing foreign exchange exposure, but also the factors which should be considered before selecting a method. As noted by the examiner in his report, some pre-planning of the answer to part (a) is desirable. You are not told enough about the group to recommend a specific method, so you must write in more general terms, making clear what further information would be needed in order to select the best method.

(a)   Likely future exchange rates should be considered. If it could be predicted that changes in the rate were very likely to be favourable, there would be little point in protecting the group against risk. However, as the rate has been very volatile, it is very unlikely that such a prediction can be made. Some protection against future adverse fluctuations is almost certainly desirable.

BPP Publishing

Likely future cash flows, beyond the next six months, should be considered. It may be that there will be a clear trend in net receipts or payments, which can be taken account of in devising a strategy.

The position of any other companies in the group may give opportunities for protection. If other companies have business denominated in the Freimark or in any other currencies which move in line with the Freimark, receipts by one company might be netted off against payments by another.

The group's own resources may limit the options available. Temporary funding is needed for several methods of protection, and specialised skills are needed for some methods. Such skills can of course be obtained by relying on a bank's services, but at a price.

Finally, the group's approach to risk should be considered. It may be that potential losses are not large enough to be of real concern, or that the directors prefer to take risks to obtain the chance of high rewards. On the other hand, the directors may prefer to take every opportunity to minimise risk.

(b) *Three techniques of exposure management*

(i)   The company could open a Freimark bank account, possibly making an initial deposit so as to avoid having an overdraft in months 2 and 3. All transactions would be conducted through this account. Any planned withdrawals for conversion into sterling could be protected by forward exchange contracts.

(ii) Forward exchange contracts could be entered into for each of the next six months. For example, the company could contract with a bank now for the conversion of Fm 2,400,000 into sterling at the end of month 1, at a pre-arranged rate. As the cash flow forecasts may prove to be inaccurate, forward option contracts may be appropriate. These are binding contracts, but with some flexibility as to the completion date.

(iii) The company could use leading and lagging. This involves timing receipts and payments so as to take advantage of exchange rate movements. For example, if a payment in Freimarks is required, the currency should be bought and the payment made when sterling is strong against the Freimark.

(c) *Economic exposure and transaction exposure*

Economic exposure is the risk that a business's value and competitiveness will suffer through the impact of exchange rate movements on its future cash flows. Transaction exposure arises on individual transactions, whereas economic exposure may affect the prosperity of a business for several years into the future. A company may be affected by exchange rate movements in several ways. The domestic currency value of its receipts will clearly be affected directly. The company's competitive position in foreign markets will suffer if the domestic currency strengthens, though on the other hand imports will be cheaper, as will future capital investment overseas.

Economic exposure should be assessed using any available information, but long-term forecasts are unreliable. Simulation techniques may be needed to assess the level of risk.

61   EXCHANGE RATES

Tutorial note. The following comments of the examiner for this question relate to part (b).

'With rare exceptions, candidates proved unable to distinguish between forward and spot rates or between buying and selling rates, or to realise which country's loan interest rate was appropriate in each instance. Some substituted their own scenarios. Others, having collected a normal commercial debt, decided that they had to reinvest instead of using the proceeds in the business. It would appear that candidates do not understand foreign exchange arithmetic!'

(a) (i)   The European Monetary System (EMS) is a system embracing the member states of the European Community. There is an extra currency, the European Currency Unit (ECU), the value of which is based on a weighted average of the values of the currencies of member states. The ECU is used for certain Community purposes, and is accepted for commercial transactions in some states. There is also an exchange rate mechanism (ERM), which the UK joined in October 1990, later suspending membership in September 1992. Under this mechanism, currencies can only fluctuate in value between specified limits. Central banks cooperate by buying and selling currencies to keep them within these limits, but if a currency cannot be kept within its limits the members of the ERM may agree to allow a movement to a new pair of limits. The standard ERM bands were ±2¼%, until raised to 15% from August 1993.

Under a managed float, there are no pre-set limits, but governments intervene to prevent sharp fluctuations in a currency's value.

A policy of fixed exchange rates commits a government to ensure that its currency does not change in value at all. This may be accomplished by market operations, or by legislation forbidding transactions other than at the official rate.

(ii) Businesses want both certainty and an exchange rate which will make them competitive. Fixed exchange rates offer the greatest certainty, followed by a system such as the ERM, and then a managed float. However, rigidity of exchange rates could rapidly damage the competitiveness of exporting businesses in a country such as the UK, which has historically had comparatively high inflation and interest rates. While importers might benefit in the short term from fixed exchange rates if UK inflation remained comparatively high, they could in the longer term find that foreign currency was simply not available.

Overall, a managed float might seem to be best. However, it could be that joining the ERM imposes the discipline needed to bring down inflation and interest rates to those of the UK's major European competitors, thus bringing greater stability both in exchange rates and in other fields.

(b) (i) Borrowing $300,000 now for one year at 6.65% and converting now to sterling will yield:

	£
$300,000 \div 1.8402$ (spot)	163,026
Assuming interest is paid at the end of one year this will be	
$300,000 \times 0.0665 \div 1.7915$	<u>11,136</u>
Net proceeds by this method	<u>151,890</u>

(ii) Taking out a 12 month forward exchange contract to sell $300,000 when received from USA and meanwhile borrowing an equivalent amount in sterling:

	£
Contract and borrowing = $300,000 \div 1.7915$	167,457
Assuming interest paid at end of one year this will be	
$167,457 \times 0.0925$	<u>15,490</u>
Net proceeds by this method	<u>151,967</u>

There is very little difference between the amounts of sterling obtained by the two methods. This is to be expected, because if the results were markedly different there would be scope for arbitrage, which would bring the results back into line. The difference between spot and forward exchange rates reflects the difference in interest rates between the two countries involved.

BPP Publishing

62 OXLAKE

(a) *Receipts from export sales*

   (i) *Sales to Singapore*

      The value of the sales at the spot rate is

$$250,000 \times \text{Singapore } \$2.862 \times \frac{1}{3.1800} \text{ (W1)}$$
$$= £225,000$$

      If Oxlake enters into a contract to sell $250,000 \times 2.862 = $ Singapore $715,000, delivery between two and three months,

      Anticipated sterling proceeds   = Singapore $715,500 \div 3.1592$
                                     = £226,481

      Tutorial note. Oxlake can take out a forward option contract to sell Singapore dollars forward, for delivery between two and three months. This will hopefully overcome the uncertainty surrounding the timing of the receipt from Singapore. The exchange rate used is the least favourable quoted rate for delivery during the period (in this case the three month rate).

      Alternatively, Oxlake can cover its foreign exchange risk via the money markets, as follows.

      (1) Borrow Singapore $703,194 for three months (W2).

      (2) As required, convert to sterling at spot rate of 3.18 (W1).
           The proceeds will be $703,194 \div 3.18 = £221,130$.

      (3) Invest sterling in the Eurosterling market for three months at 6½% pa.
           The Eurosterling deposit will grow to £224,723.

  (ii) *Sales to Indonesia*

      The value of the sales at the spot rate is $100,000 \times \dfrac{2246}{2481} = £90,528$.

      The first alternative is to compute the eventual proceeds using the £/US $ forward market, since payment has been offered in US dollars and no forward market exists in Rupiahs/£.

      Using the US $/£ forward market, the contracted receipts from selling US $ 125,000 for delivery in three months are $\dfrac{125,000}{1.5105} = £82,754$

      The second alternative is to use the money markets, as follows.

      (1) Borrow US $ 121,359 for three months (W4)

      (2) Convert US $ 121,359 into sterling at the spot rate of US $ 1.4875/£, giving
           $\dfrac{121,359}{1.4875} = £81,586$

      (3) Invest the sterling proceeds of £81,586 on the Eurosterling deposit market for three months at 6½% pa, yielding $£81,586 \times 1.01625 = £82,912$.

      Conclusion. The protection should be effected through the foreign exchange market for the sale to Singapore and through the money market for the sale to Indonesia.

(b)
		Rupiahs
Sales value = $100,000 \times 2,246 =$		224,600,000
Less 5% discount		(11,230,000)
Discounted sales value		213,370,000

     Proceeds of sales $= \dfrac{213,370,000}{1,667.9 \text{(W5)}} = \$127,927$

The best US $ deposit rate of interest is 8% pa in a US domestic bank.

The yield after three months is $127,927 × 1.02 = $130,486.

Converted into sterling, using the three month forward market, this is $\frac{\$130,486}{1.5105} = £86,386.$

Alternatively, the US dollar proceeds could be converted immediately into sterling and then invested for three months in Eurosterling. The calculation is as follows.

(i)   Conversion of US $127,927 (see above) into sterling yields

$$\frac{127,927}{1.4875} = £86,001$$

(ii)

	£
Yield of Eurosterling 3 month deposit = £86,001 × 6.5%/4 =	1,398
Add principal	86,001
	87,399

Conclusion. The best yield without the offer of immediate payment was £82,912. Both the forward foreign exchange market and the money market yield better returns, with the money market's £87,399 as the better of the alternatives.

Workings

W1   *Cross rates, Singapore $/£*

	Singapore $/US$	US $/£	Singapore $/£
Spot	2.1378	1.4875	3.1800
1 month forward	2.1132	1.4963	3.1620
2 months forward	2.0964	1.5047	3.1545
3 months forward	2.0915	1.5105	3.1592

W2   *Required Singapore $ borrowings*

The interest rate in Singapore $ is 7% pa or 1.75% for three months.

Thus the maximum borrowing which can be repaid from export sale proceeds is

Singapore $ $\frac{715,000}{1.0175} = 703,194$

W3   *Eurosterling deposit*

The interest rate for three months is 1.625%.

Thus the yield on the deposit is £221,130 × 1.01625 = £224,723.

W4   *Required US $ borrowings*

US $ interest rates (Eurodollars) are 12% pa or 3% for three months.

Thus, the maximum borrowing which can be repaid from the sale proceeds is

$\frac{\$125,000}{1.03} = \$121,359$

W5   *Cross rate, Rupiah/£*

	US $/£	Rupiah/US $	Rupiah/£
Spot	1.4875	1667.90	2,481

(c)   When a company invoices sales in a currency other than its own, the amount of 'home' currency it will eventually receive is uncertain. There may be an advantage or a disadvantage, depending on changes in the exchange rate over the period between invoicing and receiving payment. With this in mind, invoicing in a foreign currency has the following advantages.

(i) The foreign customer will find the deal more attractive than a similar one in the exporter's currency, since the customer will bear no foreign exchange risk. Making a sale will therefore be that much easier.

(ii) The exporter can take advantage of favourable foreign exchange movements by selling the exchange receipts forward (for more of the home currency than would be obtained by conversion at the spot rate).

(iii) In some countries, the importer may find it difficult or even impossible to obtain the foreign exchange necessary to pay in the exporter's currency. The willingness of the exporter to sell in the importer's currency may therefore prevent the sale falling through.

The disadvantages of making export sales in foreign currency are the reverse of the advantages.

(i) The exporter (rather than the foreign customer) bears the foreign exchange risk.
(ii) If the exchange movement is unfavourable, the exporter's profit will be reduced.

63 BID

Tutorial note. The first part of this question simply required you to run through possible sources of finance, commenting on each. There was no need to produce an integrated essay, so you should have started to write as soon as you had thought of a source and something to say about it. However, as the examiner pointed out, the sources suggested should not be unrealistic. For example, Eurobonds, rights issues and other long-term sources would not normally be used for export finance.

The calculations in the second part of the question might have seemed complex, but if you took each transaction in turn the individual computations would have been quite short. To guard against getting rates the wrong way round, you should always ask yourself 'Is this answer sensible?'

(a) An exporter may often have to wait several months for payment. The following methods of finance may be appropriate.

(i) The company could obtain loans or overdraft facilities from its own bank. If the risk of non-payment is high, the bank may require insurance to be obtained from the Export Credit Guarantee Department.

(ii) The company could take out loans in the currency in which it will eventually be paid, converting the amounts borrowed into sterling immediately. This method of finance offers some protection against exchange rate fluctuations.

(iii) The company could factor its debts, obtaining payment of most of the amount owed immediately. Factoring of overseas debts tends to be more expensive than factoring of domestic debts, because of the greater difficulty of collection and because of the exchange risk involved.

(iv) The importer could issue bills of exchange to the exporter. These will be paid by the importer at their full face value in (for example) 90 days time. Meanwhile, the exporter can discount the bills. That is, he can sell them immediately for less than their face value. The discount represents the cost of obtaining finance. The importer must be regarded as financially sound for discounting to be possible.

(v) Acceptance credits could be used. An arrangement is made between the exporter and a bank, under which the bank will 'accept' (guarantee payment of) bills of exchange. These bills can then be sold at a lower rate of discount than would otherwise be the case.

(vi) An export merchant could be used. The goods would be sold to the merchant, who would pay promptly and would export the goods and sell them on his own account.

(b) Each transaction must be considered separately, in each case hedging the net receipt or payment through either the money market or forward exchange contracts.

Australia, 31 March

The sterling payment need not be hedged. The receipt could be hedged by borrowing in A$ and converting the loan into sterling (to be put on deposit) immediately. The loan would be such as to have grown (with interest) to A$120,000 by 31 March. The sterling receipt with interest to 31 March would be

$$\frac{120,000}{1 + 0.16/4} \times \frac{1 + 0.105/4}{2.1425} = £55,269$$

Alternatively, a forward contract could be taken out, yielding sterling at 31 March of 120,000/(2.1425 + 0.025) = £55,363.

The forward contract method is clearly preferable.

Italy, 31 March

The money market method is not available. A forward contract would yield 180 million/ (2,210 + 6) = £81,227.

North Africa, 31 March

The money market method would yield, at 31 March,

$$\frac{565,000}{1 + 0.09/4} \times \frac{1 + 0.105/4}{10.39} = £54,579$$

A forward contract would yield 565,000/(10.39 − 0.03) = £54,537.

The money market method is preferable.

Australia, 30 June

The money market method for net payments involves borrowing immediately in sterling, converting the sterling into the foreign currency and placing the foreign currency on deposit, so that the deposit plus the interest equals the net amount payable by the due date. In this case, however, there is no need to borrow sterling. The sterling proceeds of using the money market method to hedge the receipt from North Africa on 31 March are available.

The sterling required on 31 December is

$$\frac{80,000}{1 + 0.13/2} + \frac{1}{2.14} = £25,102$$

The cost of this up to 30 June, taking account of deposit interest lost, is £35,102 × (1 + 0.105/2) = £36,945.

The cost as at 30 June using a forward contract would be 80,000/(2.14 + 0.035) = £36,782.

The forward market method is preferable.

Italy, 30 June

We can suppose that the receipt due between 31 March and 30 June will be delayed by the payer for as long as possible, so that a net payment of lire 200 million will be needed on 30 June.

Using the money market method, the company can borrow £83,870 at 15% for six months, repaying £90,160 in 6 months. Converting £83,870 to lire at 2,208/£ spot gives 185,185 million lire.

Hedging by a forward contract would cost 200 million/(2,208 + 5) = £90,375.

The cheaper method is to use the money market.

E Europe/West Africa

The coffee will yield 70 × £860 = £60,200 on 30 June.

BPP Publishing

Calculation of the sterling position

	Receipts	*Payments*	*Net*
3 months	£	£	£
A$	55,363	40,000	15,363
Lire	81,227	-	81,227
Francs	54,579	-	54,579
			151,169

£151,169 invested for 3 months at 10.5% per year yields £155,137 at the end of six months.

6 months			
A$	-	36,782	(36,782)
Lire	-	90,160	(90,160)
Coffee	60,200	-	60,200
			(66,742)

The expected cash surplus at the end of June is £155,137 − £66,742 = £88,395.

64 TUTORIAL QUESTION: INTEREST RATE RISKS

(a) (i) A forward rate agreement is an agreement between a company and a bank about the interest rate on future borrowings (or deposits). A company can make a FRA with a bank that fixes the rate of interest to be paid at a certain time in the future. If the actual interest rate at the time is higher than that agreed, the bank pays the difference; if it is lower than the rate agreed then the company pays the difference. A FRA does not involve the movement of the principal sum. The actual borrowing itself must be arranged separately.

   A FRA could be useful to Omniown since the treasurer will know in advance what the loan is going to cost. The minimum amount is usually £500,000 so would not be a problem in this case. However, if it is expected that interest rates are going to rise, the treasurer might have difficulty in negotiating a FRA at the current rate of 14%.

   (ii) A financial future is an agreement on the future price of a financial variable, in this case the interest rate. It takes the form of a contract between buyer and seller on an interest rate at an agreed price on an agreed date. The contract will require a small initial deposit. Interest rate futures are similar in effect to forward rate agreements, except that the terms, amounts and periods are standardised. The maximum period is one to two years. They are traded on the London International Futures and Options Exchange (LIFFE).

   An interest rate futures contract should allow Omniown to hedge against most of the risk of interest rate movements.

   (iii) An interest rate guarantee (or option) provides the right to borrow a specified amount at a guaranteed rate of interest. The option guarantees that the interest rate will not rise above a specified level during a specified period. On the date of expiry of the option the buyer must decide whether or not to exercise his right to borrow. He will only do so if actual interest rates have risen above the option rate. Interest rate options are more expensive than FRAs since the buyer of the option cannot lose on the interest rate. A premium must be paid regardless of whether or not the option is exercised. Specific interest rate guarantees can be negotiated direct with the bank, or can be traded in standardised form on the LIFFE.

   Omniown could use an interest rate guarantee to ensure that it does not pay more than a certain rate of interest, and at the same time benefit from any beneficial movements in rates. However it may consider that the premium to be paid is too expensive in relation to the expected benefits and in view of the other methods of interest rate management that are available.

(b) The value of a tick on a three month contract is:

   £500,000 × 0.01% × 3/12 = £12.50

The company needs to borrow £5m for six months. If the interest rate rises by 2%, this will mean that the company incurs additional interest costs of:

£5m × 2% × 6/12 = £50,000

It therefore needs to use enough futures contracts to make a profit of £50,000 to cover this cost.

If the futures market moves by 2%, this means that it moves by 200 ticks (2% = 200 × 0.01%). The gain on a single contract would therefore be £2,500 (200 × £12.50). Omniown therefore needs to take out twenty futures contracts to make a gain of £50,000 (£2,500 × 20 = £50,000).

(i)   If interest rates and the futures market both move by 2% as the treasurer predicts, then the loss of £50,000 on the interest rate will be matched by a gain of £50,000 on the twenty futures contracts. This is therefore a hedge with 100% efficiency.

(ii)   If the futures market moves by 1.5%, this means that it moves by 150 ticks. The gain on a single contract would therefore be £187.50. The gain on twenty contracts would be £37,500 (20 × £187.50).

In this case Omniown has not generated the full £50,000 needed from the futures market to cover the 2% rise in interest rates. The efficiency of the hedge is therefore 37,500/50,000 = 75%.

(iii)   If interest rates fall by 1%, Omniown will make savings of £25,000 (£5m × 1% × 6/12).

If at the same time the futures market falls by 0.75%, this means that it moves by 75 ticks with a loss of £18,750 on twenty contracts.

In this case, Omniown has lost less on the futures market than it has gained on the interest rate movement. The efficiency of the hedge is therefore 133.33% (25,000/18,750).

(c) The premium payable on the interest rate guarantee (IRG) is:

£5m × 0.2% = £10,000

This will be payable regardless of whether the IRG is exercised.

	(i) £	(ii) £	(iii) £
Cost of futures hedge			
Interest at 14%	350,000	350,000	350,000
Additional/(saved) interest	50,000	50,000	(25,000)
Loss/(gain) on futures	(50,000)	(37,500)	18,750
Total cost	350,000	362,500	343,750
Cost of IRG			
Interest *	350,000	350,000	325,000
Premium	10,000	10,000	10,000
Total cost	360,000	360,000	335,000

* (i): 14%; (ii): 14%; (iii): 13%.

(i)   The IRG would be more expensive than the futures hedge.
(ii)   The IRG would be less expensive than the futures hedge.
(iii)   The IRG would be less expensive than the futures hedge.

65   CAPIT

(a) The most important principle of project finance is that a reliable source of funds should be available for the duration of the project. The company should not leave itself open to the risk of finance suddenly becoming inordinately expensive during the course of the project. For that reason, a preponderance of fixed rate debt would seem to be preferable.

On the other hand, the fixed rate loan is initially more expensive than the variable rate loan. The company should try to predict the future trend of interest rates as far as possible, while recognising the unreliability of such predictions. If there is clear evidence that over the life of the project average rates will be significantly below the rate on the fixed rate loan, the company should seriously consider taking the larger variable rate loan and the smaller fixed rate loan. The directors' attitude to risk will of course be relevant.

(b) We will first find out which is the cheaper alternative, in the sense of finding which has the lower expected total interest cost over the first 18 months.

The possible interest rates for months 7 to 12 and 13 to 18 on the variable rate loan, and their probabilities, are as follows.

Months 7 to 12		*Months 13 to 18*			
Rate	*Probability*	*Rate*	*Probability*		
13%	0.5	11%	0.5×0.6	=	0.30
		15%	$1 - (0.18 + 0.42)$	=	0.40
17%	0.5	19%	0.5×0.6	=	0.30
					1.00

The expected cost per £1,000 of variable rate loan is therefore as follows.

	£
Interest for months 1 to 6:	
$1,000 \times 0.15 \times 6/12$	75.00
Interest for months 7 to 12:	
$1,000 \times (0.5 \times 0.13 + 0.5 \times 0.17) \times 6/12$	75.00
Interest for months 13 to 18:	
$1,000 \times (0.30 \times 0.11 + 0.40 \times 0.15 + 0.30 \times 0.19) \times 6/12$	75.00
Fees $(1,000 \times 0.01 \times 4)$	40.00
Cost before tax relief	265.00

The expected cost of using mainly fixed interest finance is as follows.

	£
Interest on fixed interest loan $(150,000 \times 0.17 \times 18/12)$	38,250
Fee for fixed interest loan	800
Cost of variable interest loan (50×265.00)	13,250
	52,300
Less tax relief $(16,500 \times 25\%)$	(4,125)
Net after-tax cost	48,175

The expected cost of using mainly variable interest finance is as follows.

	£
Interest on fixed interest loan $(50,000 \times 0.17 \times 18/12)$	12,750
Fee for fixed interest loan	800
Cost of variable interest loan (150×265.00)	39,750
	53,300
Less tax relief $(15,500 \times 25\%)$	(3,875)
Net after-tax cost	49,425

The first alternative, to use mainly fixed interest finance, is slightly cheaper.

If the first alternative is chosen and interest rates rise every six months, the cash flows to service the loan will be as follows.

170

	After 6 months £	After 12 months £	After 18 months £
Interest	16,500	17,000	17,500
Fees (including initial fees)	1,800	500	500
Less tax relief			(4,125)
	18,300	17,500	13,875
Cash available (including surpluses brought forward)	19,500	19,700	17,700
Surplus/(deficit)	1,200	2,200	3,825

As there will be no deficit even on the most pessimistic assumption about interest rates, the probability of the company being unable to service the debt is zero.

If the second alternative, using mainly variable interest debt, is chosen, then on the same assumption about interest rates the cash flows would be as follows.

	After 6 months £	After 12 months £	After 18 months £
Interest	15,500	17,000	18,500
Fees	3,800	1,500	1,500
Less tax relief			(3,875)
	19,300	18,500	16,125
Cash available	19,500	18,700	15,700
Surplus/(deficit)	200	200	(425)

There will therefore be a deficit after 18 months on the basis of the most pessimistic assumption about interest rates. There will not be such a deficit if interest rates follow any other course, because the deficit is so small.

The probability of the company being unable to service the debt is therefore $0.5 \times 0.6 = 0.3$.

66 MANLING

> *Tutorial note.* This question covers three fairly technical aspects of financial management. However, you should note that the three parts are independent of one another. If you found that one part was difficult, that should not have affected your answers to the other parts.

(a) *Disintermediation* involves dispensing with intermediaries. Thus trading companies may borrow and lend directly between each other, without using banks or other institutions. Intermediaries have traditionally performed the important functions of term matching and aggregating deposits to make large loans, but at a price. Where large sums and only a few lenders are involved, the parties may well be able to save money by cutting out the middleman. As well as giving these direct savings, disintermediation gives companies an alternative source of finance. One ordinary trading company may be more aware of the needs of another than a bank would be.

Securitisation is the packaging of a debt or several debts in a marketable security. This has the advantage that if the lender needs to recover the loan, he can do so by selling the security (though possibly at a loss, depending on market conditions), without the borrower having to repay the loan early. Indeed, it is this option which allows many companies to consider disintermediation. The term matching function of the bank is effectively taken over by the markets for securitised debt.

An important example of both disintermediation and securitisation is the commercial paper market. Companies can raise or invest funds through this market quickly, at reasonable rates of interest.

It should be said that these developments are not necessarily beneficial. A bank's specialist advice is lost if the bank is not used, and the safety for lenders of some securitised debt is not as great as that of bank deposits.

171

(b) (i) With LIBOR at 10% for the next year, the cost with the swap would be as follows.

	£
Interest: 14,000 × (12 – 11⅝ + 10 + 1½)%	1,662,500
Fee	20,000
	1,682,500
Less tax relief 35%	588,875
	1,093,625

With LIBOR at 10% for six months and at 9% thereafter, the cost with the swap would be as follows.

	£
Interest: 14,000 × (12 – 11⅝ + (10 + 9)/2 + 1½)%	1,592,500
Fee	20,000
	1,612,500
Less tax relief 35%	564,375
	1,048,125

Without the swap, the cost would be £14,000,000 × 12% × (100 – 35)% = £1,092,000.

The swap would therefore be slightly disadvantageous to Manling plc if LIBOR were to remain at 10% throughout the year, but advantageous were LIBOR to fall to 9% after 6 months.

(ii) Possible new terms would be for Manling plc to receive 11⅝% as at present and pay LIBOR + 1⁵/₁₆% (ie LIBOR + 1½% – ³/₁₆%). Fixed interest received is 11⅝%, as at present. The net cost is LIBOR + 1¹¹/₁₆%, which is ⁵/₁₆% less than the rate at which the company could raise floating rate debt.

The other company would then effectively have fixed rate debt at 11% + (1⅛ – 1⁵/₁₆)% = 11⁷/₁₆%, which is ⁵/₁₆% less than the rate at which it could otherwise have such debt.

(c) The following might be appropriate investments for a substantial sum for a fixed period of three months.

(i) Treasury bills.
(ii) Certificates of tax deposit.
(iii) Short-term local authority debt.
(iv) Bank and building society fixed term deposits.
(v) Certificates of deposit issued by banks.
(vi) Commercial paper.
(vii) Eligible bills of exchange and trade bills.

The choice will depend on the company's attitude to risk. As a general rule, the higher the risk, the higher the return. The above list is roughly in order of increasing risk.

BPP Publishing

67 SWAPS

Tutorial note. The first part of the question required a straightforward explanation of the features of swaps and their potential benefit to a company.

In part (b) it was more helpful and little more time consuming to compare the effects of using the currency markets and using the swap under each of the three inflation scenarios, rather than to use expected values.

You should first have calculated the exchange rates at the end of six months and twelve months using the purchasing power parity theory. These could then be applied to determine the sterling values of the transactions. You should have made clear all assumptions about interest calculations and payments, and about the rates at which the receipts will be priced and the effect on the interest calculation if the swap is used.

(a) *Interest rate swaps*

An interest rate swap is a transaction which allows a company to exploit different interest rates in different markets for borrowing, and thereby reduce or alter the timing of interest payments. The parties to a swap may be either two companies, or a company and a bank. In the former case the companies may arrange the agreement themselves or a bank may act as a broker.

The parties to a swap exchange their interest rate commitments with each other. In doing this they simulate each others' borrowings but retain their obligations to the original lenders. Thus they must accept a degree of counterparty risk since if the other party defaults on the interest payments, the original borrower remains liable to the lender.

The benefits are that the company can obtain interest rates which are lower than it could get from a bank or from other investors, and may be able to structure the timing of payments so as to improve the matching of cash outflows with revenues. Swaps are easy to arrange and are flexible since they can be arranged in any size and are reversible. Transaction costs are low, only amounting to legal fees, since there is no commission or premium to be paid.

Interest rate swaps also provide a means of financial speculation, the worst consequences of which have been widely reported in the financial press.

Currency swaps

In a currency swap, two parties agree to swap equivalent amounts of currency for a given periods. This effectively involves the exchange of debt from one currency to another. As with interest rate swaps, liability on the principal is not transferred and the parties are liable to counterparty risk.

The benefit to the company is that it can gain access to debt finance in another country and currency where it is little known, and consequently has a poorer credit rating, than in its home country. It can therefore take advantage of lower interest rates than it could obtain if it arranged the loan itself.

A further purpose of currency swaps is to restructure the currency base of the company's liabilities. This may be important where the company is trading overseas and receiving revenues in foreign currencies, but its borrowings are denominated in the currency of its home country. Currency swaps therefore provide a means of reducing exchange rate exposure.

A third benefit of currency swaps is that at the same time as exchanging currency, the company may also be able to convert fixed rate debt to floating rate or vice versa. Thus it may obtain some of the benefits of an interest rate swap in addition to achieving the other purposes of a currency swap.

(b) The first step is to calculate the exchange rate in each of the different inflation scenarios. The rates can be found using the purchasing power parity theory.

$$\text{Rate after a year} = \text{current spot rate} \times \frac{100 + \text{SA inflation rate}}{100 + \text{UK inflation rate}}$$

173

$$\text{Rate after six months} = \text{current spot rate} \times \sqrt{\frac{100 + \text{SA inflation rate}}{100 + \text{UK inflation rate}}}$$

Month	*Inflation* SA %	UK %	*Exchange rate*
0			25.00
6	40	4	29.00
12	40	4	33.65
0			25.00
6	60	5	30.86
12	60	5	38.10
0			25.00
6	100	7	34.18
12	100	7	46.73

The expected values will not be calculated since these have little real meaning. Instead, the swap will be evaluated against using the currency markets for each of the three scenarios.

The effects of the exchange rate on the investments and returns can now be calculated. It is assumed that Calvold will have to borrow funds in the UK to finance the deal, and therefore interest will be calculated at the opportunity cost of funds, 12%. The interest rate for six months will be $\sqrt{1.12} - 1 = 0.0058 = 5.8\%$.

(i) *Using the currency markets*

(1) Inflation rates 4% and 40%:

	Pm	£m	*Interest* £m
Investment - month 0	(1,000.00)	(40.00)	(4.80)
Investment - month 6	(500.00)	(17.24)	(1.00)
		(57.24)	(5.80)
Interest		(5.80)	
Total cost		(63.04)	
Price received	2,000.00	59.44	
Net profit/(loss)		(3.60)	

(2) Inflation rates 5% and 60%:

	Pm	£m	Interest £m
Investment - month 0	(1,000.00)	(40.00)	(4.80)
Investment - month 6	(500.00)	(16.20)	(0.94)
		(56.20)	(5.74)
Interest		(5.74)	
Total cost		(61.94)	
Price received	2,000.00	52.49	
Net profit/(loss)		(9.45)	

(3) Inflation rates 7% and 100%:

	Pm	£m	Interest £m
Investment - month 0	(1,000.00)	(40.00)	(4.80)
Investment - month 6	(500.00)	(14.63)	(0.85)
		(54.63)	(5.65)
Interest		(5.65)	
Total cost		(60.28)	
Price received	2,000.00	42.80	
Net profit/(loss)		(17.48)	

BPP Publishing

(ii) *Using the currency swap*

Calvold will have to borrow sterling funds in the UK to finance the swap. The cost of funds in the UK is 12%. However, swaps involve the transfer of interest rate liabilities as well as of principal, and therefore the interest cost will be calculated at the swap rate of 10%.

It is assumed that no interest will be earned on the 500 million pesos which will be lying idle until month 6.

The sterling investment required before interest is £1,500,000/20 = £75,000.

The price received will depend on the inflation rates. 1,500,000 million pesos will be at the swap rate of 20 pesos to the pound, yielding £75,000, equal to the initial sterling outlay; the balance (500 milliion pesos) will be at the prevailing year end rate. The sterling value of interest payments (150 million pesos) will also depend on the exchange rate. It is assumed that no interest will be paid until the end of the year.

Inflation rates	Spot rate receipts £m	Interest £m	Profit £m	Profit/(loss) without swap £m
4% & 40%	14.86	4.46	10.40	(3.60)
5% & 60%	13.12	3.94	9.18	(9.45)
7% & 100%	10.70	3.21	7.49	(17.48)

The calculations show that due to the fact that the price Calvold will receive is denominated in pesos and will not be received until the end of the year, any profit on the deal is eroded by inflation if currency is traded on the market. If the swap is used, only a part of the receipts will be paid at the floating rate, and therefore the effects of inflation are diminished. Thus it appears that it would be beneficial for Calvold to use the currency swap.

68 TUTORIAL QUESTION: MULTINATIONAL INVESTMENT APPRAISAL

(a) The proposed investment will be worthwhile to either party if the return on the investment equals or exceeds the cost of capital to the company. It is assumed that since the subsidiary is paying a dividend and has its own cost of equity, it also has local shareholders and is not wholly owned by Rippentoff. The element of borrowing in the investment is therefore considered to be irrelevant to Rippentoff.

(i) The situation from the point of view of Rippentoff must be evaluated in US dollars. It is assumed that the exchange rate is expected to remain stable throughout the life of the project.

Rippentoff's initial investment can be calculated as follows.

	Gross cash payment LCU m	$m	Offset $m	Net cash $m
Capital funds supplied	30	6	0	6
Plant: due for scrap	(10)	(2)	0.1	(1.9)
due for replacement	(10)	(2)	1.5	(0.5)
new machine	(10)	(2)	1.9	(0.1)
Stock	(5)	(1)	0.75	(0.25)
Total	(5)	(1)	4.25	3.25

In the case of the plant, the opportunity cost has been offset to calculate the net cash inflow to Rippentoff. For the first machine this is the amount that would have been received had the item been scrapped. For the second two machines this is the amount that will have to be spent on replacement and purchase.

In the case of the stock, the effective net cash inflow is the contribution on the cost of materials.

In return for its investment, Rippentoff will receive each year a management fee of $1m, together with a contribution of 25% on materials supplied amounting to $0.5m ($20 \times 0.5 \times 0.25 \times 0.2$).

Thus Rippentoff will earn an annual return of $1.5m on its initial investment of $3.25m which amounts to 46.15%. This exceeds 15% which is the cost of capital, and therefore the investment is worthwhile.

(ii) From the point of view of the subsidiary, the capital invested is equal to the assets employed in the project ie LCU50m. The investment must in this case be evaluated in local currency.

The return on the investment can be calculated in two ways.

(1) *Net profit plus management fee to Rippentoff*

This is included since there is no consideration for the payment, and it is merely a means of extracting cash from the subsidiary. In this case the return is LCU10m. This represents a return of 20% which is equal to the cost of equity. The investment is therefore worthwhile unless there are alternatives available with a more beneficial risk/return profile.

(2) *Net profit plus management fee plus interest*

It can be argued that since the investment is being evaluated against the cost of capital, the cost of financing the project in terms of interest should be excluded. In this case the return is LCU13m. This represents a return of 26% which is in excess of the cost of equity, and therefore the investment is worthwhile.

However it could also be argued that since the investment is being evaluated against the cost of equity (and presumably the return required by the shareholders) and not the combined cost of capital, interest should be included as a relevant cost.

(b) Rippentoff would also have to take into account the following factors.

(i) *Exchange rate risk.* The calculations assume that the exchange rate remains constant throughout the life of the project. It would be useful to calculate the sensitivity of the return to movements in the exchange rate, and to form a view of the likelihood of such movements occurring. Exchange rate movements could impact on the project in two main ways.

(1) The value of the assets employed may go down due to a fall in the value of the local currency against the dollar.

(2) Payments received for materials and the management fee may be affected by the exchange rate ruling at the date of the transaction. This risk can be averted to some extent by hedging through timing the payments judiciously, and through the use of the option and currency markets. However these methods will not avert the consequences of a long term downward movement in the local currency, or of a deterioration in the local economy. An example is Peru where inflation has been spiralling out of control and the currency has become almost worthless.

(ii) *Political risk.* Rippentoff must assess the political situation and take account of the likelihood of the government taking action that would jeopardise its ability to extract cash from Penuria, and even its ownership of the assets. Possible government actions include the following.

(1) Import quotas which might restrict the volume of materials being purchased from Rippentoff and the contribution earned from them.

(2) Import tariffs on the materials supplied.

(3) Exchange control regulations which might restrict the ability of Rippentoff to obtain regular payments of the management fee.

(4) Nationalisation of assets.

176

(5) Legislation restricting the granting of work permits to foreigners might cause Rippentoff a problem in the management of the investment.

Alternatively, it is possible that the government might look favourably on foreign investment as a means of developing the local economy. If this is thought to be likely, then Rippentoff should aim to time its investment to take maximum advantage of any government support that will be available.

(iii) *Geographical separation.* Management and control are likely to be more difficult due to the geographical separation of parent and subsidiary, and communication problems may be enhanced by language barriers. This may mean that the actual return achieved on the investment is less than the potential performance assumed in the calculations.

69 TRANSFER PRICING

The objective of a transfer pricing policy is to set prices which will give the separate divisions incentives to act in such a way as to maximise the profits of the company as a whole. Where there is an external market for the products to be transferred, market prices are likely to be the best transfer prices, with perhaps some adjustment for savings in selling and delivery costs. Where there is no such external market, or only a market in which there is a monopoly or an oligopoly, some other method of setting transfer prices is needed. For multinational companies, restrictions on remittances from overseas subsidiaries and tax planning considerations may influence the setting of transfer prices.

The first sentence of the statement is certainly correct. There is great scope for dysfunctional behaviour in pricing policy. The managers of separate divisions, influenced by incentive schemes, are likely to set selling prices so as to maximise the profits of their own divisions. These prices may then lead the buying divisions to make quantities and set prices for external sales which fail to maximise profits for the company as a whole, simply because the buying divisions have been misled as to the true marginal cost (to the company as a whole) of their finished products.

If divisional managers are left to argue about such transfer prices, the likely result is that managers with strong personalities will get their way, and the other managers will resent the outcome. It is therefore appropriate, as the statement says, to have such prices fixed centrally, subject to the following.

(a) The department setting transfer prices must be seen to be acting fairly and in the interests of the company as a whole. It should not be involved in setting bonus rates or the basis on which bonuses as calculated.

(b) Head office should not be tempted to encroach further on divisional managers' responsibilities. Transfer prices should be set so as to encourage production at the appropriate levels. There should be no need to tell mangers what quantities to produce.

70 BRITISH COMPANY IN RURITANIA

> *Tutorial note.* The question asks for a report, but you should begin by showing your workings and assumptions. There is a lot of data to digest and sort out! The problem of depreciation charges in the subsidiary is particularly tricky, and you may need to think carefully about how the project's cash flows should be calculated, to take the depreciation into account.

(a) The cash benefits to the parent company from the project are the sterling cash flows from Ruritania. Since these occur at each year end, it is appropriate to use the end-of-year expected exchange rates for converting Rm into pounds.

The exception to this 'rule' is the purchases of goods from the parent company. The cash profits to the parent company are 40% (100 − 20 − 40) of the selling price, and since the goods are paid for immediately in cash, the Rm should be converted into sterling at the expected mid-year exchange rate.

Capital expenditure - relevant costs

(i)   Start of 19X0 (year 0). Relevant cost in sterling.

	£m
New machinery	6.0
Scrap value of surplus machinery	0.2
Replacement cost of machinery currently in use*	2.5
	8.7

* It is assumed that replacement machinery will have to be purchased to continue this current operation.

(ii)   End of 19X1 (year 2). Since the machinery is surplus to requirements, its relevant cost is its scrap value, £500,000.

(iii)   End of 19X3 (year 4). The break-up value of Rm 13 million has a sterling value of (÷ 13) £1 million.

Profit analysis and depreciation in the subsidiary

	Profits Rm	Dividends (75%) Rm		Dividends £	Profits invested in stock (25%) Rm
19X0 (Year 1)	21,000,000	15,750,000	(÷ 7)	2,250,000	5,250,000
19X1 (Year 2)	22,500,000	16,875,000	(÷ 9)	1,875,000	5,625,000
19X2 (Year 3)	22,000,000	16,500,000	(÷ 11)	1,500,000	5,500,000
19X3 (Year 4)	26,000,000	19,500,000	(÷ 13)	1,500,000	6,500,000
					22,875,000

The stock will have a conversion value into sterling of (÷ 13) £1,760,000 approx at the end of 19X3.

We are not given sufficient information about depreciation charges in the subsidiary company. Depreciation is a non-cash expense, and so the cash profits of the subsidiary will be Rm 10,000,000 higher each year (because of this) than the reported accounting profits. Presumably, the cash is built up within the business, since it is *assumed* that it cannot be paid as dividend nor invested in Ruritanian stock.

It is therefore *assumed* that Rm 40,000,000 will be available in cash at the end of the project, within the subsidiary, for paying back to the UK. It is *assumed* that this Rm 40 million is additional to the Rm 13 million break-up value of the subsidiary's fixed assets. This will have a conversion value into £ of (÷ 13) £3,077,000 approx at the end of 19X3.

Purchases from parent company by subsidiary

The relevant cash costs to the parent company are the labour and materials costs (60% of sale price) and the cash profits are 40% of the sales price.

Year		Sales Rm ('000)	Cash profits for parent Rm ('000)		Cash profits £
19X0	(Year 1)	12,000	4,800	(÷ 6)	800,000
19X1	(Year 2)	16,000	6,400	(÷ 8)	800,000
19X2	(Year 3)	24,000	9,600	(÷ 10)	960,000
19X3	(Year 4)	30,000	12,000	(÷ 12)	1,000,000

Management fees and royalties paid by the subsidiary

		Rm ('000)		£
End of 19X0	(Year 1)	14,000	(÷ 7)	2,000,000
End of 19X1	(Year 2)	15,300	(÷ 9)	1,700,000
End of 19X2	(Year 3)	17,600	(÷ 11)	1,600,000
End of 19X3	(Year 4)	19,500	(÷ 13)	1,500,000

Cash flows of the project	Start of 19X0 £'000	19X0 £'000	19X1 £'000	19X2 £'000	19X3 £'000
Capital cost	(8,700)		(500)		1,000
Dividends		2,250	1,875	1,500	1,500
Ruritanian stock					1,760
Cash built up within subsidiary (depreciation)					3,077
Profits from intercompany trading		800	800	960	1,000
Income from fees, royalties		2,000	1,700	1,600	1,500
Cost of management services		(100)	(100)	(100)	(100)
Net cash flows	(8,700)	4,950	3,775	3,960	9,737

NPV analysis

Year	Cash flow £'000	Discount factor at 20%	Present value £'000
0	(8,700)	1.000	(8,700)
1	4,950	0.833	4,123
2	3,775	0.694	2,620
3	3,960	0.579	2,293
4	9,737	0.482	4,693
		Net present value	+5,029

REPORT

To: Board of Directors
From: Company Secretary
Date: 14 June 19W9

Subject: The Ruritanian project

1. The Ruritanian project appears to be worthwhile, because it will be expected to earn a return in excess of 20%, and has an estimated net present value of approximately £5 million. (See figures above).

2. Certain factors ought to be taken into account before a final decision is made.

    (a) The value of the Ruritanian mark is expected to fall very sharply against sterling over the 4 year period. If its fall in value exceeds expectation, the NPV of the project will be less.

    (b) A large portion of the project cash flows will not occur until the end of 19X3, and these will be particularly vulnerable to a very sharp fall in the Ruritanian mark's value.

    (c) A closer consideration ought to be given to the assumption that the accumulated depreciation charges of Rm 40 million will be convertible into cash at the end of 19X3.

    (d) There will be a potential risk, due to the declining value of the Ruritanian mark, that the Ruritanian government will impose even stricter exchange controls, making it difficult or even impossible for our company to extract cash from Ruritania.

(b) Control of remittances by a government is a form of exchange control which stops the currency being fully convertible. Such measures imposed by government as a form of protection in order to rectify, or avoid, a balance of payments deficit and to prevent a depreciation in the nation's currency. Such controls were imposed in 1939 in the UK as a wartime measure and the last controls were finally abolished in 1979. Exchange controls are discouraged by the OECD but are still imposed by many developing countries.

BPP Publishing

The foreign investor will suffer from the problem that it will be difficult to 'repatriate' dividends from the investment. Faced with this difficulty, the investor may respond in different ways. If the investor is less concerned about the flow of dividends, he may not see the controls as a major impediment, but ultimately the value of the investment must depend upon the ability to receive distributions of profits. One response of the foreign investor is to avoid investments in countries in which controls over remittances exist. This could hamper investment in the local economy but on the other hand it may allow local entrepreneurs to operate more easily. However, this may mean that enterprises in the country are less efficient than they would be if there was foreign competition, to the possible detriment of consumers in the country.

Another possible response of the foreign investor is to find ways of avoiding the exchange controls, for example by seeking returns through royalties or by setting transfer prices for part-processed goods at non-market levels. The government exerting the controls will have to close such 'loopholes' through further control and regulation if it wants the controls to have an effect.

71 RANEK

> *Tutorial note.* The examiner commented that candidates' answers to this question were very poor. Although there is a lot of detail in this question, part (a) should have helped you to sort it out. In part (a), you had to list the costs without being concerned about the time value of money. You should thus have obtained a good grasp of the question, ready to tackle part (b).

(a)

		£'000
Materials	715×15	10,725
Labour	380×15	5,700
Other direct costs	50×15	750
Leasing costs	620×5	3,100
Plant	$1,800 - 900$	900
		21,175
20% mark up		4,235
Sterling price		25,410

The present exchange rate is Z$46.0 to the pound, and this will change to Z$46.0 × 1.25 to the pound, or Z$57.5 to the pound, over the duration of the project. The tender price in Z$ based on a 20% markup is therefore found as x from

$$\frac{x \times 0.3}{46} + \frac{x \times 0.7}{57.5} = \quad 25.41 \text{ million}$$

$$(0.00652174 + 0.01217391) x = \quad 25.41 \text{ million}$$

$$x = \quad 25,410,000 \div .01869565 \cong Z\$1,359 \text{ million}$$

(b) To find the net present value of the project, we must first work out the tax cash flows and then include these, along with all other relevant costs, in a discounted cash flow computation.

	Tax year 1 19X2 £'000	Tax year 2 19X3 £'000
Materials (4:11)	2,860	7,865
Labour (3:12)	1,140	4,560
Other direct costs (3:12)	150	600
Leasing costs	620	2,480
Capital allowances[1]	450	450
	5,220	15,955
Sales 1,359,000 × 30%/46	8,863	
1,359,000 × 70%/57.5		16,544
Taxable profit	3,643	589

	Tax year 1 19X2 £'000	Tax year 2 19X3 £'000
Tax cash flow at 35%	1,275	206

¹   Year 1: £1.8m × 0.75 = £1.35m WDV, £450,000 allowance.

    Year 2: £1.35m × 0.75 = £1.0125m WDV, £337,500 + £112,500 balancing allowance.

Net present value computation

Month	Item	Amount £'000	Discount factor (1%)	NPV £'000
0	Sales	8,863	1.000	8,863
15	Sales	16,544	0.861	14,244
1 - 15	Labour	(380)	13.870	(5,271)
0 - 14	Materials	(715)	14.000	(10,010)
1 - 15	Other direct costs	(50)	13.870	(693)
0	Lease	(620)	1.000	(620)
3	Lease	(620)	0.971	(602)
6	Lease	(620)	0.942	(584)
9	Lease	(620)	0.914	(567)
12	Lease	(620)	0.887	(550)
9	Taxation	(1,275)	0.914	(1,165)
21	Taxation	(206)	0.811	(167)
0	Plant not sold	1,936	1.000	(1,936)
15	Final sale of plant	900	0.861	775
				1,717

Plant not sold represents the opportunity cost of not selling the plant and equipment immediately. On immediate sale, a balancing charge of £2m − £1.8m = £200,000 would arise, with tax of £70,000 payable in Month 9. The present value of the tax payment is therefore £70,000 × 0.914 = £64,000. £2,000,000 − £64,000 = £1,936,000.

The net present value of the project at the suggested tender price is approximately £1,717,000.

The minimum tender price

Unless there are special factors, such as a need to succeed at almost any cost because of the prestige and future business which this project would bring, the company should not tender at a price below that which will yield a net present value of zero. The price which will yield such a result may be estimated as follows.

Each Z$1,000,000 reduction in the tender price has the following effects.

Month	Item	Amount £'000	Discount factor (1%)	NPV £'000
0	Fall in sales (300/46)	6.52	1.000	6.5
15	Fall in sales (700/57.5)	12.17	0.861	10.5
9	Fall in taxation (35% × 6.52)	(2.28)	0.914	(2.1)
21	Fall in taxation (35% × 12.17)	(4.26)	0.811	(3.5)
Fall in net present value				11.4

The net present value would therefore fall to zero at a tender price of approximately 1,359 − (1,717 + 11.4) = 1,208 million Z$, and this should be the minimum tender price.

This estimate assumes that the cash flow estimates are accurate. However, they could all be subject to considerable error. No account has been taken of inflation in the costs payable in sterling, and it has been assumed that payment for the project will be received in full on time. This in turn depends on the project being completed on time to an acceptable standard. It has

BPP Publishing

also been assumed that the project's risks are such that the company's usual cost of capital is an appropriate discount rate.

72 PASSEM

> *Tutorial note.* It is helpful to structure the body of the report required in part (a) with reference to the different areas of company performance. This helps to focus attention on the key areas and improves clarity. State clearly all assumptions made in computing the ratios, particularly where different methods of calculation are available (as with the gearing ratio).

(a) REPORT

To: Board of Directors
From: Financial Director
Date: 28 August 19X3

Subject: Evaluation of shareholding in Passem plc

Introduction

The group holds 2,000,000 shares in Passem which at current market prices are worth £3.1 million (0.62% of the group's share portfolio). This holding amounts to 4.34% of Passem's equity. If Passem is a potential acquisition target, then these shares should continue to be held by the group unless it is anticipated that the share price is likely to fall, in which case the shares could be sold and later bought back at a lower price.

If however the investment is held purely for financial reasons to provide quick access to liquid funds, then the merits of disposal should be considered since the current 'Z' score suggests that Passem does not lie in the survival zone. The body of this report comprises a more detailed evaluation of Passem's financial position with the aim of determining whether or not the holding should be sold. It is assumed that the group wishes to maintain a shareholding in the retail sector. Detailed financial analysis may be found in the Appendix to this report.

Performance: 19W8 - 19X2

Sales and profits (19X1 - 19X2)

Sales in 19X2 fell by £50 million as compared with 19X1. This represents a fall of 6.1% and compares with an average fall in the retail sector as a whole of 10%. Sales performance is therefore relatively encouraging. Gross profit has fallen by £3 million (6.7%) leaving the margin virtually unchanged at 5.45%, indicating that sales have not been maintained at the expense of margin.

Return on capital employed has fallen from 17.3% to 14.9%. This reflects the fact that while profits have fallen, the asset base has increased, although the increase in fixed assets and stocks has been offset to a large extent by the increase in short term creditors, particularly trade creditors.

To summarise, although trading performance has deteriorated, the decline appears to be less bad than that of the sector as a whole. On this basis there is no good reason to dispose of the holding in Passem given that the group wishes to maintain a presence in the retail sector.

Liquidity and working capital (19X1 - 19X2)

The liquidity ratios have not worsened over the period, although in absolute terms they are very low. The quick ratio stands at around 0.07:1 where a ratio in excess of 1:1 is considered necessary for safety. However it is likely that this partly reflects the fact that ratios are generally low in the retail sector since sales are for cash whereas purchases are made on credit.

Falling sales have impacted significantly on the working capital ratios. Stock and debtor turnover rates have both reduced, and interest cover has fallen from around 2.4 times to 1.5 times. This latter figure is very low and may indicate a substantial risk of failure.

182

Financial structure (19X1 - 19X2)

There has been little change in the level of gearing (based on book values) from 1.56 to 1.71, mainly due to the increase in the overdraft from £68 million to £84 million. This seems to be a very high level of overdraft to be running and it would be helpful to know the borrowing limits and security held by the bank. It would be interesting to know if Passem has any plans to convert this to a cheaper longer term form of finance. It is not clear how the company intends to source the £40 million that will be needed to repay the 10% fixed rate term loan which matures in three years' time.

Market performance (19W8 - 19X2)

Passem's share price has performed well over the period 19W8 to 19X2 compared with the market averages, and it has not fallen by as much as the average in the last year of difficult trading conditions. This may indicate that the market believes that Passem is well placed to pull out of the recession ahead of its rivals. Similarly, the price/earnings ratio in 19X1 and 19X2 was higher than the industry average, but this also reflects Passem's low earnings per share in 19X2.

Dividend yield is lower than the industry average, reflecting the reduced dividend for 19X2, and this might be significant in deciding whether it is worth continuing to hold the shares.

Given the level of systematic risk of the company as measured by the beta value, the shares have so far yielded a good return given their level of risk.

Conclusions

The main indicator of risk to Passem's continued survival is the very low level of interest cover. In the event of the company going into liquidation, there would be more than sufficient assets based on book values to repay the creditors (£330 million) and there would be £103 million left over for the shareholders (224 pence per share). If the fixed assets undervaluation can be realised, then the payment to shareholders could be as high as 415 pence per share. Since this is well in excess of the current market price of the shares, the group would still be able to recoup its investment in the event of failure.

In other areas, Passem appears to be performing well when compared with the sector as a whole. Given that the group wishes to continue to hold shares in the retail sector, it is recommended that the holding in Passem be retained, unless a better investment can be found.

Appendix (amounts in £ million)

Sales and profits

	19X1	19X2
Gross profit : sales	45/820	42/770
	5.49%	5.45%
Return on capital employed		
Earnings before interest and tax	33	29
Capital employed	191	195
	17.3%	14.9%

Liquidity and working capital

Current ratio		
Current assets	139	159
Current liabilities	210	238
	0.66	0.67
Quick ratio		
Current assets excluding stock	14	17
Current liabilities	210	238
	0.07	0.07

BPP Publishing

	19X1	19X2
Stock turnover (times)		
Total sales	820	770
Closing stock	125	142
	_6.56_	_5.42_
Debtor turnover (times)		
Total sales	820	770
Closing debtors	12	16
	_68.3_	_48.1_
Interest cover		
Operating profit	33	29
Interest payable	14	19
	_2.36_	_1.53_

Financial structure

	19X1	19X2
Gearing		
Long-term debt + overdraft	158	176
Equity	101	103
	_1.56_	_1.71_

Market performance

	19X1	19X2
Price/earnings ratio		
Profit after tax	15	5
EPS (E)	37.5	10.87
Average market price (E)	175	150
	_4.67_	_13.8_
Industry average	_4.0_	_3.1_
Dividend yield		
Gross dividend per share (E)	15	6.5
Average share price	175	150
	_8.57%_	_4.33%_
Industry average	_10.0%_	_11.1%_

Average CAPM return for period
Risk-free rate of return (R_f) = 7.0%
Beta = 1.2
Market rate of return (R_m) = 12.0%
CAPM required rate of return = $R_f + \beta(R_m - R_f)$ = 13.0%

Actual rate of return (capital gain/loss + dividend yield)

Year	Capital gain %	Dividend yield %	Total %
19W9	4.0	9.2	13.2
19X0	44.6	6.9	51.5
19X1	(6.9)	8.6	1.7
19X2	(14.3)	4.3	(10.0)
			_56.4_

Average for period = 56.4% ÷ 4 = 14.1%

(b) Other useful information would include the following.

(i) Recent copies of the full annual and interim reports and accounts.

(ii) Any press comment and analysts' reports that are available.

(iii) More details about the nature of Passem's properties and the basis on which a possible revaluation is calculated.

BPP Publishing

(iv) Accounts of comparable companies in the retail sector.

(v)   Economic forecasts dealing with the likely duration of the recession and interest rate movements.

(vi) Details of Passem's future investment plans.

73 CASH WITH ORDER

(a) In the case of cheques drawn in sterling by European buyers, it would be possible to speed up payment by means of:

(i)   banker's draft, although this is still fairly slow;

(ii)   mail transfer, which is quicker and as cheap;

(iii) telegraphic transfer (TT) or priority SWIFT message (EIMT), which is the quickest method of the three, but more expensive.

If the company is worried about cost, it might be able to persuade its customers to pay the costs involved in any of these arrangements.

(b) In the case of cheques drawn in US dollars, there is the problem that the customers are unwilling to change the current system, and want to carry on sending cheques drawn in dollars. In this case, the UK bank can help its customer by *negotiating* the cheques (ie purchasing the cheques, but with recourse to the customer in the event of non-payment). The customer's account will be credited straight away (in sterling).

The customer does not receive any notification of the eventual payment of the cheques, because payment is kept by the bank. However, if a cheque is unpaid, the customer will be notified and must 'repay' the bank in dollars. This means that the UK bank will debit the customer's account with the sterling equivalent of the dollars value of the cheque, plus interest charges.

74 THE TREASURY FUNCTION

REPORT

To: The Board of Directors
From: B Brown, Finance Director
Date: 20 May 19X9
Subject: Proposed responsibilities of the treasury function and the advantages of having a specialist treasury department

Following the decision at the group board meeting of 15 May 19X9, I present this report on the responsibilities and advantages of a treasury function.

(a) *Proposed responsibilities of the treasury function*

A treasury function's responsibilities can be usefully divided into four areas.

(i)   *Funding management* - advising the finance director and the board on appropriate sources for the group's capital. The treasurer will advise on the cost of different types of capital, anticipated future changes, and where such funds can be obtained, in the light of the overall strategy for the group's capital structure.

(ii)   *Liquidity management* - co-ordinating the group's cashflows to ensure that:

(1) transaction costs are minimised;
(2) short-term cash deficits and surpluses amongst group companies are set off;
(3) banking relationships are properly managed.

(iii) *Investment management* - ensuring that surplus short-term funds awaiting investment in the group's businesses are obtaining the best possible yield, subject to the group's risk strategy.

BPP Publishing

Where surplus funds are held on a longer term basis, the treasury department will also co-ordinate investment to yield maximum return, consistent with realising the investments for planned group expenditure.

(iv) *Currency management* - co-ordination of group policy as regards:

    (1) transaction risk in foreign currency;

    (2) hedging and matching currency exposure;

    (3) minimising the political risks of international investment;

    (4) transacting the group's foreign currency requirements and establishing a sound system of control over these.

(b) *Advantages of a separate treasury function*

Four advantages can be claimed for establishing a separate treasury function rather than using the general finance department to deal with treasury matters.

(i) Attention will be focused on the importance of good cash management. Efficient use of cash is vital in optimising the overall group performance.

(ii) Treasury management is a distinct area of expertise and personnel with the required expertise are more likely to be attracted to the group as an employer if their importance is recognised through the establishment of a separate function.

(iii) The additional expertise which will be available can be used to advantage in providing advice to other departments. In particular, export marketing will profit from increased knowledge of ways to reduce the risks of international trade.

(iv) Through having a separate profit centre, attention will be focused on the contribution to group profit performance that can be achieved by good cash, funding, investment and foreign currency management.

BPP Publishing

TEST YOUR KNOWLEDGE

1   What is assumed to be the financial objective of a company? How is this objective modified in the case of nationalised industries?

2   What are the problems in the relationship between a company's management and its shareholders?

3   What is the Yellow Book?

4   A company has 200,000 £1 ordinary shares in issue which have a current market price of £2. The company is making a 2 for 5 rights issue at a price of £1.50. What is the theoretical ex rights price?

      A   £1.50
      B   £1.64
      C   £1.75
      D   £1.86

5   What factors will influence the market price of convertible debentures?

6   What is semi-strong form efficiency in a market?

7   (a)   What is LIBOR?
      (b)   What is a floating rate loan?

8   Name three of the London money markets.

9   In the context of financial futures, what is a 'tick'?

10   In the context of options:

      (a)   What is a negotiated option?
      (b)   What is a delta value?

11   (a)   What is an interest rate swap?
      (b)   What is a swaption?

12   What is the formula for calculating the cost of equity using Gordon's Growth Model?

13   How is the effective real cost of capital established in times of inflation?

14   Data of relevance to the evaluation of a particular project are given below:

Cost of capital in real terms	5% per annum
Expected inflation	4% pa
Expected increase in the project's annual cash inflow	7% pa
Expected increase in the project's annual cash outflow	3% pa

      Which one of the following sets of adjustments will lead to the correct NPV being calculated?

BPP Publishing

	Cash inflow	Cash outflow	Discount percentage
A	4% pa increase	4% pa increase	9.2%
B	7% pa increase	3% pa increase	9.0%
C	7% pa increase	3% pa increase	9.2%
D	unadjusted	unadjusted	5.0%

15 A project has the following cash flows.

Cash flow	Timing of cash flow	Value
Purchase of equipment	Now	£40,000
Sale of equipment	Three years from now	£7,000
Sales revenue	At the end of each of the next three years	£90,000
Variable costs	At the end of each of the next three years	£60,000
Taxation on revenue profit	One year after the end of the period to which it relates	35%

The equipment costs are not allowable as a deduction from revenue profit and no capital allowances are available.

Fixed overheads of £10,000 a year have been allocated to the project based on labour hours used.

What is the net present value (to the nearest thousand pounds) of the project cash flows using an after tax cost of capital of 10% pa?

A   £14,000
B   £16,000
C   £25,000
D   £64,000

16 Four projects, P, Q, R and S, are available to a company which is facing a shortage of capital over the next year but expects capital to be freely available from then on.

Project	P	Q	R	S
	£'000	£'000	£'000	£'000
Total capital required over the life of the project	10	60	20	20
Capital required in the next year	10	20	15	16
Net present value of the project at the company's cost of capital	30	80	50	30

In what sequence should the projects be selected if the company wishes to maximise the total net present value?

A   P, R, S, Q
B   Q, P, R, S
C   Q, R, P, S
D   R, S, P, Q

17 Easy Does It Ltd is considering three projects I, II, III with the following estimated cash flows:

Project	Year 0	Year 1	Year 2
	£	£	£
I	(15,000)	9,000	10,500
II	(30,000)	21,000	15,000
III	(45,000)	15,000	42,000

If the cost of capital is 10%, the amount available for investment is restricted to £64,000, and the projects are divisible, which projects should be undertaken:

BPP Publishing

A   I and II completely with the remainder invested in project III
B   I and III completely with the remainder invested in project II
C   II completely with the remainder invested in project III
D   III completely with the remainder invested in project II

18   What are the steps needed to find the APV of a project?

19   The market value of an all equity company, Unlevered plc is £240,000,000. Another company in the same industry and with the same business risk, Levered plc, is identical in every respect to Unlevered plc with the exception that it is geared, with £50,000,000 of 12% debenture stock helping to finance it.

(a)   The debenture stock is valued at par on the stock market.
(b)   The rate of corporation tax is 35%.
(c)   Both Unlevered plc and Levered plc have annual profits before interest and tax of   £55,000,000.

Required

According to Modigliani and Miller, what should be the price of Levered plc's equity?

A   £207,500,000
B   £222,500,000
C   £240,000,000
D   £257,500,000

20   What is Modigliani and Miller's theory regarding the effect of gearing on the cost of capital when there is no taxation?

21   If a company has a beta factor of 1.2, the risk-free rate of return is 10% and the current average market return is 15%, what is the company's cost of equity using the CAPM?

22   From the data given below, what is the beta factor for shares in Evan Elpus plc?

A   2.5
B   3.7
C   5.8
D   6.9

	Stock market index	Evan Elpus plc Share price	Dividend for the year
		£	£
31.12.X0	1,800	2.00	Nil
31.12.X1	1,830	2.40	Nil
31.12.X2	1,770	1.50	Nil
31.12.X3	1,960	2.60	Nil
31.12.X4	2,091	3.00	Nil

The formula for calculating β is $\dfrac{(\text{Cov x, m})}{\text{Var m}}$

where m is the market rate of return and x is the return on the shares of the company.

23   The standard deviation of market returns is 40%, and the expected market return (R_m) is 14%. The risk free rate of return is 7%. The covariance of returns for the market with returns on shares in Portfolio plc over the same period has been 20%. Calculate a cost for Portfolio plc equity.

24   Two companies are identical in every respect except for their capital structure. One company ABC plc has a debt: equity ratio of 1:4 and its equity has a β value of 1.10. The other company, XYZ plc, has a debt:equity ratio of 3:4. Corporation tax is 35%. Estimate a β value for XYZ plc's equity from these data.

25   Greedy plc's shares are quoted at a market price which gives the shares a P/E rating of 10. The company has just made a takeover bid for Target plc. The offer price is £6 cash per share, and the most recently quoted EPS for Target plc is 40p. Target plc shares stood at a market price of £4.50 before the offer.

What are the implications of the offer price by Greedy plc?

26   Harrow Ltd has budgeted the following for a month:

	£
Accounting net profit after tax	40,000
Increase in debtors (before provisions)	20,000
Increase in inventory	15,000
Increase in creditors	15,000
Depreciation	30,000
Increase in provisions	
Doubtful debts	5,000
Taxation	18,000

What is the budgeted increase in cash balances for the month?

A   £7,000
B   £33,000
C   £43,000
D   £73,000

27   What is overtrading?

28   What are the three main aspects of factoring?

29   What is the ECGD and what does it do?

30   What are the two uses of a documentary credit facility?

31   If you saw currency rates quoted as US$ 1.7335 - US$ 1.7535, what would this mean?

32   What is a forward exchange contract?

33   You are given the following information about currency rates for sterling spot and forward.

Germany (DM)
Spot   2.95-2.965
One month forward   2 - 1½ pf pm

What would be the value in sterling if you sold DM 6,000 one month forward?

BPP Publishing

34   A UK company has just despatched a shipment of goods to France. The sale will be invoiced in French francs and payment is to be made in 3 months' time. Neither the UK exporter nor the French importer uses the forward foreign exchange market to cover exchange risk.

If the pound sterling were to strengthen against the French franc, what would be the effect upon the UK exporter and the French importer?

	UK exporter	French importer
A	Gain	No effect
B	No effect	Gain
C	Loss	No effect
D	Loss	Gain

35   On 1 June, a UK importer purchased goods with an invoice value of $90,000 from the USA. The importer has to pay for the goods by 1 September. The spot rate of exchange on 1 June was 1.80 $/£ and the three month forward rate was 2.00 $/£. The importer has £50,000 available on 1 June to pay the invoice. The importer could invest in either the UK at a three-monthly interest rate of 4% per quarter or in the USA at 3% per quarter.

If the spot rate of exchange on 1 September was 1.95 $/£, which of the following courses of action would have minimised the UK importer's costs? (Ignore taxation and any transaction costs.)

A   Invest £50,000 in the UK on 1 June and at the same time enter a forward currency deal to purchase $90,000 on 1 September and use this $90,000 to pay the invoice.

B   Pay the $90,000 on 1 June

C   Invest £50,000 in the UK on 1 June and pay the $90,000 on 1 September

D   Invest $90,000 in the USA on 1 June and pay the $90,000 on 1 September

36   A bank's quoted exchange rate for sterling against the dollar is

Spot	1.6645
1 month forward	0.55 cents pm
3 months forward	1.50 cents pm

What is the cost, as an interest percentage, of forward cover from 1 March to 1 June?

A   3.57% pa
B   3.60% pa
C   3.64% pa
D   3.97% pa

37   What is a Z score?

38   What is a eurobond?

39   TST is a UK company that is planning a joint venture in Poland with a French company. Each of the two companies has agreed to inject £2 million of capital, to finance the following assets.

	£
Plant and equipment	3,500,000
Working capital	500,000
	4,000,000

TST plc will provide plant and equipment to the value of £1,800,000. Of this, one half will be second-hand. Some of this would have to be replaced for £500,000, but the remainder would be scrapped and sold off for £80,000.

What is the relevant Year 0 cash flow to TST plc for the project, with respect to the capital injection of £2,000,000, that should be used in a DCF evaluation?

A   £1,400,000
B   £1,480,000
C   £1,600,000
D   £1,680,000

40   Data of relevance to the evaluation of a particular capital project are given below.

Cost of capital in *real terms*	5% per annum
Expected inflation (general rate of inflation)	4% pa
Expected rate of increase in project's benefits due to inflation	3% pa
Expected rate of increase in project's costs due to inflation	5% pa

Which one of the following sets of adjustments will lead to the correct NPV being calculated?

	Cash inflow adjustment	Cash outflow adjustment	Discount rate
A	3% pa increase	5% pa increase	9.2%
B	4% pa increase	4% pa increase	9.2%
C	1% pa reduction	1% pa increase	5.0%
D	unadjusted	unadjusted	5.0%

BPP Publishing

1   The financial objective of a company is assumed to be to maximise the market value of the company and therefore to maximise the wealth of its owners, the shareholders.

In a nationalised industry the owners are the government or the general public, therefore the same objective would not be practical. However, the objective in a nationalised industry may still be to earn sufficient profit to provide some or all of its investment needs from its own resources but it will be restricted by the need to maintain a standard of service and to fulfil social needs.

2   Although ordinary shareholders are the owners of the company to whom the board of directors is accountable, the actual powers of shareholders tend to be restricted in practice (except in those companies where shareholders are also directors of the company).

The day-to-day running of a company is the responsibility of the management, and although the company's results are submitted for shareholders' approval at their annual general meeting, there is often marked apathy. Shareholders are often ignorant about their company's current situation and future prospects.

The relationship between management and shareholders is sometimes referred to as an agency relationship, in which managers act as agents for the shareholders, using delegated powers to run the affairs of the company in the shareholders' best interests.

The problems in this relationship are that if managers hold none or very little of the equity shares of the company they work for, they may:

(a)   work inefficiently;
(b)   not bother to look for profitable new investment opportunities;
(c)   give themselves excessively high salaries and perks.

3   The Yellow Book 'Admission of Securities to Listing' contains the Stock Exchange rules.

4   D

	£
5 shares valued at £2 each	10.00
2 shares issued at £1.50 each	3.00
7	13.00

The theoretical ex rights price is:

$$\frac{£13.00}{7} = £1.86$$

5   When convertible loan stock is traded on a stock market, its minimum market price will be the price of straight debentures with the same coupon rate of interest. If the market value falls to this minimum, it follows that the market attaches no value to the conversion rights.

The actual market price of convertible stock will depend not only on the price of straight debt but also on the current conversion value, the length of time before conversion may take place, and the market's expectation as to future equity returns and the risk associated with these returns. If the conversion value rises above the straight debt value then the price of convertible stock will normally reflect this increase.

6   If the stock market displays semi-strong efficiency, current share prices reflect:

(a)   all relevant information about past price movements and their implications; and
(b)   all knowledge which is available publicly which is relevant to the valuation of the share.

BPP Publishing

7   (a)   LIBOR is the London Inter-Bank Offered Rate. This is the rate of lending between banks on the London money markets.

    (b)   A floating rate loan is a loan at a variable rate of interest (such as 2% above base rate or 2% above LIBOR). With these loans, the rate of interest payable might be reviewed periodically, such as every three months. Alternatively, interest rates might be altered whenever and as soon as the base rate or LIBOR changes.

8   The money markets include the inter-bank market, the eurocurrency market, the inter-company market, the discount market and the Certificate of Deposit market.

9   A tick is the minimum price movement for a financial future.

10 (a)   A negotiated option is the right to buy or sell shares (or other financial instruments) at a known price within a stated period which is arranged individually for the investor by his stockbroker.

    (b)   A delta value (or hedge ratio) is a measure of the change in price of the option relative to the corresponding change in the price of the underlying instrument.

11 (a)   An interest rate swap is an arrangement to exchange a debt at a fixed rate of interest for a debt at a variable rate of interest, or vice versa. For example, A Ltd might borrow £20,000,000 at a fixed rate of 12%, and B Ltd might borrow £20,000,000 at an interest rate of 1% over LIBOR. They might then swap interest rates, with A Ltd arranging to pay the 1% over LIBOR variable rate and B Ltd arranging in return to pay the 12% fixed rate.

    (b)   A swaption is an instrument which is traded on a market in the writing/purchasing of options to buy an interest rate swap. For example, A Ltd might buy a swaption from a bank, giving A Ltd the right, but not the obligation, to enter into an interest rate swap arrangement with the bank at or before a specified time in the future.

12 $$r = \frac{D_0(1 + g)}{MV} + g$$

    Where   r   =   the cost of equity
            D_0 =   the dividend at time 0
            g   =   the annual estimated growth rate
            MV   =   the current ex-div market value.

13 $$1 + r = \frac{1 + m}{1 + i}$$

    Where   m   =   the money rate
            i   =   the inflation rate
            r   =   the real rate.

14 C

    $1.05 \times 1.04 = 1.092$

BPP Publishing

15   B

Time	£'000	DCF factor	PV
			£
0	(40)	1.000	(40,000)
3	7	0.751	5,257
1-3	30	2.487	74,610
2-4	(10.5)	2.261	(23,741)
			16,126

16   C

NPV/£ outlay

P	£3	(3)	R	£3.33	(2)
Q	£4	(1)	S	£1.875	(4)

17   B

I	1,095/15,000 = 0.127	(1) Invest £15,000
II	1,560/30,000 = 0.052	(3) Invest remainder
III	3,510/45,000 = 0.078	(2) Invest £45,000

18   In essence, the APV method consists of three steps.

(a)   Establish the cost of equity, as if the investment were entirely financed by equity.

(b)   Use this cost of equity to calculate a project NPV.

(c)   Adjust this NPV to allow for the benefits or costs of the method of financing used.

   (i)   Benefits include the tax shield on interest costs.
   (ii)   Costs include the issue costs of any new capital issue or loan for financing the project.

   These adjustments to the NPV bring us to the project's APV.

19   A

V_g = V_u + Dt
V_g = £240,000,000 + £(50,000,000 × 0.35)
   = £257,500,000

The total market value of Levered plc should be £257,500,000 and since the market value of its debt is £50,000,000, the market value of its equity should be £207,500,000.

20   Modigliani and Miller theorise that the cost of equity rises as the level of gearing becomes greater in such a way as to cancel out exactly the benefits of having extra, cheaper, debt capital. Therefore the WACC is constant at all levels of gearing.

21   R_s = K_e = 10 + 1.2 (15 − 10) = 16%

BPP Publishing

22 D

Calculation of Var m

Year	Stock market index	Change	Return as a proportion of start-of-year index		
			m	$(m-\bar{m})$	$(m-\bar{m})^2$
19X0	1,800	-	-	-	-
19X1	1,830	+30	0.0167	−0.0228	0.0005
19X2	1,770	−60	−0.0328	−0.0723	0.0052
19X3	1,960	+190	0.1073	0.0678	0.0046
19X4	2,091	+130	0.0668	0.0273	0.0007
		$\Sigma m =$	0.1580		0.0110

$$\bar{m} = \frac{0.1580}{4} = 0.0395$$

$$\text{Var } m = \frac{\sum (m - \bar{m})^2}{(n-1)} = \frac{0.0110}{(4-1)} = 0.0037$$

Calculation of (Cov x, m)

Year	Evan Elpus share price	Return	Return as a proportion of start-of-year price		
	pence		x	$(x-\bar{x})$	$(x-\bar{x})(m-\bar{m})$
19X0	200				
19X1	240	+40	0.2000	0.0220	−0.0005
19X2	150	−90	−0.3750	−0.5530	0.0400
19X3	260	+110	0.7333	0.5553	0.0376
19X4	300	+40	0.1538	−0.0242	−0.0007
		$\Sigma x =$	0.7121		0.0764

$$\bar{x} = \frac{0.7121}{4} = 0.1780$$

$$\text{Cov}(x,m) = \frac{\sum (x - \bar{x})(m - \bar{m})}{n-1} = \frac{0.0764}{3} = 0.0255$$

$$\beta = \frac{0.255}{0.0037} = 6.9$$

23   The variance of market returns is $(0.40)^2 = 0.16$

$$\beta = \frac{0.20}{0.16} = 1.25$$

The cost of Portfolio plc equity is 7% + 1.25(14% − 7%) = 15.75%

BPP Publishing

24 *Stage 1* Estimate an ungeared beta from ABC plc data

$$\beta_u = \frac{1.10}{\left[1 + \dfrac{1(0.65)}{4}\right]} = \frac{1.10}{1.1625} = 0.9462$$

Stage 2 Estimate a geared beta for XYZ plc using this ungeared beta

$$\beta_g = 0.9462[1 + \frac{3(0.65)}{4}] = 1.41$$

25 Target plc shares had a P/E ratio of 11.3 just before the offer, which is just a bit higher than Greedy's P/E ratio. The offer price gives a P/E ratio of 15.

(a) This, if the bid is successful, would dilute the EPS of Greedy plc.

(b) Target plc might be expecting earnings growth which would offset this dilution.

(c) Greedy might buy Target plc and then sell off some of Target's assets and business, in order to recover some of the cash paid out and to improve EPS.

(d) The offered P/E ratio of 15 might not be high enough to persuade Target's shareholders to accept the offer.

(e) Greedy plc must raise the cash to buy the shares, if the offer is successful.

26 D

Increase in net assets = profit = 40,000

Debtors + Stock – Creditors – Depreciation – Provisions = (33,000)

Increase in cash = 73,000

27 Overtrading arises when a company tries to conduct a volume of trade above that for which it is financially equipped. This leads to a reduction in net current assets over a period of time resulting in serious problems for management in finding cash to meet its commitments as they fall due. This can result from internal factors, such as using cash or short-term borrowings to acquire longer-term assets such as tangible fixed assets, investments or loans, or from building up stock levels in anticipation of future large orders. Overtrading can also result from external factors, such as inflation or a general increase in taxation levels levied by the government.

28 The three main aspects of factoring are:

(a) administration of the client's invoicing, sales accounting and debt collection service;
(b) purchase of a client's debts either with or without recourse;
(c) making payments or advances to the client in advance of collecting the debts.

29 The ECGD is a government body, the Export Credit Guarantee Department, which, up to December 1991:

(a) provided insurance to cover the risks of bad debts from overseas trading (both commercial and political risks);

(b) provided credit support for exporters and sometimes for overseas buyers.

ECGD's short-term credit insurance activities were privatised when the Insurances Services Division was sold to NCM UK in December 1991. ECGD continues to provide credit support in the form of guarantees to banks.

BPP Publishing

30 A documentary credit facility acts as:

   (a) a method by which an exporter receives payment from a foreign buyer, when the payment is also guaranteed by a bank;

   (b) a method by which the exporter can receive immediate payment, or if required, an advance from a bank against a term bill of exchange.

31 This would mean that the bank would sell US dollars at $1.7335 and therefore the customer would buy at that price. The bank would buy US dollars at $1.7535 and therefore a customer could sell at that price to the bank.

32 A forward exchange contract is:

   (a) an immediately firm and binding contract between a bank and its customer;
   (b) for the purchase or sale of a specified quantity of a stated foreign currency;
   (c) at a rate of exchange fixed at the time the contract is made;
   (d) for delivery and payment at a future time which is agreed upon when making the contract.

33 The rate to be used is DM 2.965 – 1½ pf = 2.95

   DM 6,000 at DM 2.95 = £2,033.90

34 C

   For example, suppose goods are sold for FF 1,000

   The current spot rate is FF10 = £1, say.

   In three months time, the spot rate is FF10.2 = £1, say.

   The French importer pays FF 1,000: no effect.

   The exporter receives only £98 (instead of £100), a loss.

35 A

		£	
A	£50,000 × 1.04 =	52,000	on 1 September
	Forward contract cost $90,000 ÷ 2	45,000	
		7,000	net return on 1 September

		£	
B	Available on 1 June	50,000	
	Cost $90,000 ÷ 1.80	50,000	
		0	net return on 1 September

		£	
C	£50,000 × 1.04	52,000	
	Cost $90,000 ÷ 1.95	46,154	
		5,846	net return on 1 September

		$	
D	$90,000 × 1.03	92,700	
	Payment on 1 September	90,000	
	Surplus in $ on 1 September	2,700	

   ÷ 1.95
   = £1,385   net return on 1 September

BPP Publishing

A is best.

36 C

$$\frac{0.0150 \times 12 \times 100}{3 \times (1.6645 - 0.0150)} = 3.64\% \text{ pa}$$

37 It is a score calculated by a corporate failure prediction model, based on a formula and applied to available financial data about a company. In many models, a Z score below 0 indicates a very strong likelihood that the company is about to collapse.

With Altman's Z score, a market below 1.8 indicates a potential failure, using the formula

$Z = 1.2X_1 + 1.4X_2 + 3.3X_3 + 0.6X_4 + 1.0X_5$

where X_1 = working capital/total assets
        X_2 = retained earnings/total assets
        X_3 = PBIT/total assets
        X_4 = market capitalisation/book value of debts
        X_5 = sales/total assets

Altman's Z score test is not valid for all types of companies (for example, it cannot be applied to retail companies).

38 A eurobond is a bond or loan denominated in a currency which often differs from that of the country of issue, and sold internationally.

39 D

	£
Cost of new plant and equipment	900,000
Replacement cost of second-hand plant that will be replaced	500,000
Scrap value of unwanted plant	80,000
Working capital injection (2,000,000 – 1,800,000)	1,680,000

40 A

The cash inflows and outflows should be increased by the expected rate of price/cost increase, which is 3% per annum for benefits and 5% per annum for costs. The money rate of discount is

$(1.04 \times 1.05) - 1 = 0.092$ or 9.2%

This should be used to discount the 'out-turn' or 'money-value' cash flows.

PAPER 14
FINANCIAL STRATEGY

Time allowed - 3 hours

Number of questions on paper - 3

Answer all 3 questions

Formulae and present value and annuity

tables are to be found on pages (xxiv) to (xxvi)

DO NOT OPEN THIS PAPER UNTIL YOU ARE READY TO START

UNDER EXAMINATION CONDITIONS

1 (a) The managers of Axmine plc, a major international copper processor are considering a joint venture with Traces, a company owning significant copper reserves in a South American country. If the joint venture were not to proceed Axmine would still need to import copper from the South American country. Axmine's managing director is concerned that the government of the South American country might impose some form of barriers to free trade which put Axmine at a competitive disadvantage in importing copper. A further director considers that this is unlikely due to the existence of GATT.

Required

Briefly discuss possible forms of non-tariff barrier that might affect Axmine's ability to import copper, and how the existence of GATT might influence such barriers. **(8 marks)**

(b) The proposed joint venture with Traces would be for an initial period of four years. Copper would be mined using a new technique developed by Axmine. Axmine would supply machinery at an immediate cost of 800 million pesos and ten supervisors at an annual salary of £40,000 each at current prices. Additionally, Axmine would pay half of the 1,000 million pesos per year (at current prices) local labour costs and other expenses in the South American country. The supervisors' salaries and local labour and other expenses will be increased in line with inflation in the United Kingdom and the South American country respectively.

Inflation in the South American country is currently 100% per year, and in the UK 8% per year. The government of the South American country is attempting to control inflation, and hopes to reduce it each year by 20% of the previous year's rate.

The joint venture would give Axmine a 50% share of Traces' copper production, with current market prices at £1,500 per 1,000 kilogrammes. Traces' production is expected to be 10 million kilogrammes per year, and copper prices are expected to rise by 10% per year (in pounds sterling) for the foreseeable future. At the end of four years Axmine would be given the choice to pull out of the venture or to negotiate another four year joint venture, on different terms.

The current exchange rate is 140 pesos/£. Future exchange rates may be estimated using the purchasing power parity theory.

Axmine has no foreign operations. The cost of capital of the company's UK mining operations is 16% per year. As this joint venture involves diversifying into foreign operations the company considers that a 2% reduction in the cost of capital would be appropriate for this project.

Corporate tax is at the rate of 20% per year in the South American country and 35% per year in the UK. A tax treaty exists between the two countries and all foreign tax paid is allowable against any UK tax liability. Taxation is payable one year in arrears and a 25% straight-line writing down allowance is available on the machinery in both countries.

Cash flows may be assumed to occur at the year end, except for the immediate cost of machinery. The machinery is expected to have negligible terminal value at the end of four years.

Required

Prepare a report discussing whether Axmine plc should agree to the proposed joint venture. Relevant calculations must form part of your report or an appendix to it.

State clearly any assumptions that you make. **(18 marks)**

BPP Publishing

(c) **If the South American government were to fail to control inflation, and inflation were to increase rapidly during the period of the joint venture, discuss the likely effect of very high inflation on the joint venture.** **(4 marks)**

(30 marks)

2 Extracts from the 19X9 annual report of Noifa Leisure plc are shown below.

Chairman's report
'The group's financial position has never been stronger. Turnover has risen 209% and the share price has almost doubled during the last four years. Since the end of the financial year the company has acquired Beddall Hotels for £100 million, financed at only 9% per year by an ecu (European Currency Unit) floating rate loan which has little risk. Our objective is to become the largest hotel group in the United Kingdom within five years.'

PROFIT AND LOSS ACCOUNT SUMMARIES
FOR THE YEARS ENDING 31 DECEMBER

	19X6 £m	19X7 £m	19X8 £m	19X9 £m
Turnover	325	370	490	680
Operating profit	49	60	75	92
Investment income	18	10	3	1
	67	70	78	93
Interest payable	14	16	24	36
Profit before tax	53	54	54	57
Taxation	20	19	19	20
Profit after taxation	33	35	35	37
Extraordinary items[1]	(3)	-	-	4
Profit attributable to shareholders	30	35	35	41
Dividends	12	12	12	12
Retained earnings	18	23	23	29

[1] Loss/gain on disposal of fixed assets

BALANCE SHEET SUMMARIES AS AT 31 DECEMBER

	19X6 £m	19X7 £m	19X8 £m	19X9 £m
Fixed assets				
Tangible assets	165	260	424	696
Investments	120	68	20	4
	285	328	444	700
Current assets				
Stock	40	45	70	110
Debtors	56	52	75	94
Cash	2	3	4	5
	98	100	149	209
Less current liabilities				
Trade creditors	82	94	130	176
Taxation	18	19	19	20
Overdraft	-	-	42	68
Other	15	24	28	42
	115	137	219	306
Total assets less current liabilities	268	291	374	603

BPP Publishing

	19X6 £m	19X7 £m	19X8 £m	19X9 £m
Financed by:				
Ordinary shares (10 pence nominal value)	50	50	50	50
Share premium	22	22	22	22
Revaluation reserve	-	-	-	100
Revenue reserves	74	97	120	149
Shareholders' funds	146	169	192	321
Bank loans	42	42	102	102
13% debenture 19Y6-8	80	80	80	180
	268	291	374	603

Analysis by type of activity

	19X6 Turnover £m	Profit[1] £m	19X7 Turnover £m	Profit £m	19X8 Turnover £m	Profit £m	19X9 Turnover £m	Profit £m
Hotels	196	36	227	41	314	37	471	45
Theme park	15	(3)	18	(2)	24	3	34	5
Bus company	24	6	28	8	38	14	46	18
Car hire	43	7	45	8	52	12	62	15
Zoo[2]	5	(1)	6	(1)	9	0	10	(1)
Waxworks	10	1	11	3	13	4	14	5
Publications	32	3	35	3	40	5	43	5
	325	49	370	60	490	75	680	92

[1]Operating profit before taxation.
[2]The zoo was sold during 19X9.

	19X6	19X7	19X8	19X9
Noifa Leisure plc average share price (pence)	82	104	120	159
FT 100 Share Index	1,500	1,750	1,800	2,300
Leisure industry share index	178	246	344	394
Leisure industry PE ratio	10:1	12:1	19:1	25:1

Required

In his report the chairman stated that 'the group's financial position has never been stronger'. From the viewpoint of an external consultant appraise whether you agree with the chairman. Discussion of the group's financing policies and strategic objective, with suggestions as to how these might be altered, should form part of your appraisal. Relevant calculations must be shown.   (30 marks)

3   It is now 31 December 19X2. The corporate treasurer of Uniprod plc is concerned about the level of cash flows of the company during the next six months, and how the company might be protected from the adverse effects of changing interest rates. Interest rates are widely expected to change in late April when a General Election is due, but the size and direction of the change is dependent upon the result of the election which is forecast by opinion polls to be very close. Current interest rates for Uniprod are 11% per year for short-term borrowing, and 8% per year for short-term investment. Sales of the company in December 19X2 were 824,180 units at a price of £10.60 per unit. Sales have been recently increasing at the rate of 1.5% per month, and this trend is expected to continue. Two months' credit is given to all customers and one month's credit is received on all purchases. Materials, with a unit variable cost of £3.71, are purchased to meet expected sales in two months' time. Direct

labour costs £3.18 per unit and wages are payable one month in arrears. Production levels are based upon expected sales in one month's time. Overheads, payable one month in arrears, are expected to be £1,950,000 per month (invoice value) for the next three months, and £2,010,000 per month for the following six months. Sales price, material and labour costs are expected to rise by 5% in early March 19X3. No other changes in price or costs are expected. Other forecast cash flows are:

(a) March: replace 150 salesmen's cars at a net cost of £900,000.

(b) May

    (i)   Purchase new machinery for planned expansion at a cost of £2,381,000.
    (ii)   Disposal of a plot of land for the sum of £1,990,000, £1,300,000 receivable in May and £690,000 receivable in June.

(c) A dividend of £1,817,000 is payable in June, and taxation of £5,700,000 is payable in April.

There will be an opening cash balance of £800,000 at the beginning of January 19X3.

Apart from an overdraft facility to finance short-term cash shortages, the company has no other form of floating rate debt.

June sterling three month time deposit futures are currently priced at 90.25. The standard contract size is £500,000 and the minimum price movement is one tick (the value of one tick is 0.01% per year of the contract size).

Interest rate guarantees at 11.5% per year for a two month period from May are available to Uniprod for a premium of 0.2% of the size of the loan to be guaranteed.

Forward rate agreements are available for periods of up to four months from May at 11.88-11.83%.

Required

(a) Prepare a report discussing the advantages and disadvantages of alternative strategies that the managers of Uniprod might adopt to protect the company from interest rate risk associated with the company's expected cash flows during the next six months. The company does not wish to seek speculative profits from interest rate movements. State clearly any assumptions that you make and include relevant calculations as part of your report.   (24 marks)

(b) If at the end of April rates have moved as follows:

Scenario (1)
Borrowing rate for Uniprod 13% per year
Investment rate for Uniprod 10% per year
June sterling three month time deposit futures 88.05

Scenario (2)
Borrowing rate for Uniprod 9.5% per year
Investment rate for Uniprod 6.8% per year
June sterling three month time deposit futures 91.75,

evaluate with hindsight, separately for *each* of scenarios (1) and (2) above, the results of *four* alternative strategies that the company might have adopted towards its interest rate risk. Taxation, margin requirements and the time value of money may be ignored.   (16 marks)

(40 marks)

BPP Publishing

TEST PAPER
SUGGESTED SOLUTIONS

DO NOT TURN THIS PAGE UNTIL YOU
HAVE COMPLETED THE TEST PAPER

1

Tutorial note. For parts (b) and (c) it is helpful to establish clear steps in the process of analysing the financial implications of the project. Firstly, realise that since the project is to be undertaken in the foreign country the actual cash flows will be denominated in pesos even though they may be calculated on the basis of sterling figures. Once the project cash flows have been established these can be used to calculate the tax liability in the foreign country. When tax has been deducted, the net cash flows can be translated into sterling at the appropriate year end rate which is calculated on the basis of the relative inflation rates of the two countries for the year. The incremental UK tax payable can then be found, but take care to base this on the taxable income, and not the translated figure including WDAs. The net sterling cash flow can then be discounted to find the NPV of the project. In the report, take into account non-financial factors that could influence the outcome of the project.

(a) Non-tariff barriers of the following types might be imposed.

   (i) Complex bureaucratic procedures, for example in passing exports through customs, or licensing requirements which must be met before trading. Such measures will delay the trading process for overseas buyers of copper and increase their costs.

   (ii) Regulations which prohibit trade with particular countries.

   (iii) A quota system on copper exports, which would maintain higher prices if the country is a major copper supplier or if quotas are also agreed by other copper-exporting countries. Quotas on quantities exported might also help to prevent overexploitation of copper reserves.

   (iv) Setting of minimum or raised prices for copper through regulations fixing exchange rates for copper sales at non-market levels.

Trade protection measures are often imposed in order to create a favourable balance of trade position and are therefore more often imposed on imports than on exports. If the South American country has a need for foreign exchange to finance imports, for example of oil and machinery, it may in fact wish to encourage exports.

The General Agreement on Tariffs and Trade (GATT) has been successful in reducing the general level of tariffs over the past 30 years, but many non-tariff barriers to trade remain. Non-tariff barriers are more difficult to identify than tariffs, for example where they appear under the guise of health and safety regulations. However, the reduction of non-tariff barriers has been an important aim of the Uruguay round of GATT negotiations.

It may be that GATT has no effect on the South American country, if it is not a GATT member. If the country does belong to GATT, it may be able to impose non-tariff barriers of some of the types for which examples are given above, either covertly or more overtly evading GATT requirements.

(b) REPORT

To: Board of Directors
From: Accountant
Date: 14 December 19X2

Subject: Proposed joint venture with Traces SA

Introduction

This report addresses the financial implications of the proposed joint venture with Traces SA. A detailed financial analysis can be found in the Appendix to this report.

Financial implications

On the basis of the assumptions made about market conditions, likely costs and revenues and macroeconomic forecasts, the joint venture should produce a positive net present value of

---

£4,722,000 at the lower discount rate of 14%. However, it is likely that this result will be sensitive to changes in the key variables, notably the price of copper over the period, to the relative rates of inflation in the two countries and to other factors influencing the exchange rate. It would be useful to investigate these sensitivities further.

Other considerations

Axmine plc should also consider some of the wider issues surrounding the proposed joint venture. These include the nature of the relationship with Traces SA. Can Traces be trusted to fulfil all their obligations with regard to the project? It is assumed that they will be managing the operation and selling the copper - do they have the expertise to do this efficiently and successfully?

A further area of risk concerns the political stability of the country. Axmine should consider what its position might be and whether it would be able to extract cash from the operation in the event of a change of government.

It would be useful to make some evaluation of Axmine's position at the end of the four year period. If it is likely that the joint venture could be extended on favourable terms, then this could further enhance the attractiveness of the project.

Conclusions

On financial grounds, the project appears to be well worth undertaking since it yields a large positive NPV. However the sensitivities should be calculated and some of the wider issues surrounding the joint venture addressed before Axmine finally commits itself to the project.

APPENDIX

Annual cash flows (pesos m)

Year	0	1	2	3	4	5
Sales		1,925	3,215	4,952	7,109	
Costs:						
Machinery	800					
WDA		200	200	200	200	
Supervisors		101	165	250	352	
Local expenses		900	1,476	2,232	3,146	
Taxable	(800)	724	1,374	2,270	3,411	
SA tax (20%)			(145)	(275)	(454)	(682)
Add back WDA		200	200	200	200	
Net cash	(800)	924	1,429	2,195	3,157	(682)

Annual sterling cash flows (£'000)

Year		0	1	2	3	4	5
	£'000	£'000	£'000	£'000	£'000	£'000	
Net cash	(5,714)	3,960	4,033	4,425	4,876	(857)	
UK tax (15%)			(465)	(582)	(686)	(790)	
	(5,714)	3,960	3,568	3,843	4,190	(1,647)	
Discount (14%)	1.000	0.877	0.769	0.675	0.592	0.519	
NPV	(5,714)	3,473	2,744	2,594	2,480	(855)	

Total expected NPV = £4,722,000

Notes

1 The WDAs are added back to the cash flow after the tax has been calculated and deducted because they do not involve any movement in cash terms.

2 UK tax is calculated on the taxable revenue arising in the previous year, translated at the exchange rate ruling at the end of that year ie tax in year 2 is calculated on the total of 724 million pesos, translated at 233.33 pesos/£. The tax rate used is the incremental rate of 15% (35% – 20%), since tax has already been paid in the country where the income arises and, because of the tax treaty, all foreign tax paid is allowable against UK tax. No adjustment has to be made to the WDAs since the rate is the same in both countries.

Workings

The exchange rate at the end of each year can be calculated using the purchasing power parity theory (P'm = millions of pesos).

New rate = old rate × $\dfrac{1 + \text{SA inflation}}{1 + \text{UK inflation}}$

Year	SA infl'n %	UK infl'n %	Exchange rate
0	100.00	8.00	140.00
1	80.00	8.00	233.33
2	64.00	8.00	354.32
3	51.20	8.00	496.05
4	40.96	8.00	647.44
5	32.77	8.00	795.92

Supervisors' salaries payable in pesos will be:

Year	Infl'n %	£'000	P'm
0	8.00	400.00	
1	8.00	432.00	101
2	8.00	466.56	165
3	8.00	503.88	250
4	8.00	544.20	352

Copper revenues in pesos will be:

Year	Prod'n '000 kg	Infl'n %	Price £/1000kg	Revenue £'000	Revenue P'm
0			1,500.00		
1	5,000	10.00	1,650.00	8,250.00	1,925
2	5,000	10.00	1,815.00	9,075.00	3,215
3	5,000	10.00	1,996.50	9,982.50	4,952
4	5,000	10.00	2,196.15	10,980.75	7,109

Local labour costs and expenses will be:

Year	Infl %	P'm
0	100.00	500
1	80.00	900
2	64.00	1,476
3	51.20	2,232
4	40.96	3,146

(c) If inflation increases rapidly during the life of the project, provided that the purchasing power parity theory holds good, the exchange rate should move in such a way that local costs (when translated into sterling) effectively only increase at the rate of inflation in the UK (8%). Since it is predicted that copper prices (fixed in sterling) will increase at 10% per year, the project should continue to be attractive.

One adverse effect would be that the value of the writing down allowances would be diminished since they are fixed at 200m pesos per year. However, this should be more than offset by the fact that tax is payable a year in arrears. The net effect of this should be to increase the expected NPV of the joint venture.

BPP Publishing

2

> *Tutorial note.* This question has a fairly brief requirement, not divided into sections, and so careful planning of your answer is vital. Several different answers could be equally good, but any good answer will make good use of the detailed information given in the question, supporting general conclusions with specific calculations.

APPRAISAL OF THE FINANCIAL MANAGEMENT AND STRATEGIC OBJECTIVE OF NOIFA LEISURE PLC

The chairman clearly foresees that the group's rapid growth in turnover over the past four years (an average annual rate of growth of $\sqrt[3]{[680/325]} - 1 = 28\%$) will be sustained into the future, leading to the group becoming the major force in its industry. While the growth in turnover has indeed been remarkable, it is debatable whether this objective of growth is in fact appropriate, both in general and for this group. The main financial objective of any company should be to increase the wealth of its shareholders. To do that, profits must be made, and preferably increased. A rise in turnover may be to the shareholders' disadvantage if it leads to a fall in profits, and it is noticeable that profits after tax for this group have shown little of the remarkable growth in turnover. Furthermore, if growth becomes the sole aim, other important financial considerations, such as the need to maintain a safe capital structure, may be ignored. This group has raised significant amounts of debt but has made no new equity issues recently, and this should give rise to concern. These general concerns are borne out by a detailed study of the accounts.

The profit and loss account

Operating profit has risen along with turnover, suggesting reasonable control over operating expenses, which have remained stable at around 85% of turnover. The failure of net profit to rise in line with turnover can be explained by the marked fall in investment income (caused by the disposal of investments) and by the sharp rise in interest payable (caused by a sharp rise in borrowings). The consequence has been that the profit before tax as a percentage of capital employed (taken as shareholders' funds plus non-current liabilities) fell from 20% in 19X6 to 9% in 19X9. (The 19X9 figure is 11% if the asset revaluation is ignored.)

The tangible fixed asset turnover gives further information. It was $325/165 = 1.97$ times in 19X6, and $680/696 = 0.98$ times in 19X9. This low turnover suggests that the group has been buying new assets and funding their purchase with borrowings, without sufficient attention being paid to the scope for improved use of existing assets.

The analysis by activities

The analysis clearly shows that performance has not been uniform across the group. Hotels have remained the mainstay of the business, with 60% of the turnover in 19X6 and 69% by 19X9. However, in 19X6 hotels had above average profitability, contributing 74% of the group's operating profit, while by 19X9 they only contributed 49% of the operating profit. Publications, by contrast, have done very well. In 19X6 they contributed 9.8% of the turnover and 6.1% of the profit, but by 19X9, although only contributing 6.3% of the turnover, they still contributed 5.4% of the profit. This division is perhaps being managed in the way that the group as a whole ought to be managed. The growth in turnover has been good, if not spectacular, but profitability has grown. Of course, we cannot tell how the group's rising burden of debt interest should be apportioned between the divisions, and making an allowance for that interest might have a significant impact on the distribution of profit between the divisions.

It does seem that the decision to sell the zoo was correct. Turnover was static and losses were being made. Nevertheless, it may be that careful attention to the details of management, rather than exclusive concern with turnover, could have made this division profitable and worth retaining.

The balance sheet

The growth in fixed assets has, as already remarked, been very rapid. We can also see from the balance sheet the fall in investments which has caused the fall in investment income. Presumably the investments were sold to help fund the purchase of fixed assets. To the extent that this reflected a decision to concentrate on trading rather than on investing, this was no doubt sensible. If, however, the sales were made merely because equity and debt finance proved hard to obtain, this should cause concern. Perhaps warning signs, in the form of the difficulty of obtaining finance, were not being heeded.

Current assets were kept under reasonable control, being 30%, 27%, 30% and 31% of turnover in the years 19X6 to 19X9 respectively. We cannot compute stock turnover, because we do not know the mark-ups on stock, and we cannot compute the debtors collection period, because we do not know what proportions of sales were on credit. However, it can be noted that the ratio of stock to turnover has risen from 12% to 16% between 19X6 and 19X9, perhaps indicating a need for improved stock management.

The group's liquidity position is very worrying. There were net current liabilities in every year, and in the latest year (19X9) the current ratio was 0.68 and the quick ratio was 0.32. The company is at serious risk of insolvency, particularly as it has come to rely on a substantial and growing bank overdraft. While overdrafts are in practice often allowed to remain outstanding for long periods, they are repayable on demand, and a bank concerned about the safety of the funds could well demand repayment.

The need for more funds, and the choice of loan finance to provide them, is even more apparent from the second section of the balance sheet. Shareholders' funds have risen only by the retained profits, and by a revaluation which may or may not be justified, while an additional £60,000,000 bank loan was raised in 19X8 and a £100,000,000 debenture issue was made in 19X9. The gearing percentage, defined as the ratio of total loans (including overdraft) to equity, was 83% in 19X6, 72% in 19X7, 117% in 19X8 and (ignoring the asset revaluation) 158% in 19X9. Gearing has increased to reach a level at which total loans far exceed equity: the trend is clearly unsatisfactory given the immediate liquidity problems.

The share price and the P/E ratio

The share price has, as the chairman says, risen substantially over the period 19X6 to 19X9. However, if the price is deflated by the rise in the industry share index, the trend looks rather different. The results are as follows.

Noifa Leisure plc price	Deflation factor	Deflated Noifa Leisure plc price
p		p
82	× 178/178	82
104	× 178/246	75
120	× 178/344	62
159	× 178/394	72

It is clear that Noifa Leisure plc has actually gone down in the market's estimation relative to other companies in the industry since 19X6. The P/E ratio of the company has similarly performed badly relative to that of the industry. In 19X6 it was 12.4, or 124% of the industry average. In 19X9, it was 21.5, or 86% of the industry average. In what appears to be a booming industry, the group's management is failing its shareholders.

Conclusion

The group does appear to be achieving the chairman's declared objective of substantial growth. However, it is not at all clear either that that should be the overriding objective, or that the group will be able to continue on its chosen path for much longer. The main changes which would seem appropriate are as follows.

(a) The strategic objective should be reformulated, with more weight being given to profitability.

(b) A plan should be formulated for the next two years, concentrating on consolidation of the group's existing position rather than on further growth.

(c) Immediate attention should be given to the group's liquidity, with detailed cash flow projections being made. It should not be assumed that any more overdraft or loan finance will be available, and if any problems are foreseen urgent consideration should be given to the raising of new equity.

3

Tutorial note. The answer is required in the format of a report to management. Detailed numerical analysis can be included as an appendix to the report.

The first step is to construct a cash flow forecast for the six months in question. This can then be used to assess the level of interest rate exposure that Uniprod is likely to face. In discussing the options available to Uniprod, do not forget that there are other methods available beyond those mentioned in the question, and that one valid option might be to do nothing.

In part (b) state clearly the assumptions used in calculating the interest costs, for instance whether the calculation is based on the opening balance for the month or on the average balance. It is helpful to provide a summary of your results.

(a) **REPORT**

To: Managers of Uniprod
From: Accountant
Date: 31 December 19X2
Subject: Interest rate risk management - January to June 19X3

Introduction

Uniprod is likely to enjoy cash surpluses for the period from January to March; however after that, shortfalls will arise due to payments of taxation and dividend and to fixed asset purchases. Detailed cash flow projections are contained in Appendix 1 to this report.

The maximum amount available for short term investment is likely to be £2.6m and the largest shortfall should be £2.413m. This means that the absolute level of interest rate exposure is likely to be relatively small - even a 3% change in rates would only affect the maximum monthly liability by £6,028 and the maximum receipt by £6,500.

Possible strategies for interest rate risk management

Since the size of the risk in terms of the company's overall cash flows is small, one option is to do nothing and to accept the effects of any movement in the rates which occurs.

If Uniprod does wish to hedge, there are a number of alternative strategies available. It is probably most appropriate to concentrate on the months of May and June, given that it is unlikely that there will be significant rate changes in advance of the general election.

The possible strategies available are described below.

Forward interest rate agreements (FRAs)
There are agreements made between the company and the bank concerning the interest rate on future borrowings or deposits. They fix the interest rate to be charged for a certain period into the future. If the actual interest rate on borrowings is below the rate fixed, then the company will pay the bank the difference; if the reverse situation applies, then the bank will pay the company the difference. A FRA is simply an agreement about rates - it does not involve the movement of the principal sum. The actual borrowing must be arranged separately. FRAs are usually only available on transactions in excess of £0.5m.

Thus Uniprod could take out an FRA to cover £2.413m for three months from April onwards at a guaranteed annual rate of 11%. This will then be the effective rate charged regardless of the outcome of the election. Uniprod will therefore know in advance exactly what its interest rate commitments will be, and it will be protected from any adverse movements in rates. However it will not be able to take advantage of any reduction in interest rates following the election.

Such a strategy is dependent upon the bank's willingness to lend at the agreed rate. The rate which will be negotiated with the bank will take account of market expectations of how rates may be likely to move in the period in question.

Interest rate futures
A financial future is an agreement on the future price of a financial variable. Interest rate futures are similar in all respects to forward rate agreements, except that the terms, sums involved, and periods are standardised. They are traded on the London International Futures and Options Exchange (LIFFE). Their standardised nature makes them less attractive to corporate borrowers because it is not always possible to match them exactly to specific rate exposures. Each contract will require the payment of a small initial deposit.

Since Uniprod will have a maximum borrowing requirement of £2.413m, it will not be able to match amounts exactly. If the company believes that rates may rise following the election, then it should sell contracts now in order to buy them back at a lower price following the rise in rates. The profit on the futures deal can then be used to offset the increased cost of borrowing. It is unlikely that an exact match (perfect hedge) can be made. If rates fall rather than rise, then the loss on the futures contracts should be offset to some extent by the saving made on actual interest payments.

Interest rate options
An interest rate guarantee (or option) provides the right to borrow a specified amount at a guaranteed rate of interest. The option guarantees that the interest rate will not rise above a specified level during a specified period. On the date of expiry of the option the buyer must decide whether or not to exercise his right to borrow. He will only exercise the option if actual interest rates have risen above the option rate. The advantage of options is that the buyer cannot lose more as a result of unfavourable interest rate movements and can take advantage of any favourable rate movements. However, a premium must be paid regardless of whether or not the option is exercised. Options can be negotiated directly with a bank or traded in a standardised form on the LIFFE.

BPP Publishing

Uniprod could therefore gain full protection from an adverse movement in rates and not forfeit its ability to take advantage of a fall in rates following the election. It may however decide that the premium to be paid for this is too expensive.

Caps and collars
These can be used to set a floor and a ceiling to the range of interest rates which might be incurred. A premium must be paid for this service. Thus Uniprod could buy a cap to give a maximum rate of interest that will be payable regardless of how actual rates move. It could reduce the premium for this by selling an interest rate floor to fix the minimum interest rate for the company.

These agreements do not provide a perfect hedge, but they do limit the range of possibilities and thus reduce the level of exposure.

Conclusion

A number of methods are available which Uniprod could use to hedge against interest rate movements. These provide differing degrees of protection and differing opportunities to take advantage of beneficial movements in rates. The cost of such methods varies. Uniprod must decide whether it is happy to accept its exposure, which appears to be low in relation to its cash flow, or whether it would prefer to pay for greater stability in its interest rate commitments.

APPENDIX
CASH BUDGET FOR THE PERIOD JANUARY TO JUNE 19X3

	January £'000	February £'000	March £'000	April £'000	May £'000	June £'000
Cash inflows						
Debtors	8,607	8,736	8,867	9,000	9,592	9,736
Land sale					1,300	690
Net inflow	8,607	8,736	8,867	9,000	10,892	10,426
Cash outflows						
Materials	(3,150)	(3,197)	(3,245)	(3,459)	(3,511)	(3,563)
Labour	(2,660)	(2,700)	(2,741)	(2,921)	(2,965)	(3,009)
Overheads	(1,950)	(1,950)	(1,950)	(1,950)	(2,010)	(2,010)
Fixed assets			(900)		(2,381)	
Taxation				(5,700)		
Dividend						(1,817)
Net outflow	(7,760)	(7,847)	(8,836)	(14,030)	(10,867)	(10,399)
Opening balance	800	1,652	2,552	2,600	(2,413)	(2,410)
Interest	5	11	17	17	(22)	(22)
Movement	847	889	31	(5,030)	25	27
Closing balance	1,652	2,552	2,600	(2,413)	(2,410)	(2,405)

Notes

1. It is assumed that overheads payable in January will be £1.95m.

2. Interest has been calculated on the opening balance for the month at the rate of 8% on cash surpluses and 11% on cash deficits.

BPP Publishing

Workings

	Nov	Dec	Jan	Feb	Mar	Apr	May	Jun	Jul
Sales units	812,000	824,180	836,543	849,091	861,827	874,755	887,876	901,194	914,712
Unit price (£)	10.60	10.60	10.60	10.60	11.13	11.13	11.13	11.13	11.13
Sales (£'000)	8,607	8,736	8,867	9,000	9,592	9,736	9,882	10,030	10,181
Receipts		8,607	8,736	8,867	9,000	9,592	9,736	9,882
Prod'n units	824,180	836,543	849,091	861,827	874,755	887,876	901,194	914,712	928,433
Mat'ls purchased	3,104	3,150	3,197	3,245	3,459	3,511	3,563	3,617
Payment to creditors		3,104	3,150	3,197	3,245	3,459	3,511	3,563	3,617
Labour		2,621	2,660	2,700	2,741	2,921	2,965	3,009

(b) The following strategies will be evaluated:

    (i) No action

    (ii) Hedge using futures contracts

    (iii) Hedge using interest rate guarantee

    (iv) Hedge using forward rate agreement

    (i) *No action*

	May	June	Total
Opening borrowings	£2,413,000	£2,410,000	
(1) Interest at 13%	£26,141	£26,108	£52,249
(2) Interest at 9.5%	£19,103	£19,079	£38,182

    (ii) *Futures contracts*

To hedge for May and June using three month deposit futures, Uniprod will need the following number of contracts:

$$(£2,413,000/£500,000) \times 2/3 = 3.21$$

To hedge fully therefore four contracts will be needed.

(1) 1 January 19X3: sell four June sterling three months time deposit futures at 90.25.

1 May 19X3: buy four June three month time deposit futures at 88.05.

A profit has been made on the hedge of:

$$90.25 - 88.05, \text{ ie } 220 \text{ ticks}$$

One tick is worth £0.5m × 0.01% × 3/12 = £12.50

The profit on four contracts is therefore:

$$£12.50 \times 220 \times 4 = £11,000$$

This can then be offset against the actual cash cost of borrowing calculated in (i) above:

$$\text{Net cost} = £52,249 - £11,000 = £41,249$$

(2) 1 January 19X3: sell four June sterling three months time deposit futures at 90.25.

1 May 19X3: buy four June three month time deposit futures at 91.75.

A loss has been made on the hedge of:

$$90.25 - 91.75, \text{ ie } 150 \text{ ticks}$$

One tick is worth £0.5m × 0.01% × 3/12 = £12.50

The loss on four contracts is therefore:

$$£12.50 \times 150 \times 4 = £7,500$$

This must be added to the actual cash cost of borrowing calculated in (i) above:

$$\text{Net cost} = £38,182 + £7,500 = £45,682$$

(iii)   *Interest rate guarantee*

If an interest rate guarantee is used, it will only be exercised in scenario (1) when interest rates rise. However, the premium must be paid regardless of whether the guarantee is exercised. The net cost can be calculated as follows.

				£
(1)	Interest cost:	£2,413,000 × 11.5% × 2/12	=	46,249
	Premium:	£2,413,000 × 0.2%	=	4,826
		Total cost		51,075
(2)	Interest cost:	£2,413,000 × 9.5% × 2/12	=	38,206
	Premium:	£2,413,000 × 0.2%	=	4,826
		Total cost		43,032

(iv)   *Forward rate agreement*

If a forward rate agreement is used the net interest cost will be the same regardless of the actual rate. In this case the rate will be 11.88%. The net cost can be calculated as follows.

$$£2,413,000 × 11.88\% × 2/12 = £47,777$$

This cost is arrived at differently in the two scenarios. In scenario (1), the actual interest rate is higher than the FRA, and the difference will be paid to Uniprod by the bank. In scenario (2) the reverse situation applies and Uniprod must pay the additional costs to the bank to bring the effective rate up to 11.88%.

The results can be summarised as follows.

	Scenario (1)	Scenario (2)
	£	£
No hedge	52,249	38,182
Futures	41,249	45,682
Interest rate guarantee	51,075	43,032
Forward rate agreement	47,777	47,777

In scenario (1), Uniprod would gain the most from the use of futures contracts, while in scenario (2) the best course of action is to do nothing. The use of a forward rate agreement or futures contracts minimises the possible variation in interest costs.

BPP Publishing

FURTHER READING

If you have not already used the BPP companion Study Text, you may now wish to do so. Published in August 1993, it contains full, structured coverage of the ACCA's new syllabus and teaching guide, plus plenty of opportunity for self-testing and practice.

You may also wish to test your grasp of the subject by tackling short questions in multiple choice format. BPP publish the Password series of books, each incorporating a large selection of multiple choice questions with solutions, comments and marking guides. The Password title relevant to *Financial Strategy* is called *Financial Management*. This is priced at £6.95 each and contains about 300 questions.

To order your Study Text or Password book, ring our credit card hotline on 081-740 6808. Alternatively, send this page to our Freepost address or fax it to us on 081-740 1184.

To: BPP Publishing Ltd, FREEPOST, London W12 8BR   **Tel: 081-740 6808**
                                                          Fax: 081-740 1184

Forenames (Mr / Ms): _____

Surname: _____

Address: _____

_____

Post code: _____

Please send me the following books: Quantity   Price   Total

Password *Financial Management*   ....   £6.95   ....

Financial Strategy Study Text   ....   £17.95   ....

Please include postage:

UK: Texts £2.50 for first plus £1.00 for each extra book.   ....

        Password £1.50 for first, 50p for each extra   ....

Europe: (inc ROI): Texts £5.00 for first plus £4.00 for each extra book.   ....

        Password £2.50 for first, £1.00 for each extra   ....

Rest of the World: Texts £7.50 for first plus £5.00 for each extra book.   ....

        Password £4.00 for first, £2.00 for each extra   ....

I enclose a cheque for £ _____ or charge to Access/Visa

Card number ☐☐☐☐☐☐☐☐☐☐☐☐☐☐☐☐☐☐

Expiry date _____ Signature _____

On the reverse of this page there is a review form, which you can send in to us (at the Freepost address above) with comments and suggestions on the Kit you have just finished. Your feedback really does make a difference: it helps us to make the next edition that bit better.

Name: _____

How have you used this Kit?

Home study (book only) ☐   With 'correspondence' package ☐

On a course: college_____ ☐   Other_____ ☐

How did you obtain this Kit?

From us by mail order ☐   From us by phone ☐

From a bookshop ☐   From your college ☐

Where did you hear about BPP Kits?

At bookshop ☐   Recommended by lecturer ☐

Recommended by friend ☐   Mailshot from BPP ☐

Advertisement in _____ ☐   Other _____

Have you used the companion Study Text for this subject?   **Yes/No**

Your comments and suggestions would be appreciated on the following areas

'Do you know?' checklists

Tutorial questions and content of solutions

Quiz and Test Paper

Errors (please specify, and refer to a page number)

Structure and presentation

Please return to: BPP Publishing Ltd, FREEPOST, London W12 8BR